REA

362.
ROBINSON
WORKING WITH CHILDREN OF
ALCOHOLICS

FRIENDS
OF ACPL

P9-DBT-889

ALLEN COUNTY PUBLIC LIBRARY
FORT WAYNE, INDIANA 46802

You may return this book to any location of
the Allen County Public Library.

DEMCO

Working with
Children of Alcoholics

Working with Children of Alcoholics

The Practitioner's Handbook

Bryan E. Robinson
University of North Carolina at Charlotte and
The Randolph Clinic, Inc.

Foreword by
Migs Woodside

LEXINGTON BOOKS
An Imprint of Macmillan, Inc.
NEW YORK

Maxwell Macmillan Canada
TORONTO

Maxwell Macmillan International
NEW YORK   OXFORD   SINGAPORE   SYDNEY

Allen County Public Library
900 Webster Street
PO Box 2270
Fort Wayne, IN 46801-2270

Copyright © 1989 by Lexington Books
An Imprint of Macmillan, Inc.

All rights reserved. No part of this book may be reproduced
or transmitted in any form or by any means, electronic or
mechanical, including photocopying, recording, or by any
information storage and retrieval system, without permission
in writing from the Publisher.

Lexington Books
An Imprint of Macmillan, Inc.
866 Third Avenue, New York, N.Y. 10022

Maxwell Macmillan Canada, Inc.
1200 Eglinton Avenue East
Suite 200
Don Mills, Ontario M3C 3N1

Macmillan, Inc. is part of the Maxwell Communication
Group of Companies.

Printed in the United States of America

printing number
2   3   4   5   6   7   8   9   10

Library of Congress Cataloging-in-Publication Data

Robinson, Bryan E.
  Working with children of alcoholics.

   1. Children of alcoholics—United States.   2.   Social
work with children—United States.   3.   Alcoholics—
United States—Family relationships.   I.   Title. [DNLM:
1. Alcoholism.   2.   Child Development Disorders—
etiology.   3.   Child Guidance.   4.   Parent-Child Relations.
5.   Stress, Psychological—in infancy & childhood.
WM   274   R658w]
HV5132.R63   1989   362.2'92   87–45558
ISBN 0–669–16638–3 (alk. paper)

To the staff of the Randolph Clinic, Inc., in Charlotte,
North Carolina; to children who have received treatment
there; and to children everywhere who have experienced
the misery, pain, and suffering when a parent is
addicted to alcohol.

Contents

3 1833 02583 2277

Figures and Tables

Figures

Tables

Foreword

Migs Woodside
President, Children of Alcoholics Foundation

Until recently, children of alcoholics were neglected, overlooked, and ignored. Few were aware of the millions of Americans who grew up with parental alcoholism. Few realized youngsters were watching, listening, and deeply affected by the harmful effects of their parents' drinking. Hardly anyone knew children of alcoholics need and deserve help for themselves. For far too long, children from alcoholic families remained out of sight, unseen, and nearly invisible.

In the last few years, professionals and the general public have begun to recognize this huge and vulnerable group. At last they have begun to emerge from the shadows. Buttressed by research findings pointing to an inherited predisposition to family alcoholism and to the increased likelihood of other emotional, physical, and mental-health-related problems, practitioners, scientists, and others are beginning work to educate service providers about the pain and suffering endured in an alcoholic home. As a nation, our knowledge and understanding has begun to blossom.

We know that 28 million Americans—one out of every eight—are children of alcoholics. Seven million are youngsters under the age of eighteen who face the fear and problems caused by parents who drink too much. Twenty-one million are adults burdened by long-lasting negative consequences of their parents' behavior. We also know that with information, education, and help from others, children of alcoholics can lead happier, more productive lives.

Research scientists and clinicians have found that alcoholism runs in families. Children of alcoholics are four times more likely than others to become alcoholics and grandsons of alcoholic grandfathers are at three times' greater risk. Daughters of alcoholics are also more prone to marry alcoholic men, thereby perpetuating the painful cycle into future generations. All too often, problems related to parental alcohol abuse are passed on from parent to child and grandparent to grandchild as the cycle of family pain continues.

Parental alcoholism often results in lifelong injury and harm. Fetal alcoholism syndrome, resulting from maternal alcohol abuse, can cause prenatal central nervous system damage, mental retardation, microcephaly, hypotonia, and a host of other abnormalities. Other infants may have feeding problems, vomiting, and incessant crying. Babies with alcoholic mothers may be especially harmed because of inconsistent handling and neglect.

As youngsters, children of alcoholics are more likely to complain of stomachaches, headaches, sleep problems, nervous tics, and nausea, although no physical causes for these complaints can be found. As teenagers, they are more likely than others to be truant or delinquent, abuse alcohol or other drugs, drop out of school, or even attempt suicide. As adults, they may have more interpersonal and work-related problems, as well as higher rates of alcoholism.

However, it is important to note that some children of alcoholics appear to do very well. They clean the house, pay the bills, and cover up when irate employers demand to know the whereabouts of their absent employee. These children also take care of their siblings, do well in school, and shine in sports and other extra-curricular activities. But deep inside, these superstars experience little satisfaction or self-worth. They feel like failures; after all, they are unable to stop their parent's drinking.

A tragedy of parental alcoholism is the way it makes children feel. Almost always, youngsters are fraught with guilt, believing they are responsible for the alcohol abuse. They do not know that alcoholism is a disease they cannot cause, control, or cure. Instead, they truly believe if they got better marks in school, were more polite, mowed the lawn, or cleaned up their room, their parent would stop drinking. This unspoken belief is underscored by parents who blame youngsters and tell them their behavior makes them drink. Children believe what they are told. They are crushed by guilt and drive themselves to become better, to become perfect.

Life with an alcoholic parent is filled with tension and insecurity. Youngsters never know what to expect. They do not know when it is safe to ask for money for new sneakers or a school trip. They do not know when they will be abused. The household rules and emotional climate change abruptly according to the level of alcohol in the parent's bloodstream. Consistency is always inconsistent. It is difficult for these youngsters to trust, to be emotionally involved with others, to rely on anyone else. Parental alcoholism breeds isolation and fear.

Because the entire family revolves around the alcoholic's behavior and moods, their children are always second best. They wait patiently for love, attention, or simple help with practical matters. They feel rejected and worthless. Their life experiences make them feel they are second-class citizens.

Later on, as adults, children of alcoholics are often tense, unable to relax, inflexible, and wary. Some react by trying to maintain tight control over events and relationships at home and at work. They long for a static world without surprise or change. Although most adult children of alcoholics do not become alcoholic, their childhood produces deeply rooted feelings of dissatisfaction, disappointment, failure, and depression. When they apply some of the coping behaviors used as survival skills in childhood, they may find these techniques no longer serve them appropriately or well.

Because alcoholism is a family secret, it is very difficult for children and adults to obtain the help they need and deserve. Youngsters learn that alcoholism is a secret so terrible and shameful it cannot be shared. Parents' admonitions are common and children are warned, "Don't tell Mom you saw me stop at the bar for a couple of beers" or "When Grandma comes to visit, don't tell her Dad's drinking again." The ingrained need to guard the family secret keeps children apart. It inhibits their ability to make friends and share the confidences critical for growth to adulthood. Both youngsters and adults keep their pain and suffering, and the family secret, hidden, locked inside.

Other factors also made it difficult for children of alcoholics to get help. Until recently, few professionals have been concerned for this underserved group or their problems. Most alcoholism treatment programs and agencies exist to provide help to active alcoholic adults. Usually, they are untrained or uninterested in handling youngsters' problems. Additionally, program staff and financial resources are usually limited. While health insurance policies may cover treatment for alcoholism, most coverage does not include services to family members. Finally, even when children are brought into family treatment, little meaningful attention is paid to them. They are usually included in one or two sessions, if at all. Or, if children try to get help on their own, they are often barred by laws that require parental permission before programs provide them services.

In addition, a myth exists that in order to help children of alcoholics, one must start by helping the alcoholic. This theory is based on a false premise that if parents get help and recover, their children also will be fine. But that is not so. The effect of difficult and frightening situations children live with can carry over into later life as hurtful, permanent scars. Children of alcoholics badly need to recognize and understand their feelings, to sort out the complexities of alcoholic family life, and to know their increased risk for alcoholism and related problems. Furthermore, because only 10 to 15 percent of the nation's alcoholics come into treatment in any one year, their children would be forced to wait a very long time. In fact, most would never get the help they need and deserve.

Another barrier is that other kinds of practitioners outside the alcoholism field have not yet been mobilized or educated to provide services. Because their numbers are so great—28 million—children of alcoholics can be found in all systems and bureaucracies. Yet, most practitioners do not know they are among their caseloads, much less what needs to be accomplished or how to provide appropriate help.

Professional schools teach very little about alcoholism and far less, if anything, about children of alcoholics issues. For example, there has been no curriculum for use by medical students, practicing physicians, hospitals, or on grand rounds. Yet the medical profession could be a prime resource for help. There is an urgent need for educational materials and tools to teach medical practitioners how to identify and provide services for children from alcoholic families.

Another huge group of potential care providers already exists, including teachers, social workers, court personnel, mental health specialists, health care practitioners, youth workers, and human resources professionals. Although efforts to inform them about children of alcoholics are under way, much more needs to be done. Routinely, professionals need to ask questions during intake interviews and to put family alcoholism high on their lists of causes for all physical, emotional, or mental health problems. And we need a new way of thinking. Practitioners need to learn more about children of alcoholics issues. They need to realize parental alcoholism is often not just a symptom but, in fact, the root cause of problems for millions in this country.

This book makes an important contribution in educating the millions of helping professionals who can make improvements for children from alcoholic families. In simple, clear, and direct terms, Bryan E. Robinson, Ph.D., describes their feelings, experiences, how they can be identified and practical ways for practitioners to help. He tells us what we need to know. He also includes a valuable section on resources for working with children of alcoholics, including books, periodicals, audiovisuals, games, and curriculum materials.

Children of alcoholics are prime candidates for education, prevention, intervention, and treatment. They are the key to preventing future alcoholism. In this book, Dr. Robinson provides many of the tools to help professionals reduce the pain and suffering millions now bear. Children of alcoholics are a face of alcoholism that has been anonymous too long. With this volume, their special problems and needs can become visible to the sensitive, caring professional and help can be provided, at last.

Acknowledgments

I want to acknowledge a number of people without whose help my words would never have seen the printed page. I have dedicated this book to the children and staff at the Randolph Clinic, who have nurtured me and helped me grow enormously. Through my work at the clinic, the staff and children have given me much more than I could ever return. I appreciate the administrative support of Henry Finch, executive director, and Bettie Dibrell, clinical administrator. Thanks to Mebane Dowd, Candace Flanagan, and Katherine Townsend for their patient assistance as I learned the ropes and for making me feel at home.

I appreciate the contributions of Lorraine Penninger, who gave me hours of time with computer searches and other library support. I extend a heartfelt thanks to Debbie Turbyfill, Bettie Dibrell, Kathryn Smith, Trina Cassell, Andrea Kepley, Judy Watson, and Patti Young for contributing case material for this book and all the anonymous children in treatment who shared their past experiences living with chemically addicted parents.

Gratitude is also extended to Mebane Dowd, Mickey Estridge, Jamey McCullers, Dr. Patsy Skeen, Linda Hamilton, Lauren Stayer, and Glenda Loftin for reading drafts of the manuscript and giving me valuable feedback. My appreciation to Judy Lynn for taking the photograph on the back cover of the book, and to Barbara Jordan and Lauren Stayer for their help in manuscript preparation. Special recognition is given to Vicky White, who shared her gold mine of resources and was so generous with her valuable time. I also want to specially thank Mary Williams, who was instrumental in fostering my personal and relationship growth and to Jamey McCullers for getting me started in my recovery.

My colleagues at the University of North Carolina have continued to nourish me with encouragement and with moral and administrative support: Dr. Bobbie Rowland, professor of Child and Family Development; Dr. Mary Thomas Burke, chair of the Department of Human Services; and Dr. Harold W. Heller, dean of the College of Education and Allied Professions.

I wish to thank Migs Woodside, president of the Children of Alcoholics

Foundation in New York City, who agreed to read the manuscript and contribute a foreword to this book. Finally, I thank Dr. Claudia Black for her inspiration and cooperation in allowing me to use some of her material, and the staff at Lexington Books—especially my editor Margaret Zusky—whose vision and enthusiasm helped me get the many drafts of this manuscript into print.

Before Reading This Handbook:
The Children of Alcoholics
Information Test (COAT)

Before reading this book, answer true or false to the following statements about children of alcoholics. Respond to the statements *before* and *after* your reading to see if your thinking has changed. After you have completed the book, check the appendix at the back for the answers and for information on computing and interpreting your score.

True   False

_____ _____ 1. There are an estimated two million children of alcoholics in the United States.

_____ _____ 2. While children can be affected by parental alcoholism, the effects generally are not long-lasting.

_____ _____ 3. Children usually get better once their alcoholic parents stop drinking or enter a treatment program.

_____ _____ 4. Reared in homes fraught with problems, children of alcoholics tend to be repelled by overindulgence in drugs or alcohol, or overeating or overworking.

_____ _____ 5. It is not a bad idea for kids to help parents stop drinking if they are willing to take some stress off parents that may be preventing them from stopping drinking.

_____ _____ 6. It is easy to spot children from alcoholic homes because the effects of alcoholism are pretty much the same.

_____ _____ 7. It is unlikely that children would blame themselves for their parents' drinking problems.

_____ _____ 8. Upbringing in alcoholic households is not as inconsistent and unpredictable as most people think.

_____ _____ 9. Parent-child relationships are actually closer in alcoholic homes than in nonalcoholic homes.

_____ _____ 10. Because of a rough home life, children of alcoholics ordinarily look outside the home for close and trusting friendships and intimate relationships.

_____ _____ 11. A common myth is that alcohol abuse and child abuse usually go hand in hand.

_____ _____ 12. Poor school performance is unrelated to parental alcoholism.

_____ _____ 13. Given an opportunity, children of alcoholics are likely to talk to teachers or counselors about their parents' alcoholism, since they have few outlets at home.

_____ _____ 14. One helpful approach for children of alcoholics is to minimize the bad things at home and help them look on the bright side.

_____ _____ 15. Generally, preschool children from alcoholic homes are easier to spot than older kids because they are less inhibited.

_____ _____ 16. School personnel recognize most children of alcoholics because they have problems in school or become delinquent.

_____ _____ 17. As grownups, children raised in alcoholic homes are likely to enter jobs that deal with things instead of people or their problems.

_____ _____ 18. Alcohol and drug treatment programs in this country generally have special programs for children of alcoholics.

_____ _____ 19. Adults brought up in alcoholic homes tend to abstain from alcohol and drug abuse and to avoid friendships and marriages where alcohol is involved.

_____ _____ 20. Armed with proper information, practitioners can help children gain control over their parents' alcoholism.

Introduction: The Little Hostages

There are an estimated 28 million children of alcoholics in the United States—seven million of whom are under eighteen years of age (Russell, Henderson & Blume 1985). The approximately 21 million adult children of alcoholics (ACOAs) are finding that even though they have left home and established their own families, they are still suffering from their alcoholic upbringing. During recent years, media attention has focused on ACOAs and an avalanche of self-help books and support groups has emerged. Services for adults are more readily available and they are free to choose from a variety of help options.

But the seven million children who are dependent on grownups to make decisions for them have few choices. They are hostages of alcoholism in which they are forced to live in misery and despair. They are hostages of one or both parents who do not know they are alcoholic or deny it. And worst of all, they are hostages of a society in which they have few services available to them. Overlooked, ignored, hidden, silent, forgotten, neglected. Every adjective in the dictionary has been used to describe society's negligence. As responsible adults look the other way, the little hostages spend their youth struggling to survive the psychological battleground of their own families. It is utterly impossible for a child to escape a chemically dependent family unscathed. Hostage children draw their battle lines, erect barricades, and fight to survive the incredible odds of a powerful adult world. They are frequently ambushed by abrupt alcoholic mood swings when they least expect it. They are crippled by the psychological warfare of mixed messages, inconsistency, unpredictability, betrayal, and deception. They are emotionally battered and bruised by the violence they witness, and many suffer the scars of physical and sexual abuse. Practically all suffer the psychological wounds of shell shock and battle fatigue, and as adults, have the same symptoms of Post Traumatic Stress Disorder as soldiers of war (Cermack 1985).

All children in the family contribute their part to survive the waging war. The oldest children usually become the war heroes (family heroes), the little generals who plan the survival strategies, give the orders, and even make it look as if they are winning the war. The second children are the foot soldiers (scapegoats), waging hand-to-hand combat on the front lines. They advance against the enemy and frequently carry their battle outside the home into school and society. Middle children aren't much help because they get lost in combat and are missing in action (lost children). Last children typically serve as relief. They enter the battle front to entertain the troops. Their comic relief and clowning around helps family members temporarily forget about their troubles (mascot).

The sooner intervention occurs, the more hope there is for the little hostages. As professionals, we cannot fight the battle for them, but we can be their allies. This book is about them and about how significant adults who have contact with these youngsters on a regular basis can give them the ammunition they need to free themselves from their plight.

In my work with children of alcoholics, I became aware of the need for a book that helps practitioners understand the impact of chemically dependent parents upon their offspring. What emerged was a handbook that addresses questions and concerns of teachers, counselors, social workers, nurses, public health workers, physicians, health educators, the clergy, school administrators, psychiatrists, psychologists, and practitioners in the chemical dependency field.

This book is a synthesis of my clinical work with children of alcoholics in an outpatient treatment center, my life as a child of an alcoholic, and my experience in Al-Anon and Adult Children of Alcoholics groups. It combines scientific knowledge with my own personal experiences and actual case studies drawn from clinical practice. The case studies are based on real children of alcoholics in recovery. The names of all children have been changed to protect their anonymity. In some instances I have used composite examples of several children to ensure privacy and confidentiality.

My decision to write a book about children of alcoholics is a meaningful communion of my personal and professional lives. It is a culmination of having lived in an alcoholic family and having worked for twenty years in the helping professions as a teacher, counselor, family researcher, therapist, and professor of child and family development. I wanted to share my personal experiences in hopes that my alcoholic upbringing can be transformed into a positive experience for millions of other children who live in chemically dependent families. There are still many practitioners in all professions who do not understand alcoholism and the devastating effects it can have on kids.

This book is an outgrowth of my desire to help practitioners understand the family disease concept of alcoholism, how the disease is transmitted to children, and what interventions can break this deadly cycle. The aim is to help those who might not otherwise know what to look for and what to do when they know a child lives in a chemically dependent household. I hope this book will help professionals touch the lives of children in need as I once was and ultimately improve services to children of alcoholics everywhere.

1
Living and Surviving in an Alcoholic Home

> Most of their skirmishes were like games of ringolevio, with the souls
> of their children serving as the ruined captured flags in their cam-
> paigns of attrition. Neither [Mother nor Father] considered the poten-
> tial damage when struggling over something as fragile and unformed
> as a child's life.
>
> —Pat Conroy, *Prince of Tides*

Case 1–1

All about Me: Confessions of a Ringmaster

Flames engulfed our tiny wood-frame house. I was five years old. I remember standing, paralyzed by fear, as the fire roared and swelled. My older
sister and I huddled together in terror as neighbors worked frantically to
retrieve household belongings from the raging inferno. A gas kitchen stove
had exploded, I heard someone say. Minutes before I had witnessed flames
leaping up the kitchen wall and my mother's sharp demands for me to hurry
for sand as she desperately tried to douse them. The fire continued to rage
out of control until our house burned to the ground. In many ways that fire
symbolized my entire childhood. The volatility, rage, and chaos of the burning house was a prelude to what was to come in the next five years as my
father became progressively sicker from the disease of alcoholism.

Within two years my hard-working and resourceful father had managed
to finance the rebuilding of that house on the same plot of land where it had
burned. But the wonderful memories in the old house burned along with our
personal belongings. My dad began to drink outside the house at first. Then
he began hiding beer and liquor bottles around the house. Eventually, he
started drinking in the open at home, despite my mother's bitter protests, and
finally began to stay out drinking all night.

On weekends my little sister and I waited for our father outside the movie
theater as the marquee darkened, the sidewalks emptied of people, and the

street traffic hushed. Underneath the big-screen excitement of James Dean and Marilyn Monroe, a ten-year-old boy's worst fear had come true. Dad had abandoned us once again. We either walked the three-mile trek in the dark or the police took us home. I preferred the walk because riding in the patrol car scared and embarrassed me. I always felt like I had done something wrong, and I didn't want neighbors and friends to see the officers pull up in front of my house. Many repetitions of these nights forced me into the care-taker role of my younger sister. Sometimes she would cry and, although I wanted to, I had to make her think I was in charge. I was scared and mad because of the cold and the dark, empty streets. My feelings of abandonment were expressed through anger that camouflaged deeper emotions of hurt and rejection.

Saturdays would be different, we convinced ourselves, because that was the day we always went into town to buy things. By the time we would get inside the department stores to try on outfits or shop for special things, Dad would be stumbling and slurring his words. The stares from clerks and other shoppers would embarrass me so badly I wanted to disappear. At restaurants he would humiliate us by loud and obnoxious behaviors. He would insult our waiters, knock over glasses of water, or drag his coat sleeve through his rice and gravy. I was embarrassed by the way he behaved and was afraid people wouldn't like me because of it. He seemed to care more for his bottle than he did for his family. That made my sense of self-worth nosedive. I reasoned that if he couldn't remember to pick me up at the movies, then I must not be very important. I became shy and withdrawn and felt all alone. I bottled my feelings up inside and never let anybody know how bad I felt.

Things got progressively worse between my parents. They had explosive arguments and violent physical fights. That's when I took center stage, trying to stabilize an out-of-control family. I refereed verbal bouts that lasted for hours, hoping and praying they wouldn't hurt or kill each other. My house was an arsenal of weapons. Kitchen knives, dishes, frying pans, knickknacks, mirrors, pictures off the wall, hair brushes—even furniture—were heaved, thrown, slung, and slammed during weekly angry outbursts between my parents. It became routine for me to stand between my father's threatening fist and defiant stare and my mother's raised arm. I tried to conceal the family battle from neighbors by closing doors and windows and drawing all the cur-tains in the house. I cleared tables of fragile figurines, hid breakable items, and removed wall hangings to prevent their destruction during the domestic war.

Sweeping up shattered glass, plastic, and debris became a weekly ritual in the aftermath. My sister and I were left to survive as best we could on our own in a world we didn't understand. Our house became a battleground, and we became the spoils of war. I became ringmaster of our family circus—the protector, the peacemaker, the referee, the family hero—in short, the one who ran the show. Although I couldn't stop the violence, I could control the scenario so that neighbors wouldn't see, the house wouldn't be destroyed, and no one would be killed or sent to the hospital or prison. It was a role no ten-year-old child would choose; it was one I took by default, out of necessity, out of a will to survive.

I continued to carry my role of ringmaster into adulthood although I no longer lived in a chaotic family. After years of seeing my parents out of control, I began to deplore any situation in which people could not control themselves. I learned very early to always be in control. As a grownup, the need to control everything and everyone around me became an obsession. Things had to be done my way or not at all. But the old survival skills that saved me as a child no longer worked as an adult and caused me many problems in my interpersonal relationships at work, at home, and at play. I carried my ringmaster role into my work and became a workaholic. I received my self-worth from work and it became my life. Through years of hard self-inventory and the help of Al-Anon and Adult Children of Alcoholics groups, I gained insight into my feelings and perceptions. I realized that I didn't have to continue on the same self-destructive course of my alcoholic upbringing. Using my childhood background as a transformational experience from which to learn, I began to reinterpret my life in a much more positive and constructive way. As a recovering adult child of an alcoholic, I have discovered, through extensive personal inventory and hard work, that life can be quite satisfying.

—Bryan Robinson

Living and Surviving in an Alcoholic Home

Many politicians, writers, comedians, and entertainers (for example, Ronald Reagan, Carol Burnett, Jonathan Winters, Chuck Norris, and Suzanne Somers) are children of alcoholics; the shorthand term is COA. Many COAs discover that, as adults, they are reliving the same destructive patterns of their families of origin. Anywhere from forty to fifty percent become alcoholics themselves; others develop eating disorders or become work-addicted, as I did. One reason for this is that COAs do not know what a healthy family is supposed to be like. They do not know what normal is. Because of their wretched early family life, they develop unrealistic expectations of the ways families function. Many times they develop a fairy tale image and when the dream isn't fulfilled, they feel like they have failed.

As a child, my vision of what a family should be like came from the television shows I watched—"Leave It to Beaver" and "Father Knows Best." I dreamed of living in a beautiful house like the Cleavers or the Andersons on a quiet and shady tree-lined street. There would be peace and tranquility and everyone would smile and talk instead of frown or yell. I would live happily ever after. Needless to say, these unrealistic expectations are sources of trouble in adulthood for anyone who expects families to be so perfect.

As you can tell from my story, the drinking parent is not the only family member who suffers from alcoholism. Children are the innocent, unseen victims. They suffer slowly and methodically every day they live in a chemically dependent family. The longer they live in the disease, the stronger grip it takes and the longer and more difficult the reversal process. Although for years treatment efforts were directed exclusively at the alcoholic parent and spouse, there is growing recognition that the entire family is affected by the disease and that all family members need treatment. Still, children of alcoholic parents continue to be the most neglected family members in terms of diagnosis and treatment.

The codependency operating in alcoholic families hampers children's efforts to separate from their parents and grow into mature, individual human beings. The sooner practitioners can recognize the problem and intervene, the quicker these negative effects can be circumvented. For intervention to be effective, however, practitioners must fully understand the family disease concept of alcoholism.

Alcoholism as a Family Disease

Alcoholism is a family disease—one that affects every member in a devastating way. Thinking of the family unit as a system helps to better understand the disease concept. Suppose I wanted to know how the cardiovascular system works (Flake-Hobson, Robinson & Skeen 1983). I might go to a medical laboratory, locate a heart and the attached blood vessels, then carefully dissect and study them. In this way I would learn something about the basic structure of the cardiovascular system, that the heart has four chambers and a number of valves. But I would still not know how these chambers and valves work because the heart would not be functioning. Only by studying the cardiovascular system while it is functioning in a living person would I see how the chambers and valves pump blood through the body. I cannot know what happens to the heart when a person is running, for example, without seeing the cardiovascular system in relationship to the whole body system. This wholistic approach informs me that, while running, the muscles of the body require more oxygen than they do at rest and the heart beats faster to supply oxygen. In other words, the total body system is affected by the running and must change to adjust to it.

The same is true of an alcoholic family. Practitioners cannot understand fully what happens to a child of an alcoholic parent without understanding the interworkings of that total family system. You must look at the family composite because each member, as part of a functioning system, is interdependent on the other. As the family works together to run smoothly, any change in one part of the family will result in changes in the other parts. A family system will always try to keep itself balanced. Alcoholic families alter how they function to accommodate the alcoholic's drastic behavior changes. As the alcoholic (also known as the dependent) gets out of kilter, the whole family is thrown off balance and must shift the way it typically functions to survive:

> Alcoholism does not burst into the family as would a heart attack; rather, it creeps slowly and silently until the time when it is finally detected and then, hopefully, faced by the family. But, by that time, it has left a mark on each family member. (Bowles 1968, 1062)

Janet is a case in point. As she continues her alcoholic binges, Janet becomes dependent upon other family members to assume her former responsibilities that helped glue the family together. She doesn't show up for work; laundry doesn't get done; meals are unprepared. Husband Sam begins putting her to bed when she collapses in the living room; he calls Janet's boss and tells him she has the flu; he straightens the previous night's mess before the kids come downstairs in the morning. As Sam scurries out the door late for work, he tells his oldest son Jamey to let Mom sleep and to help out by cooking breakfast and getting baby sister off to school, like a big boy.

As his mom's drinking continues, ten-year-old Jamey is cooking all the meals, doing the laundry, and essentially rearing baby sister while Dad takes care of Mom. The whole family system has shifted to compensate for the instability of Mom's alcoholism. Because of the denial that is such an integral part of alcoholism, members do not know the disease is eating insidiously away at the family's fabric. Everyone covers for Mom to protect the family secret, and they cannot recognize the disease for what it is.

As alcoholism progresses, the whole family becomes progressively sicker, too. Everything revolves around the dependent parent, whose behavior dictates how other family members interact inside and outside the family. Each family member adapts to the dependent's behavior by developing behaviors that cause the least amount of personal stress (Wegscheider 1976). The functioning of all family members shifts and worsens to compensate for the illness.

Because parental alcoholism is a secret within and outside of the family, children are made partners in the family's denial that a parent is drinking (Woodside 1986). It is in response to the disease of alcoholism that family members unconsciously play a role that counterbalances the alcoholic's behavior and keeps the family going.

Survival Roles in Alcoholic Families

Not all children grow up to be ringmasters like me. But every child in an alcoholic home takes on some role or combination of roles simply to survive. These roles, while appearing to function effectively in childhood, become a noose around the child's neck as he or she grows into adulthood. Working for years with chemically dependent persons and their families, Sharon Wegscheider (1976, 1979) identified the major roles that family members play in coping with chemical addictions.

These roles, each different from the others, serve the same purpose: to disguise the disease of alcoholism. Untrained eyes have difficulty detecting the disease because they get sidetracked by the roles family members play. The roles distract them from the real problems and feelings hidden behind the facade. The roles serve as a communal protection system, so the family can continue to function and individual members can achieve some security and stability for themselves. Meanwhile, the disease continues to operate incognito.

The Chief Enabler

The chief enabler is usually the alcoholic's spouse or parent. As her disease progresses, Janet becomes more dependent upon Sam, who is the enabler in this case. The duties and obligations of the dependent are transferred to the enabler, whose role is to provide responsibility within the family system. The enabler smoothes out the rough edges created by the dependent's drinking and makes everything appear okay on the surface. Sam, for instance, puts Janet to bed when she passes out, cleans up her mess, lies to her boss, and instructs the children to assume their mother's duties. As Sam protects his wife and compensates for her loss of control, he in effect enables her disease to continue. For this reason, the nonalcoholic parent is often referred to as the *codependent*.

The Family Hero

Although I called myself a ringmaster, the role that I adopted in my family is more commonly known as the family hero. There is one in every alcoholic home. The hero is usually the oldest child, who feels responsible for the family pain, as I did, and works hard to make things better. Claudia Black, who has identified role patterns that resemble those of Wegscheider, calls this the super responsible child who tries to keep the family balanced despite the odds (see box on page 8). The family hero is determined to prove to the world that everything is normal at home. My job as a child was to perform so well that others would have to think that things were okay for me to be functioning so effectively. Like all heroes, I provided self-worth to my family, yet underneath the facade, deepseated feelings of inadequacy and poor self-esteem predominated. Jamey is fast on his way to becoming the family hero.

At school, heroes excel in academics, athletics, or both. Practitioners often fail to assist these kids because they appear to be resilient and independent of a need for help (see chapter 2). Outwardly, they appear to have it all. They may be the most attentive, the most dependable, the smartest, and the most popular child in school. They follow the rules, always finish their schoolwork in the allotted time, and often are leaders in school governments and extracurricular activities. They can be the president of the student council, the star quarterback, or the homecoming queen [as was Sharon Wegscheider (1985)]. Because achievement and competition are so highly valued in our society, family heroes usually go unnoticed and, in fact, are rewarded for their super achievements. This is not to say, however, that all successful or competent children are COAs. It is the *overdeveloped* sense of accomplishment, responsibility, and perfectionism for which practitioners must look. These kids never know what it is like to play and relax and they become serious little adults. Their childhoods are filled with grave issues (such as "I wonder if Mom will be okay while I'm at school today") that are usually reserved for adulthood. While COAs dwell on their parent's drinking and welfare, their friends are playing and enjoying the carefree world of childhood.

Nina, one of two siblings in my COA treatment group, was ten years old going on thirty-five. She took care of everything around her house because her single mother was an active alcoholic. Nina had been making breakfast for herself and her little sister and getting them both off to school each morning ever since she could remember. She had great difficulty benefiting from

Table 1–1
The Survival Roles and Settings of Children of Alcoholics

Home	School	Work	Social Settings
Hero (responsible child)	Class Star	Workaholic	Social good guy/ good girl
Scapegoat (acting out child)	Problem Child	Troublemaker	Social Misfit
Lost Child (adjuster)	Class Isolate	Loner	Social Recluse
Mascot	Class Clown	Practical Joker	Stand-up Comic
Placater	Class Helper	Problem solver	Caretaker

Adopted from Wegscheider (1976) and Black (1982).

Being Responsible, Adjusting, Placating, and Acting Out

Claudia Black (1982) has found in her work with COAs that most of them adopt one or a combination of three role patterns (the responsible one, the adjuster, and the placater) that make them appear to be functioning well in early childhood.

The *responsible child* is similar to the family hero in that this role gives harmony and stability to the household. Like Jamey, the responsible child is usually the eldest, who assumes responsibilities for self and other family members. This child takes on such adult-like obligations as putting a drunk father to bed after he passes out on the front porch steps or checking little sister to make sure she has on socks that match, so people won't know the laundry isn't getting done. The responsible child, who looks after younger siblings, becomes the parent child to those brothers and sisters. Jamey is so responsible that school is a breeze. He is the little sergeant who leads the class—the one the teachers and classmates look to for decisions and leadership. His attitude is, "Yeah! I can handle it. I can handle anything!" As a grownup, Jamey more than likely will have difficulty trusting, being intimate, and relinquishing control.

The *adjuster* is the middle or younger child, who simply flows with the tides without thinking or feeling. Children like Amy usually have an older responsible sibling to do their thinking and care for them. They find it easier to follow directions and to accept and handle whatever happens. Amy can adjust to anything that comes her way because she doesn't make an emotional investment in anything. If she doesn't get emotionally involved, she doesn't get hurt. Her attitude is, "I can't do anything about it anyway." On the outside Amy appears flexible and adaptable. But on the inside, she feels low self-worth and loss of control of her life (I will discuss these two issues in more detail in chapter 2). Amy might also be called a lost child because she gives no clues to what is going on inside and never causes anyone an ounce of trouble. She does not let others know anything about her and generally gets overlooked at home, in school, and at play.

The *placater* is the family comforter. Louise takes responsibility for the family's grief, pain, and emotional well-being. Ignoring her own needs, Louise comforts others and tries to make them feel better. Attempting to fix everyone's emotional problems, she strives to ease Mom's sadness, brother's fears, sister's embarrassment, and Dad's anger. The placater is usually the most sensitive child in the family. Preoccupation with the emotions of others, outwardly at least, seems to help Louise lessen her own tension and pain, which continue to seethe beneath the placater facade. Now in her mid-twenties, Louise says:

> I don't know who I am unless I'm taking care of somebody. I'm going through an identity crisis now because for the first time in my life, there's nobody for me to take care of. My father just died, my brother's in a home for troubled boys, and I don't know what to do with myself. Here I am and I have myself to think about for the first time in my life, and I don't know what to do with it.

In contrast to these three roles that bring positive attention to children and their families, Black designates a fourth role, paralleling the scapegoat, that draws negative reactions. The *acting-out child* shows inner hurt by causing trouble at home and at school. Delinquency, unplanned pregnancies, and chemical abuse are several ways the pain is transformed and released as anger. Acting-out children can be found in correctional facilities, mental hospitals, and other societal institutions at some point in their lives. They are the ones who get the most attention and help from our society because they demand it by inappropriate behaviors.

the program because she forfeited her own needs in favor of her six-year-old sister. Her sister clung to her during group, and Nina spent most of her time parenting and protecting the little girl. During fun activities, she reprimanded her for "acting silly" or "going the wrong way in a game." She was always on the watch and chastised her for such minor infractions as taking two crackers at snacktime, instead of one. She could not relax and play or enjoy the art and puppets because she felt it was her duty to keep everything on even keel. Nina was always on guard. Once when another child complimented her sister's painting, Nina snapped, "Don't make fun of her picture!" Dismayed, the other child became angry and hurt. Nina was merely protecting her sister from what she thought had been a criticism. She spent enormous amounts of energy trying to control and change her sister. She once told me why she did not laugh or play at home: "Sometimes you don't play around an alcoholic because like my mom, she'll think you're laughing at her, and she'll knock your head off."

Once they grow up and enter the work force, family heroes encounter the greatest difficulty with their roles. They often become compulsive workers and workaholics. They become highly successful in their chosen careers and, like the corporate executive, quickly climb the ladder of success. But they pay a huge price for their overdeveloped sense of responsibility and accomplishment. Obsessed with the need to control and manage people and things around them, heroes put their own feelings and needs on hold.

Socially, they have difficulty being intimate and expressing their feelings to another person. Unable to express or identify emotions, heroes find it difficult to trust other people. They may have few or no friends and immerse themselves in their jobs to fulfill relationship needs. Heroes beat their heads against an imaginary wall to change other people and situations that are beyond their control. They become resentful and bitter adults, angry that their childhoods have passed them by. They become uptight, rigid, and inflexible and panic in spontaneous and unpredictable situations.

The Scapegoat

Harley is the scapegoat—the family's target for its problems and frustrations. Following behind the family hero is such an insurmountable task that Harley learns he cannot compete with the older sibling. He takes attention off the family by internalizing family frustrations and getting into trouble. He gets into fights and trouble with the legal system, uses drugs, or runs away from home. By acting out his family's pain, Harley—not the family—becomes the focus of the problem.

Generally in a group setting, the scapegoat will be the most disruptive, the one child that teachers never forget. Unlike family heroes, who are remembered for good things, scapegoats are remembered for the bad. How could I ever forget the twelve-year-old COA that I taught fifteen years ago? He started a fire under the propane gas container, nearly blowing up the mobile classroom it heated plus the thirty kids inside. How can I possibly forget him for the headaches he gave me, disappearing out of the room every time I turned my back, not to mention the many bloody noses and scrapes he gave the other children?

Scapegoats are the ultimate test of a practitioner's patience. Eleven-year-old Harley was usually coming off the walls within five minutes of his arrival at the COA group—pushing and shoving other children and acting out in various ways. Harley has no doors on the inside of his house. His father has removed the doors from their hinges so that the children cannot take refuge in their rooms. Harley said his father hit him, slapped him around, and yelled at him all the time. Harley said that one Christmas morning his father, in a drunken rage, chased him out of the house with a stick. Shirtless and shoeless, the child ran in the snow to a neighbor's house, where he waited for his father to calm down. "We never get any sleep around my house," Harley complained. "My dad comes in at three in the morning, waking everybody up, pulls us out of bed and makes us look at a car he just overhauled or something he just made." Harley was able to verbalize his feelings of anger and fear toward his alcoholic father and to express them in a fingerpainting. Ordinarily, these feelings are masked by a destructive Harley with whom most people are more familiar. After working with him for a period of time, I discovered that underneath his anger, Harley was a very sensitive child.

In the work world, scapegoats can never seem to do anything right. They constantly fail because of self-sabotage. Rather than following company rules, they may take shortcuts and get into trouble with the boss. Unable to get along with others, they involve themselves in destructive squabbles with co-workers. Alcohol and substance abuse may interfere with their job success.

Socially, they are misfits. In his boyhood account of an alcoholic up-bringing, novelist Harry Crews fought with everybody his whole life until he realized he was fighting himself [see Crews (1983)]. Scapegoats have diffi-culty functioning in social situations and receive social disapproval because they behave in socially unacceptable ways. As a result of their poor social skills, they become outcasts. Outwardly social jerks, scapegoats are inwardly lonely, hurt, afraid, and angry.

The Lost Child

Six-year-old Shelia has already become the lost child in her family. She is always on the outside of family squabbles, crouched in a corner playing with her doll or lying in her bed staring at the ceiling, daydreaming. Remaining in the background, Shelia never causes any trouble for the family. Quiet and undemanding, her role is to provide relief for the family. Shelia has isolated herself from the family and lives in a world of hurt and loneliness.

Lost children are often middle children who do not know where they fit in their families or at school. As adults, they do not know their place in the work world and world at large. They are the unnoticed children whom nobody sees and nobody remembers. Teachers especially have difficulty remembering these children because they demand neither positive nor nega-tive attention. They are neither troublemakers nor class leaders. Shelia spends her time on the fringes of class activities with few friends and few interactions. She is left alone and overlooked by parents, the educational sys-tem, and society in general.

Ten years later, at age sixteen, Shelia seems cut off from the COA group and spends as much time as she can by herself on the sidelines. As we talk about feelings when a parent drinks, Shelia remains quiet and listens atten-tively to the other children but never utters a sound. Given a chance to speak, Shelia says it makes her angry when her mother drinks. Although she says she is angry, she does not sound angry and has difficulty expressing it. Her verbalization of anger is emotionless—so deep down that she can not tap into it. She tells of a time her drunk mother smashed her tennis racket into a million pieces. Her father was furious because he paid so much for the racket in hopes of bringing his daughter out of her shell. Shelia's mother denied any wrongdoing and blamed her daughter for it. Ultimately, Shelia's father believed her mother's version of the story and punished the child not only for vandalizing, but also for lying to him. The well-intended act of purchasing the tennis racket backfired, sending Shelia further into her shell. Lost children deal with their feelings by locking them away inside so deeply that they are hard to retrieve. Sometimes they turn their anger inward and hurt themselves through suicide or drug abuse.

At work, lost children keep to themselves. They are always on the out-side looking in. They say little and prefer to work alone. They may have diffi-culty being a team player. They always do as they are told and never make waves. Co-workers eventually begin to leave them alone and often forget to include them in group activities. Employers may overlook them at raise and promotion time.

Sometimes they can be social wallflowers and spend their leisure time outside of large groups. They may have few friends and few long-term relationships. They prefer activities they can do alone or with few people. Outwardly shy and withdrawn, lost children feel lonely, hurt, and inade-quate.

The Mascot

Nine-year-old Jack is the family mascot. He takes the spotlight off the fam-ily's problem and puts it on himself by cutting up, being cute, and acting silly. His role is to lighten the family's burden by diversion through humor and fun. Jack's jovial nature is clearly a cover-up for the opposite feelings of fear and sadness that he harbors from his alcoholic father's daily verbal and physical abuses.

Mascots tend to be youngest children, often called the baby of the family. They make light of serious situations and try to keep the tone upbeat, every-body happy, and nothing too serious. Mascots are perhaps the most difficult children to reach because they have an impenetrable veil of laughter. Jack is the class clown, the center of attention who will go to any extreme for a laugh. He's the child who is not a serious problem but one whom a teacher might label a "nuisance." His clowning around may be disruptive at times and teachers may find themselves constantly saying to him, "settle down" or "buckle down and get serious" or "this is no laughing matter."

One night in the COA group, Jack made a joke of a time when he was small and his alcoholic father threw him against a wall. Despite the fact that he suffered a broken leg, Jack giggled through the entire story. He talked of how his drunken father embarrassed him in front of his friends who, in turn, made fun of his father when he was drunk. The only way Jack could talk

Figure 1–1. A nine-year-old girl drew what it felt like to be the lost child in her alcoholic family.

about the ordeals was to pretend he was unafraid and unbothered by them. I told him that getting smashed against a wall must have been a very scary and painful thing and that most people wouldn't think that it was funny. When I asked him if he laughed when it happened, his smile vanished and

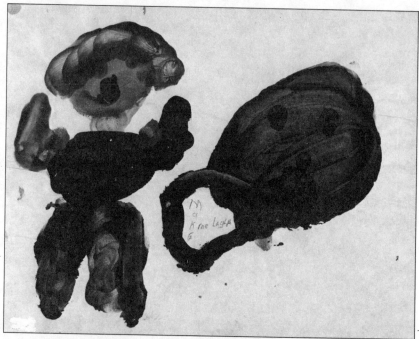

Figure 1–2. An eleven-year-old boy represented his role of family mascot by a Halloween pumpkin that demanded, "Make me laugh."

he whispered under his breath, "No, I cried." Practitioners need to know that the class clown who cuts up and laughs on the outside is crying on the inside.

At work, mascots are considered practical jokers, company buffoons. Everyone enjoys being around them because they keep everyone laughing, but nobody takes them seriously. They may even be viewed with suspicion by their employers. Jack's employer, for example, might wonder if he takes his work seriously or if he is reliable enough to make important decisions and handle responsibilities. Other family mascots turn their family roles into successes. Carol Burnett clowned her way from an alcoholic home to fame and fortune by becoming a comic in the entertainment industry [see Burnett (1986)].

Socially, mascots are the life of the party and everyone clusters around them. Like stand-up comics, they are always full of wisecracks and jokes to entertain others. Underneath, however, mascots have difficulty handling stress. They are sad, afraid, insecure, and alone. Their role as court jester keeps them out of serious and committed relationships. Chemical dependency is often their substitute for intimacy.

Tips for Practitioners

The four survival roles are often called "false selves" (Wood, 1984, 1987). They represent an unconscious attempt by the child to deal with the parents' failure to parent and to conceal and protect important aspects of inner reality. The false selves of superiority (hero), aggression (scapegoat), withdrawal (lost child), and wit (mascot) overtly contradict and deny the real covert feelings of vulnerability, need, and damaged self-esteem. The survival roles that COAs play become a rigid part of their personalities and serve as roadblocks to their recovery. Ironically, the roles serve two competing purposes. They provide a means through which children can survive the disease of alcoholism, while simultaneously camouflaging the disease from those in helping positions.

Children of alcoholics are masters at camouflaging their heartache. Noted authority Claudia Black (1982) has said children of alcoholic parents learn three unwritten rules very early: Don't talk, don't trust, and don't feel. My own childhood experience makes it difficult for me to believe the children I have worked with who laugh as they describe their parent's drunken episodes. As a fourteen-year-old boy told me, "When my stepfather comes in drunk, I don't pay him any attention when he talks to me. Now if my mother tells me to go to bed, I'll go."

His sister agreed. "It don't bother me none, because I just ignore it (her stepfather being drunk)."

"If he ever touches me, I'll knock him out," the young brother proclaims.

Even in special groups for COAs, the children's defenses are strong. The hurt and pain are buried so deeply inside it is difficult for them to reach it and the barriers are hard for counselors to penetrate. So often practitioners deal with anger, defiance, indifference, or laughter and smiles that camouflage a festering sore. Once they recognize the various roles, however, practitioners can help COAs remove false selves that stand in the way of recovery and help children face who they really are.

Helping the Family Hero

- Be on the lookout for "overly competent" children who appear to be functioning at their maximum. Make sure these potential family heroes get as much attention as other children who may have an easier time of showing their needs or asking for what they need. Helping super responsible children balance their lives between work and play is a worthy and realistic goal.

- Insist that these kids do not sacrifice or forgo potential benefits derived from activities, experiences, or interactions because they are too busy putting others' needs before their own.

- Continue to present kids with challenges that match their developmental abilities, but help them learn not to take on too much. Avoid unusually high expectations and burdening these kids with adult-like responsibilities, even when they are eager to accept them.

- Let them know it is okay to relax and do nothing. Reassure them that they do not always have to be producing to please someone else and that it is acceptable to please themselves, which can include doing nothing.

- Validate these kids for "who they are" and not just for "what they do." Provide unconditional support for them as individuals—not support for what they produce or achieve. Let them know you accept them regardless of whether they succeed or fail. Value them and hold them in esteem by letting them know they are special even when they are not producing a concrete object.

- Teach them to develop flexibility by building in spontaneous, spur-of-the-moment activities from time to time.

- Encourage them to identify their true feelings and to express them often in conversations or through creative outlets.

- Provide them with guidance when they must make significant and difficult decisions that parents have left up to them, such as how and where to spend their after-school time, whether to go to the prom with a certain date, or which career to choose.

- Encourage them in their successes and enjoy their accomplishments with them, but let them know it is acceptable to fail and that they do not have to be perfect in everything all the time.

- Be there after a big failure or letdown. Help the child understand and accept that failing is part of being human.

- Make sure they get a chance to play, relax, have fun, and enjoy their childhood with other youngsters their age rather than spend all their time with adults in adult activities. Welcome laughter, giggling, even silliness by building in funny stories or experiences during the day. The drive to achieve, succeed, and please others causes COAs to miss the experience of childhood. Despite behaviors to the contrary, COAs who are family heroes need adult guidance and supervision and time to play, learn, fantasize, and enjoy the rights of childhood. Childhood lays the bedrock for adult lives. Youngsters who have a chance to be children will become healthier, more well-rounded, and are less likely to mourn their losses in adulthood.

Helping the Scapegoat

- Consider the scapegoat's behavior a cry for help and not a personal threat against you.
- Avoid writing the scapegoat off, as there is often a tendency to do. These kids tend to be the least liked of the four roles because their sometimes violent, unlawful, and personally threatening behaviors frequently arouse fear and anger in the adult. Plus, they take the most energy.
- Take a personal inventory of your feelings toward the scapegoat. Give yourself permission to say you have difficulty liking this child, if that is how you honestly feel. Practitioners do not have to like all children the same but they are obligated to treat all children fairly and help them meet their needs.
- Reverse your behavior toward the scapegoat if you harbor negative attitudes. Sometimes you may be so angry or fearful that you find yourself saying and doing negative things to the scapegoat rather than positive things. Chances are a change in you will produce a change for the better in the scapegoat.
- Be honest with your feelings. Having come from an alcoholic home, I found it hard to admit when a child made me angry and to verbalize how I felt. Denying your true feelings only reinforces the dysfunctional denial system in the child's alcoholic family.
- Communicate your feelings to the child. If scapegoats do something to make you mad, let them know it in a caring way. But tell them that you are angry about a specific thing they did, not at them as a person. You are teaching many concepts by using this approach: (1) You are teaching COAs that they do not have to deny their true feelings as they must do at home. (2) You are teaching scapegoats that they can *talk out* their feelings constructively rather than *take them out* on someone else in a destructive way. (3) You are setting an example for mature ways of dealing with strong feelings and directing emotions.
- Avoid being overly strict or punitive with these children and attempt to communicate with the real child underneath.
- Make sure the scapegoat knows what the boundaries are. Spell out clearly for them what the rules and routines are. Reasonable, predictable, yet flexible limits and routines are important to help these children control their own behaviors.
- Take a positive approach by telling them what they are supposed to do and why, not what they are *not* supposed to do. For example, telling a child who is running in the hall, "Walk in the hall, please. You might fall

down and get hurt," gives him the "what" and "why." But merely telling that child "don't run in the hall" emphasizes the negative as well as fails to communicate the message of what you want him to be doing instead.

- Praise the scapegoat for what might seem the most insignificant positive behavior (such as turning in homework, doing one thing you ask, or showing an interest in a lesson even if only for five minutes). These kids need lots of positive attention for behaving appropriately, because most of their feedback from adults tends to be negative.

- Put them in leadership roles in which success can be assured and give them praise for a job well done. Scapegoats frequently have latent leadership abilities waiting to be tapped.

- Help scapegoats identify and express feelings through various outlets: creative activities, dramatic play, or group discussions.

- Encourage them to vent and direct feelings in appropriate ways. You can show them, for example, that it is okay to vent anger or frustration by pounding clay, kicking a tree, or batting a punching bag. But it is not permissible for them to take it out on another child or adult.

- Provide the child with individual attention through a volunteer, parent, or counselor who can work on a one-to-one basis. Both you and the child may need a breather from each other from time to time.

- Encourage them to take part in rigorous, organized sports that serve as outlets for strong emotions as well as avenues for developing positive social relationships, citizenship, and leadership skills.

- Help other children understand the scapegoat as best you can while simultaneously recognizing their feelings and rights. They should not be forced to interact with the scapegoat if they do not want to.

Helping the Lost Child

- Give them a sense of belonging and make sure they know they have an important place in the classroom and that they fit it.

- Capitalize on times when the lost child can be integrated into the larger social group. Avoid pressuring the child to be socially gregarious, however, because all kids need some time to be alone.

- Encourage the lost child to venture into pastimes that require social interaction (such as group problem solving, making a collage, painting a mural, planning a class play) rather than solitude (daydreaming or reading in a quiet corner).

- Display artwork, stories, or other items of interest on bulletin boards to build the child's self-confidence and self-worth.

- Build the child's self-concept by praising the expression of constructive ideas and thoughts.
- Choose a unit of study in which the child might be particularly interested and toward which the child could contribute something of value to the group.
- Help the child identify and express feelings through safe, nonthreatening outlets such as fingerpainting, woodworking, puppets, dictating stories, music, and other art forms.
- Present problem-solving activities and ask for help in finding solutions in ways the child would feel comfortable. Many lost children hide their exceptional intelligence along with everything else, and teachers may never realize the child's potential.
- Construct a sociogram (see chapter 6) to find out who the lost child would most like to work with in the group and the one who would be a good influence. Pair the lost child with the selected child and assign them a project or activity on which they can work cooperatively.
- Keep a checklist of how many times you interact with the lost child or make positive comments to the child. Check it at the end of the day so that you have an ongoing reminder of how you are doing as well as how the child is progressing.

Helping the Mascot

- Give the mascot lots of individual attention and get to know the child on a one-to-one basis.
- Let the child know it is okay to be the real person inside and that people will like the child even when he or she is not telling jokes.
- Help mascots open up by winning their trust. Although they may appear happy-go-lucky, they need a lot of nurturing if they are to trust you enough to drop the mask and expose the true self.
- Use storytelling as a vehicle to let the child know that real feelings are okay. A made-up story about a child who is always laughing on the outside but is crying on the inside can communicate a message to the child in a nonthreatening way.
- Use puppets to act out the clown but also describe the sadness the clown feels inside. Then let the child use the puppets to act out a similar role.
- Engage the child in other creative outlets such as art, music, and crafts.
- Mirror back to the child appropriate reactions and emotions that match the event. Indicate that we laugh at funny things, for example, but we cry

about sad things and we get mad when someone hurts us. If a child laughs when someone is hurt, define the situation for the child and express the feeling in your matter-of-fact voice tone: "That wasn't funny when John fell down. He hurt his leg and it was very painful for him."

- Let older children keep a daily or weekly journal and assure them that no one will see it but you. Tell them they can talk to you about it at any time.

Hope for COAs

Alcoholism is widespread in our society and is one of the most menacing medical and social problems in existence. The natural focus for treatment has been the alcoholic, while the family members have been neglected. The problems in chemically dependent homes cannot be resolved when treatment is provided only for the dependent parent. In most cases there is also a child who suffers quietly and desperately. COAs are the invisible victims of a ravaging illness. One of the biggest myths about alcoholism is that once the alcoholic adult stops drinking, everything else at home will be okay too. If Dad stops drinking, he and Mom will start to get along again and the kids will automatically readjust. Their school grades will improve, they will get along with their teachers and friends, and everybody will live happily ever after. This scenario is truly a myth.

Millions of children who live in alcoholic homes—even for a short period of time—can become trapped in what has been called an infinite loop of self-destructive behavior patterns (Wood 1987). As a child, for example, I learned to take control of everything around me to keep my world from coming unglued when my father drank. Ironically, these acts of self-sabotage bring some sense of predictability to chaotic families and emotions and help COAs survive the disease of alcoholism.

Although the survival roles provide temporary relief from the disease, there comes a point, usually in adulthood, when these roles become obsolete. They no longer provide the payoff they yielded in childhood and, in fact, work against the COA. The dysfunctional nature of the roles becomes ever more obvious. Adult heroes lose themselves in work and have difficulty being intimate and being in relationships with others. The scapegoat gets into all sorts of trouble, becomes a social outcast, and is shunned by others. The lost child becomes a social recluse and withdraws from people and social situations. The mascot is considered a joke—not to be taken seriously. Many COAs play more than one role. A composite of two, three, or even four of the roles may dominate the personalities of some of these children.

After many years of comfort in playing the various roles, COAs have difficulty discarding what has become an integral part of their personalities.

As adults, they are confronted with the pain and confusion of behaviors that no longer serve their original survival function. Instead, carried into adulthood, the roles contribute to their demise. In their anxiety and confusion COAs often attempt to cope with their dilemma through alcohol and other drugs, work, food, sex, and other compulsive forms of behavior (see chapter 3).

The best time for intervention is in childhood before the behavior patterns become overly rigid. Hope for breaking the patterns lies in those practitioners who interact daily with COAs. A mainstream understanding of the disease of alcoholism will enable them to help COAs by working through existing systems and by using the tools and assets already at their disposal. Regardless of whether practitioners are in the business of alcohol rehabilitation, they have a responsibility to the huge and generally neglected, vulnerable population of children from alcoholic homes. By understanding the disease and how kids are affected by it, teachers, counselors, school administrators, social workers, and other professionals can make a difference in the child's recovery.

2
Psychological Adjustment of Children of Alcoholics

Early childhood development within an alcoholic family system constitutes a stress that is clearly *outside the range of human experience usually considered to be normal.* If this statement is not accepted, then one is left believing that parental alcoholism is a normal state of affairs. God help us if we ever get to the point of believing that.
—Timmin Cermak, *A Primer on Adult Children of Alcoholics*

Case 2–1

"As I was getting ready for bed, my mom told me to sleep on the outside of my bedcovers so she wouldn't have to make up the bed. I did what she told me to do. But when my dad came into my room the next morning, he was upset that I slept on top instead of underneath the sheets. I told him what Mom had said, but when he asked her about it, she lied. She denied saying anything like that to me. She was afraid of what Dad would say and do. He didn't say anything to her because he believed her. But he beat me with a belt. Now I don't know who to listen to."

—Rex, age eleven

"My mom bought me a six-hundred-dollar set of drums. One night my grandmother got drunk and slashed them with a knife. They were brand new, too. Naturally, my mom was mad, and so was I. I told her grandmother did it, but grandmother said I was lying and blamed it on me. Mom believed her and punished me for something I didn't do. I hate grandmother for that and I hate my dad more and more as he starts to be like his bitch wife and for leaving me behind with them. He can take everything he bought me and shove it up his ass (especially the jeep). I wish I had never been born."

—Rick, age sixteen

Rick wrote the following poem about his alcoholic grandmother:

> She old and cranky, got white hair,
> She yells at me in her underwear.
> She'll attack you like a crazed bear,
> But come on in, don't be scared.
> She goes through and breaks my things.
> These are actions that anger brings.
> The things you do my family doesn't like.
> So look in the mirror and use your inner sight.
> Think about all the things you've done.
> Figure out why, when I'm around you, I want to run!
>
> —Rick, age sixteen

"My mother was always drunk, and she beat me from the time I was four years old. While she hit me she'd say, 'You're a good little girl.' How could I believe that? I remember she was on the couch and sandwiched me between her feet and the coffee table pushing me hard against it with her feet and the whole time she was telling me one thing and doing another. I remember thinking, "Well, why are you doing that if you think I'm a good girl?"

—Deidre, age twenty-one

Psychological Adjustment of Children of Alcoholics

Betrayal, deception, lies, mixed messages. Sounds like a James Bond thriller, but unfortunately it is much less glamorous than that. These are some of the interactions that occur between alcoholic parents and their children. The opening cases are real-life examples of the kinds of mixed messages children get. In the last chapter, I discussed how COAs develop survival roles in response to the disease of alcoholism. In this chapter I will take you beneath the false selves and examine the profound impact on their psychological development. All kids experience fear, anger, confusion, guilt, embarrassment, and shame. The depth, intensity, and frequency with which COAs experience these emotions are greater than that of most children. Their feelings, personalities, and behaviors are molded more by the fact of alcoholism than by any other (NIAAA 1981). Parental drinking becomes the major driving force in their young lives, and everything revolves around it. Living with an alcoholic parent, it should come as no surprise, can severely damage a child's psychological makeup.

My personal experience with alcoholism and that of hundreds of my clients lead me to agree with physician Timmen Cermak (1985), who compares the lives of COAs to those of psychologically wounded war veterans. Post Traumatic Stress Disorder (PTSD) occurs when veterans have problems readjusting to civilian life. Similar to the stress soldiers experience in battle, life as a COA constitutes stress that lies outside the range of normal human experiences. Symptoms identical to PTSD stalk children into adulthood until they seek the help of understanding that their childhoods were not normal or healthy.

Psychological Battleground

While all children must wrestle with some degree of psychological adjustment as they grow up, the slings and arrows of everyday life carry a sharper sting in alcoholic families. The presence of family conflict, for example, leads to incredible psychological stress and strain on its members. I often use the analogy of an alcoholic home to a psychological battleground. In some ways it is a fight for survival in which it is every man, woman, and child for himself or herself. Children frequently are forced to choose sides against one parent. Sometimes battle lines are drawn between adults and children, and the wounds are swift and sweeping. Ross grumbled that his mother always sided with his drinking father—even when she knew his dad was wrong. Ross saw this as betrayal and internally drew the battle lines: "Me against them." Through walls of anger, he distanced himself from both his parents. Other kids complain that their parents use them as their confidants and try to turn them against the other parent.

Because everyone who lives in it is affected by alcoholism, it is not unusual for COAs to bemoan that the nonalcoholic parent is harder to get along with than the alcoholic. One night eleven-year-old Carlos interrupted the COA group. "I want to know something," he demanded. "Why is my mother so cranky all the time? She's always on me about something—always trying to pick a fight, and she doesn't even drink."

"Does this sound familiar to anyone else?" I asked the group. A resounding affirmation from the other children brought a sigh of relief from Carlos, who learned that he was not alone. Discussing the cranky codependent parent also helped the children understand that it is part of the disease.

Codependent parents often become ill-tempered from battle fatigue. Interviews with nondrinking parents reveal that they feel worried, nervous, and tense because of their spouse's alcoholic behaviors and inadvertently transfer these emotions to their children. Irritable from their own tensions, they often find themselves getting upset with their kids over minor incidents. Some parents try to hide their distraught feelings from their children by suppressing their own problems and attending to their children's needs. Inevitably, this leads to snapping and other temper outbursts that children do not understand (Wilson & Orford 1978).

Codependent parents struggle furiously to make everything appear normal and to keep things functioning as they used to. They become so consumed that sometimes the smallest incident will ignite their temper. The seemingly indifferent attitude they often reflect to their children is, "Just do what you want, but don't bother me." Because all the attention revolves around the alcoholic, however, children feel neglected, unwanted, unloved, and unworthy. "I just want to know what I did wrong," was Carlos's refrain.

The codependent parents will go to any extreme, even psychological warfare, to keep peace in the family. Sometimes they compromise their values, tell lies, and sacrifice their children's happiness. On other occasions, as in the case of Rex, codependents lie to avoid the ire of the alcoholic, while subjecting their own children to it. Other times, as in the case of Rick, alcoholics lie to protect themselves, at the expense of their loved ones. In the more advanced stages of the disease, alcoholics suffer *blackouts*—memory losses while intoxicated that can never be retrieved. In these cases, parents may actually believe they are innocent of the charges.

The Development of Denial

Denial is the most common means alcoholic families use to cope and survive their pain. Ironically, while denial helps families survive, it also helps the disease coexist. As part of their attempts to smooth over family problems, codependents pretend everything is okay and insist that the children perceive things that way too. They accomplish this by invalidating the child's reality: "Your father isn't an alcoholic. He's depressed." Or "Your mother doesn't drink that much." During my own childhood, my mother denied my father's alcoholism by saying, "Your father is not an alcoholic; he's a drunkard."

As codependent parents deny what their children see before their very eyes, the children become confused and have difficulty trusting their own reality. They begin to repress their suspicions and to minimize their feelings about it: "If Mom says so, then things must not be as bad as I had thought." Children often split the drinking parent into a good half and a bad half and downplay the importance of their emotions about their parent's drinking. By age nine, COAs routinely doubt and deny their own perceptions and those of outsiders who try to convince them that a parent has a drinking problem. They deny and lie to their peers to cover up the painful reality with which they are forced to live:

> They are ashamed of their family secret and isolated by it; they feel anger and guilt; they are taught to deny the existence of the problem itself and their own feelings about it; they feel an intense loyalty that would make any revelation a betrayal; and they feel hopeless. (Deutsch 1982, 96)

They even pass the denial on to younger siblings or other family members. A common denial tactic I have observed in COA groups is for older children to invalidate the perceptions of their very young siblings. I have seen older siblings (age ten and older) censure a younger sibling time and time again for revealing family secrets in groups—even when all the children were from alcoholic homes and confidentiality was assured. As his younger sister spoke candidly about her innermost feelings about their family life, eleven-year-old Mallory tried several times to silence her with such nonverbal cues as raised eyebrows and hateful looks. When that did not work, he tried verbal warnings and reprimands, finally resorting to physical threats. It is through the development of denial that alcoholism spreads so that psychologically, alcoholic families develop characteristics that distinguish them from nonalcoholic families.

Psychological Profile of Alcoholic Families

Social scientists, after studying chemically dependent families, have discovered specific patterns of interaction that characterize them differently from chemical-free families. Authorities agree that more conflict and dysfunction occur in alcoholic families than in nonalcoholic ones (Moos & Billings 1982). There are greater numbers of marital disturbances and reports of unhappiness and instability (Schulsinger et al. 1986). Alcoholic families are less cohesive, less organized, less oriented toward intellectual or cultural pursuits, and more conflict-ridden (Clair & Genest 1987). The prevalence of more emotional problems in alcoholic families is attributed to frequent quarrels between parents, lack of care for the children, and the entire family's preoccupation with the alcoholic's irresponsible behaviors (Venugopal 1985). COAs are raised in more disrupted families characterized by more parental arguments, higher divorce rates, and premature parental and sibling death (Black, Bucky & Wilder-Padilla 1986).

The child-rearing practices of alcoholic fathers, compared to nonalcoholic fathers, are more likely to include ridicule, rejection, harshness, and neglect (Udayakumar, Mohan, Shariff, Sekar & Eswari 1984). Similarly, the attitudes of alcoholic mothers, compared to nonalcoholic mothers, tend to be less accepting, more rejecting, disciplinarian, or overprotecting, and they have a significantly greater degree of conflicting attitudes (Krauthamer 1979).

In her landmark study of 115 COAs between ages ten and sixteen, Margaret Cork (1969) found most families lacking solidarity and in constant turmoil. None of the teenagers in her interviews rated their families as "normal." Sibling relationships were characterized by considerable tension, fighting, and quarreling—the same kind of fighting their parents indulged in, which results in progressive damage to all family members. With some of the older COAs in her study, the apparent need to dominate their younger siblings was a result of deep aggressive and frustrated feelings. Cork also reported an abnormal amount of dissention and separation among brothers and sisters at all age levels. Instead of warmth and affection, siblings carried a deep sense of hostility and resentment.

Emotional Wounds

Typical upbringing in an alcoholic family leaves children with many emotional—and sometimes physical—wounds. Regardless of parents' motives, effects on the children are the same. They react to their parents with a flood of strong emotions, ranging from rage to despair. Carried throughout childhood and into adulthood, these feelings interfere with fully functioning relationships with friends, spouses, and loved ones.

Anger

Through clinical work, I have observed anger as the most common emotion children harbor in reaction to parental alcoholism. When children have learned that expressed anger is wrong, unexpressed anger is often veiled with false smiles. Anger is aroused for many of the reasons I have already discussed: refusal of a parent to support children during disputes, betrayal, mixed messages, and broken promises. Another common reason for anger is destruction of personal belongings. Over and over again children tell me they have no sense of personal ownership. Material items, like Rick's drums, are potential targets in violent homes and vulnerable to destruction, as the rage in his poem reflects.

Ten-year-old Carlos said his father got drunk and tore up the house. Among the destruction were Carlos's prized cassette tapes that he had been collecting for months. The child was so angry he went to his school and punched a metal caution sign until he broke one of his knuckles. Children are also angry simply because the alcoholic yells and hits family members, as the drawing in figure 2–1 indicates. Children usually use the words "mad" and "hate" to express their anger, although feelings of hurt and sadness are layered underneath.

Fear and Anxiety

COAs are kids who are afraid and terrified of what is happening at home. The seesaw existence in chemically dependent families is enough to elicit anxiety. Apprehension and fear become normal reactions for children in unpredictable situations. Coupled with violence and psychological, physical

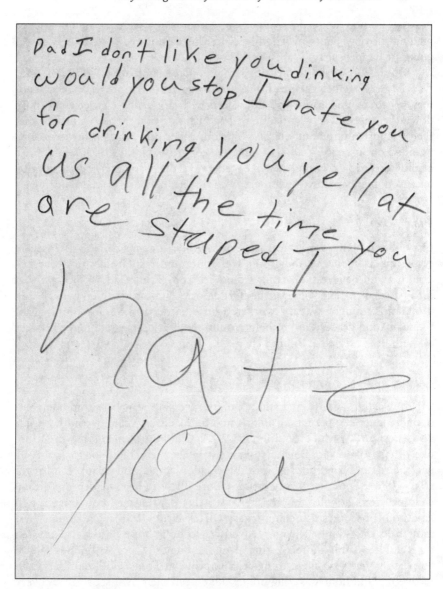

Figure 2–1. Feelings of anger toward her alcoholic father leap from the page of this drawing by an eight-year-old girl.

and sometimes sexual abuse, impending doom is the COA's silent companion. Jane said, "I lived in constant fear of when my father would get drunk again. Each time it happened it got worse. There were signs that I knew, like when he said he was happy. I knew he was going to go off the deep end because he was not a happy person. Other signs were when he stopped reading the newspaper or when he wore this certain red vest, I knew it was going to happen again."

Most COAs have witnessed parents out of control or violent in some way. Many have been slapped, hit, or thrown around more than once. They may be afraid that Mom will fall asleep with a burning cigarette and burn down the house, worry someone will be hurt in a nightly brawl, or fear that their friends will find out what is going on. Their peer relationships are often founded on insecurity, anxiety, and lack of trust (Cork 1969). Children of alcoholics are also more likely to generalize their anxiety and to develop unreasonable fears for which there is no discernible basis (Haberman 1966).

Guilt

COAs often blame themselves for causing their parent's drinking. Unaware of the disease concept, they often feel guilty and responsible for a parent's drinking and believe they can get them to stop. Trina said, "I thought that if I just tried to take some of the burden off my mom, that she would stop drinking. I thought that if I worked a little harder to keep my room clean, to make good grades, and to help around the house, it would make it easier on her. But it didn't. Nothing changed."

Sadness and Depression

Children call it sadness, and adults call it depression. They are common emotional reactions to parental drinking and to the ensuing family conflict (Clair & Genest 1987; Moos & Billings 1982). Children of alcoholics are more likely than offspring of nonalcoholics to describe their childhoods as unhappy and their home conditions as unstable (Callan & Jackson 1986; Schulsinger et al. 1986). They are also two times more likely to become depressed than children from nonalcoholic homes, and this depression, as it lingers into adulthood, becomes a lifelong legacy (Black et al. 1986). The good news, though, is that children from recovering alcoholic homes are less depressed than children from nonrecovering alcoholic homes (Moos & Billings 1982). So when parents get help, things can improve at home. Still, children from recovering and nonrecovering homes alike need their own separate recovery programs to deal with parental changes and the residue of unexpressed emotions. The tears in the drawing (figure 2–2) exemplify the sadness of one seven-year-old boy of alcoholic parents.

Confusion

Little Molly was a bouncy nine-year-old who swelled with delight when her mother beckoned to her with open arms. "Come here, sweetheart, and give

**Figure 2–2. A seven-year-old boy illustrates his feelings about his
alcoholic parents.**

me a kiss. Mommie loves you so much!" Expecting to be comforted in the
security and warmth of her mother's arms, Molly was met instead with a
sharp slap across her face and a belligerent reprimand, "You are a bad little
girl!" Then Molly smelled the alcohol on her mother's breath. She had been
duped again. It was not until the age of fourteen that Molly put a stop to her
mother's seductive abuse. Molly hit her mother on the head with all her might
and was never struck again.

Parental inconsistency and unpredictability are hallmarks of alcoholism
that propel children into a cyclone of confusion. Alcoholics are notorious for
mood swings and making and breaking promises during drinking bouts.
COAs learn early in life about the Dr. Jekyll/Mr. Hyde syndrome. I was

perplexed by my own father's personality changes and wondered how he could always act like nothing out of the ordinary had happened the morning after drunken skirmishes. While my family still carried around anger from the previous night, my father had transformed into a sweet, gentle, and caring man. It was a kind and considerate father who dropped us off at the seven o'clock movie and promised through genuine smiles to be back by nine. But it was a snarling monster who returned at twelve o'clock or never returned at all. I didn't realize at the time that his blackouts prevented him from remembering the events of the night before.

Children of alcoholics realize they have at least three different parents—the drinking alcoholic parent, the sober alcoholic parent, and the nonalcoholic parent. Sometimes when both parents are alcoholic, COAs must figure out how to get along with multiple personalities. In some ways this predicament is like living in schizophrenia, where parental mood swings are unpredictable and expectations are inconsistent. Children often find themselves walking on eggshells and desperately trying to second-guess parents in order to do what they want. This is very difficult, especially for preschool children who are starting to discriminate between right and wrong and who need consistency to trust their abilities to venture out socially, share their feelings, and show affection for others. It is equally difficult for school-age children who developmentally have learned to think concretely about their world and to understand that things in it can be categorized and ordered. There are ethical morals of good and bad, there are laws of legal and illegal, and there are school rules of right and wrong. But things are not so cut and dried at home. The order and rules do not apply. Rules, when they do exist, are switched around daily, just enough to keep children guessing and never knowing what to expect. The lives of COAs become two or three times more complicated than children from nonalcoholic homes. They grow up unsure of what "normal" is and insecure about how to act in different situations.

According to Margaret Cork (1969), 94 percent of the teens in her study reported parental inconsistency as the major problem of alcoholism. Co-dependent parents also send inconsistent and conflicting messages to their kids, who become confused and angry at their parents for deceiving and betraying them.

Embarrassment and Isolation

Roger always complained in group that the other kids made fun of his dad when he was drunk. This caused great embarrassment for Roger. The threat of embarrassment causes COAs to isolate themselves from their peers at a time when other youngsters are forming and consolidating friendships (Cork 1969). Their freedom to meet friends and to reciprocate friendships is restricted (Wilson & Orford 1978). Normal friendships are impaired because children try to hide their parent's drinking or refuse to bring friends home for fear of being embarrassed by drinking, out-of-control parents. Mac's alcoholic father ordered his friends out of the house. Patti complained that her mom would get drunk and "come on" to her teenage boyfriends. Candace said she did not like for her dad to come to school functions because he came to school drunk one day and embarrassed her. On his way out of the classroom, he stumbled and fell in full view of her classmates who giggled and snickered at him. Such experiences have left Candace so shy and withdrawn that she whispers when she talks. Deidre was taunted by her friends at school:

> My dad's drinking had a big effect on me because I was ashamed. I mean, here I was, I had a crazy dad and kids at school would tease me and say, "Give me some of that stuff your dad takes." And it was awful and I didn't want anybody to come to my house. It had a real bad effect on me. It was torture living with him. He'd stay up all night talking and laughing as if there was some demon in him.

When Deidre was finally taken out of the home and placed with her grandparents, she carried the embarrassment with her: "I remember I would lie at school when kids and teachers would ask me who I lived with. I'd say my mom, dad, and little brother. I was so ashamed of living with my grandparents because I wanted to live in a normal family like everybody else. And I remember lying so many times."

As a reaction to shame and embarrassment, children often withdraw and isolate themselves from peers. COAs also become more preoccupied with their thoughts than with those of the outside world (Fine 1976). Many of these kids build a wall around themselves for protection against the alcoholic parent. They insulate their emotions and seal their feelings in a time capsule. Many do not open that time capsule until their thirties or forties. Tragically, some never reopen it.

Grief

"Coming from an alcoholic home makes me want to be totally different from my alcoholic parents," Deidre told me. "And it makes me want to have a family because I've never had one. I've never considered myself part of a family, and I want to have a family more than anything. I don't think that would be so important to me if I had lived with my parents in a normal life."

Grief is an emotional reaction that most children of alcoholics experience on many levels. Missing out on a "normal" family life will be mourned at one time or another in the child's life. The missed experience of a magical, joyful, and carefree childhood is also a common reason to grieve. Losing a parent to alcohol can be so traumatizing to children that it has been compared to the loss of a loved one through death or divorce (Black 1987). Children of alcoholics experience loss on many levels and on a chronic basis at a time in life when they are developing a sense of worth and identity. The grief process, however, is usually not fully felt until adolescence, at which time it only adds to the teenager's confusion: "The difficulty for adolescents who experience grief around the loss of a parent to alcohol lies in the fact that the parent is physically present. This makes a grief reaction seem inappropriate and leaves teens confused as to why they feel this way, and the issue remains unresolved." (Priest 1985).

Psychological Functioning

Many problems befall children as a result of the stresses and strains of their alcoholic upbringing. Emotionally battered and bruised, many children limp through life, their psychological functioning impaired. Poor self-esteem, lack of feeling in control of their own lives, poor coping skills, and problems in interpersonal relationships all characterize their psychological functioning.

Factors Influencing Psychological Outcomes

The outlook for COAs sounds pretty dismal. But before I continue discussing their psychological functioning, it is important to note that not all children of alcoholics fit the pattern I have described. Some never succumb to these devastations. Research suggests that numerous factors operate singly or inter-act collectively to produce negative psychological outcomes: sex of child (Werner 1986); sex of alcoholic parent (Steinhausen, Gobel & Nestler 1984; Werner 1986); age of child (Werner 1986); family socioeconomic status and whether both parents drink (Parker & Harford 1987); race (Ackerman 1987); birth order (Keltner, McIntyre & Gee 1986); constitutional factors (Tabakoff et al. 1988); offsetting factors such as other people or institutions that have positive effects on the child (Ackerman 1987); and whether the parent is a recovering or active alcoholic (Callan & Jackson 1986; Moos & Billings 1982; O'Gorman 1975).

The psychiatric literature indicates a tendency for children's conduct dis-orders to correlate with paternal alcoholism and for emotional disorders to correlate with maternal alcoholism, although both types of disorders occur with the same frequency when children have two alcoholic parents (Stein-hausen, Gobel & Nestler 1984). Children with two alcoholic parents become more aggressive and seriously disturbed than those who have one alcoholic parent or none at all (McKenna & Pickens 1983). In cases where the alco-holic parent is in recovery, family relations are better than in those where the parent is still drinking. Children of recovering alcoholics, in fact, rated their families similar to nonalcoholic homes in terms of happiness and togetherness (Callan & Jackson 1986). They rated their lives as much happier than those of offspring in households where fathers still drank. The health and psychological functioning of children from recovering homes were also similar to nonalcoholic homes (Moos & Billings 1982).

In contrast, parents in families of relapsed alcoholics reported less cohesion and expressiveness, and less emphasis on independence, achievement, and moral-religious, intellectual-cultural, and active-recreational orientation than nonalcoholic families (Moos & Billings 1982). Children from relapsed homes suffered more depression and anxiety and had more serious physical and mental problems.

The combined effects of coming from low socioeconomic backgrounds and having two alcoholic parents put kids at even higher risk for alcohol-related problems (Parker & Harford 1987). Birth order also makes a difference in the child's adjustment. Research indicates that middle and later-born children are more likely to develop psychological problems from living in alcoholic homes than first-borns, who are more resilient (Keltner, McIntyre & Gee 1986). During the mid-1980s social scientists identified and began studying a group of youngsters known as resilient or invulnerable children. Additional factors associated with children who are said to be resilient to the effects of alcoholic parents are described in the box on page 36.

Self-Esteem

The self-esteem of children who grow up with alcoholism is often severely damaged. As part of the intake process in one children's program, clinical staff administer *The Rosenberg Self-Esteem Scale.* Eyeballing the simple inventory quickly shows how poorly the children feel about themselves. Social science research corroborates that COAs have more negative self-concepts than nonCOAs. One of the first such studies to examine self-esteem reported that fifty-four children of recovering alcoholics had lower self-esteem than fifty-four children of nonalcoholics (MacLachlan, Walderman & Thomas 1973). COAs, compared to nonCOAs, rated their families significantly lower in family harmony and reported a significantly more disturbed relationship with the alcoholic parent. Families in which the alcoholic parent was recovered had relationships that were significantly improved. Another study compared three groups of adolescents: twenty-nine teens from active alcoholic homes, twenty-three whose fathers were recovering alcoholics, and twenty-seven from nonalcoholic homes (O'Gorman 1975). Adolescents from both active and recovering homes had lower self-esteem than those from nonalcoholic homes. A later investigation compared fifty-four COAs with 129 peers who were not COAs (DiCicco, Davis & Orenstein 1984). Overall, the COAs scored lower in virtually all the self-image measures.

Resilient Children of Alcoholic Parents

The psychiatric literature has identified a group of youngsters known as *resilient* or *invulnerable children*—those reared under the most dire circumstances who somehow do remarkably well despite their disadvantaged surroundings. The most common characteristic of these children is their ability to cope and react to stress in exceptional ways. Despite the fact that resilient children are reared in such extremely traumatic and stressful surroundings as alcoholic homes, they are described as stress-resistant. They are said to thrive in spite of their problems (Robinson & Fields 1983).

Anthony (1978) describes the differences between children who are vulnerable and those who are invulnerable. To explain the effects, he compares children with three kinds of dolls—glass, plastic, and steel. Glass dolls are shattered by the stressful experiences in childhood. Plastic dolls are permanently dented, and steel dolls are invulnerable—resisting the harmful effects of their surroundings. Glass (vulnerable) children break down completely, plastic children sustain some serious injury, and steel (invulnerable) children thrive on the trouble and turmoil in their world.

Resilient children share a number of common characteristics. They have good social skills. They are at ease and make others feel comfortable, too. They are friendly and well liked by classmates and adults. They have positive feelings of self-regard. And they sense a feeling of personal power for influencing events around them (internal locus of control). This contrasts with the feelings of helplessness of vulnerable children. Not only do resilient children feel in control, but they also have an urge to help others needier than themselves. There is a certain sense of detachment from the stressful surroundings. Along with this self-distancing comes a greater sense of independence and a more objective understanding of what's going on around them. They are successful, usually receiving high grades in school. Later on they become high achievers in their careers. Somehow, their intellectual and creative skills are not destroyed by their misfortunes at home. Most of these children, who experience inadequate parenting and early turmoil, grow up to be competent adults and appear to suffer little or no psychological damage.

Emmy Werner (1986) followed forty-nine offspring of alcoholic parents over eighteen years. She discovered that some children developed severe psychological disorders, while others appeared resilient to their alcoholic upbringing. Children were judged resilient by their outward appearance through interviews and examination of records, showing good grades and no mental or behavioral problems. Resilient children did well in school, at work, and in their social lives, and they had realistic goals and expectations for the future. Overall, the following characteristics distinguished resilient children from the vulnerable children (who developed delinquent and mental health coping problems by age eighteen):

- They were girls.
- The alcoholic parent was the father.
- They had received more attention from their primary caregivers during the first twelve months of life.
- They had grown up in homes where little family conflict occurred during the first two years of life.
- Their mothers were steadily and gainfully employed between the child's second and tenth year of age.
- Their parents had not separated or divorced by the time the child had reached adolescence.
- They tended to have fewer serious illnesses or handicaps during adolescence.
- They had fewer problems in family relationships during adolescence.
- They had fewer problems with their mothers or fathers.
- Mothers did not become pregnant again or give birth to another sibling within the first two years of the resilient child's life.
- They had more pleasant temperaments during the first year of life.
- They reflected a greater sense of well-being, self-esteem, and psychological health.
- They appeared more responsible, more socialized, and caring.
- They projected a greater degree of self-control and tolerance of individual differences.
- They were more achievement-oriented.
- They had higher scores on tests of intellectual efficiency, which indicated high desire to use talents to the fullest.

Resilient children sound like carbon copies of the family hero (discussed in chapter 1). On the surface these kids appear to be functioning exceptionally well. But professionals must be careful making this interpretation until more is known about this special group of children. We know that the resilience of family heroes is also the source of deeper-seated, concealed problems of inadequacy and poor self-esteem. Many cases of invulnerability may be a disguise for an inner misery that resilient children are compelled to hide. It would behoove practitioners to take caution in labeling children who appear to be resilient. It is important that the helping professions not discount the resilient child simply because he or she appears to be functioning better than the more vulnerable children in a family. Resilient children may, in fact, be in greater need than those who can reveal their vulnerability. The best resource for these invulnerable children can be practitioners who make sure that, while developing their talents and skills, these kids also get a chance to balance their personal lives to the maximum.

The COA self-concept encompasses the sum total of all the events I have discussed in this chapter. The cranky, nonalcoholic parent who seems to never have time, the drinking parent who unpredictably switches personalities at the drop of a hat or who promises but never delivers, the child's guilt and self-blame for somehow causing the drinking, the betrayal and hostility that accompany parental alcoholism, the embarrassment in front of friends, and the stigma of the family's image that has been tainted by the drinking parent—all culminate in poor self-worth. When children can no longer separate these events from who they are, they internalize them as humiliation and shame. Children begin to feel that they are not worthy, and shame becomes a part of their self-concept.

But there is a good side to all of this. As the box on page 36 indicates, higher self-esteem was a major distinguishing factor between resilient boys and girls (under age eighteen) and vulnerable children who had serious coping problems by eighteen years of age (Werner 1986). As more is known about resilient children, perhaps the self-image and the lives of COAs can be further improved. Another positive finding is that the self-esteem of many adult COAs is high and for others low, depending upon whether their situations warranted treatment. Adult COAs in treatment had much lower self-worth than nonCOAs. But adult COAs not undergoing treatment had as much self-esteem and an even higher capacity for intimate contact than adults from nonalcoholic homes (Barnard & Spoentgen 1987).

Locus of Control

Control is a big issue for children of alcoholics, mainly because they have witnessed one or both parents struggling, without much success, to maintain control and to manage their own lives. Children have *internal locus of control* when they gain a sense of mastery over their difficult alcoholic environment. They believe their own actions determine the positive or negative consequences in their lives. In contrast, children with *external locus of control* do not feel in control of their lives. They believe, instead, that external forces govern their destiny. As a result, they externalize their responsibilities, resign themselves to their circumstances, and succumb to the guides of fate and chance.

Do children from alcoholic homes have control over their lives? Or are they bent and swayed at the mercy of their everyday worlds? Generally, research findings indicate that children from chemically dependent homes have greater externality than children from sober ones (O'Gorman 1975). Joseph Kern and his research associates (1981) studied forty children between the ages of eight and thirteen. The researchers administered a test that measured locus of control to half the children who lived in drinking households and another half who lived in sober homes. They concluded from the test results that the COAs in their study were significantly more externally oriented than the comparison group. The COAs felt less personally responsible for and less control over the events that shaped their daily lives. This feeling of being under the control of others generally leads to a lack of initiative and achievement in maneuvering the world to one's advantage.

Other studies have confirmed that children reared in alcoholic households lack a true sense of control over their lives, compared to children reared in nonalcoholic families (DiCicco, Davis & Orenstein 1984; Prewitt, Spence & Chaknis 1981). Authorities believe this difference in psychological functioning occurs because of deficits in childhood socialization of COAs. Paralyzed from the stresses and strains of an alcoholic upbringing, these children are unable to develop an effective ability to manage their lives. Some experts believe this factor may even contribute to the high incidence of alcoholism among COAs (Kern et al. 1981). There is a consensus among researchers that, as a rule, children from alcoholic households believe they have little say-so and control over their personal lives.

An exception to this rule, however, can be found among resilient children and children living with recovering parents. Children of recovering alcoholics tend to have more internal control and to feel greater affection from their alcoholic fathers than children with active alcoholic fathers (O'Gorman 1975). Resilient COAs score similarly to children from nonalcoholics on locus of control. They are less likely than children who developed coping problems by eighteen years of age to believe that luck and fate were decisive factors in their lives. Instead, they believe their own actions determine the positive or negative consequences in their lives (Werner 1986).

Relationship Problems

Family interaction sets the tone and quality of the kinds of relationships kids will have with others outside their homes. Unfortunately, alcoholic homes provide less than optimal training grounds for healthy human relationships. Positive parental role models are generally missing. Distrust of parents is often generalized to all adults—teachers, counselors, other parents, even the clergy—which leads to resentment toward authority and inability to accept it (Cork 1969). Sibling relationships are the first important peer interactions children have that prepare them for later relationships with the many types of people they will meet outside the home. The sibling relationships in chemically dependent families are often riddled with conflict and dissention. Consequently, COAs have little success or little experience making friends during their youth. Their friends are scared away by the bizarre behaviors of the alcoholic parent or by actual insults and ridicule (Cork 1969). Some COAs have no time to spend with friends because of their household obligations.

The battle scars from alcoholic homes make it difficult for COAs to develop intimacy and trusting relationships. So it is understandable that this difficulty spills over into adolescence and adulthood in forming companionships, expressing intimacy, and maintaining viable relationships. Studies of interactions during adolescence reveal that as many as 87 percent of the teens from alcoholic homes had ineffectual peer relationships (Booz-Allen & Hamilton 1974). Another 64 percent had trouble forming relationships with the opposite sex because of suspicion and distrust. Deidre, twenty-one years old, carried her distrust of intimate relationships into adulthood:

> My counselor said I made decisions when I was little that I had to make to survive in that situation but those decisions can ruin the rest of my life. I've got to get rid of them. One thing was that I'm unlovable and I can't trust it when somebody says they love me.

In a study of 409 adult children of alcoholics, the respondents reported significantly less communication with their parents, neighbors, friends the same age, teachers, counselors, and friends' parents than a comparison group of adult children of nonalcoholics (Black et al. 1986). Adult children of alcoholics cited "problems trusting people" as the biggest factor that distinguished them from adults from nonalcoholic homes.

Tips for Practitioners

Practitioners cannot make the alcoholism in the child's life disappear, and they cannot change the way things are at home. But they can help by first accepting the fact that they—as teachers, counselors, social workers, medical personnel, clergy, and so forth—are just as powerless over the parent's drinking as family members. No one can stop the drinking except the alcoholic. Once this is understood, professionals will realize their best avenue for helping children adjust is to help them make the best of their home situations and to take care of themselves.

Ordinarily, COAs do not reach out. They do not have emotional resources, and they do not use the social supports around them. They repress their feelings or minimize them (Black 1987). So it is up to practitioners to make the first move. The following tips will give you a head start in the right direction.

- Reserve caution with the label "resilient," because it conveys the notion that some COAs do not need special help or attention. No one lives for any length of time in a chemically dependent home without suffering some side effects.

- Be on the lookout for children you would otherwise consider resilient. Always make sure these kids get special attention as would any other child. A close, intimate relationship with just one significant adult makes a big difference in their lives.

- Assure children that alcoholism occurs because of problems the parents have. Help them understand they are not responsible for their parent's behavior and they did not cause, cannot control, and cannot cure the disease. This may even help them on the road to understanding that they should not be embarrassed by what parents do because parental behaviors are apart from them.

- Help children gain a sense of mastery over their environment. Give them choices to make and challenges that are developmentally sound and that ensure their ability to manage and control their lives. Teaching autonomy through simple decision-making processes in the classroom can help break children's fear and dependency. Making choices about which activities they want to engage in during free play (preschoolers), how they choose to spend their time on the playground (school-age children), or what theme they want to write about for the assignment (older children) are simple examples in which you can give children opportunities to make decisions about their lives.

- Establish a one-to-one relationship with the child and communicate on a feeling level. Make a special effort to love the child. Let the child know that he or she is important and worthwhile by smiling, hugging, praising, and paying attention to appropriate behaviors. But avoid "being a mother or a father." You cannot replace the alcoholic parent and should not try to do so. Allowing too much dependence on you would be a disservice, because this child must continue to deal with the alcoholism long after leaving your services.

- Avoid overprotecting children, always realizing that they must be dealt with patiently and might regress to less mature forms of behavior at times. Set firm, reasonable limits. Even though children might have problems, you should not allow them to "run wild."

- Teach children what families are like by reading children's stories. In situations where family alcoholism is complicated by separation or divorce, children may be dealing with a double whammy. These children need special attention to deal with not only the hurt of drinking but of the splitting up of their home. Help COAs and other children from homes of divorce and stepfamilies understand that there are many types of families. COAs especially need to know that there is no perfect family like the Cleavers or the Andersons. This gives them an idea of what "normal" families are like, since they have never lived in one, and gives them more realistic and less idealistic images for when they grow up. An excellent resource in this regard is *Free To Be a Family* (Marlo Thomas 1987).

- Understand that difficulties in the child's behavior do not necessarily mean that the child has become permanently damaged. If a ten-year-old, for example, has become a serious behavior problem, in school this may simply be a cry for help. The kindness of a teacher's guidance or expression of concern can make a difference. Research also shows that once the alcoholic goes into recovery and children get the help they need, family functioning improves and children are happier and better adjusted.

- Help the child recognize and express feelings, resolve conflict, and master his or her realm through creative activities, children's literature, and play (see chapter 8). Creative expression, in particular, helps children with locus of control, self-esteem, and overall psychological functioning. The opening poem that Rick wrote, for instance, gave him a constructive outlet for expressing his anger and frustration at living with an alcoholic grandmother.

- Allow children solitude and privacy when they need it. If they spend an inordinate amount of time alone, however, this may be a cause for concern. Balance is what you should look for—balance of alone time and social time.

- Help the child develop feelings of trust. The alcoholic home is often one in which promises are broken. COAs believe that they cannot trust their parents or any adult. Establishment of trust between you and the child can be the greatest gift you can give. Be consistent. Do not say one thing and do another. When you make a commitment, no matter how small it may seem to you, stick to it. Never make promises unless you plan to follow through.

- Make the classroom a sanctuary in which children feel secure, psychologically safe, relaxed, and enjoy learning. Have predictable routines and rules. If you are going to change this predictable world (because of an emergency or a special event), be sure to tell children beforehand and explain to them why the change is necessary.

- Let the children play, play, and play. As a rule, children of alcoholics do not have opportunities to play, and the time they spend with you may be their only leisure time. They may have more trouble than most children in playing with peers and just plain *having fun*. Your role may be to literally help them learn to play and to have fun doing it. Integrate fun activities, jokes, and funny stories. Laughing is therapeutic and a sense of humor is a powerful antidote against stress.

- Self-esteem building activities are important for the fragile self-concepts that so many children of alcoholics have. Chapter 10 provides some self-esteem building curricula for elementary youngsters. The books in Further Readings on p. 243 are also excellent resources for improving self-image.

3
Health and Safety Hazards

The most destructive element in an alcoholic family is chronic stress. Stress in an alcoholic home can stem from the controlling behavior of the adult child of an alcoholic or the chronically inconsistent behavior of an alcoholic parent. It is aggravated by the twin fears of violence and the fear that the family will be separated. If incest and child abuse are involved, the stresses are magnified a hundredfold.
—Patricia O'Gorman and Philip Oliver-Diaz,
Breaking the Cycle of Addiction

Case 3–1

The first time I met five-year-old Shelia was at the beginning of the school year, and I noticed how small she was compared to the other children in my kindergarten class. She weighed about twenty pounds, whereas most kindergarten children weigh forty-five pounds. She wore a size three when she should have worn a size six. Her clothes fell off her because she was so tiny. I thought perhaps she had anemia, and I referred her to the school nurse.

Not only were Shelia's clothes too big for her, but she couldn't concentrate or retain skills for very long. She could remember for a few seconds, but if I asked her the same thing again, she would draw a total blank. Her downfall was her nervousness, which at times got worse. She shook all the time, bit her fingernails, and her eyes darted from one place to another. If I held her hand, the nervousness went up my arm in a constant steady rhythm. She had a short attention span and couldn't sit or stand still for very long because of her nervous condition. She'd rather stand up to do seat work, and she preferred to do something that would allow her to move around the room, such as looking at pictures in the book center or playing in the housekeeping area. She wouldn't use manipulatives very well or very often. She couldn't hold a pencil or crayon deftly and could barely write her name. She could put down the letter *s* for the first letter of her name. But the rest of the letters were out of sequence and ill formed. From her brain to hand, she just couldn't make the correct formation of her letters. She could hold a crayon but she couldn't stay inside the lines.

While the nurse was checking into the problem, I figured out on my own that she probably had been a fetal alcohol syndrome baby because of her extremely small size, her nervousness, her emaciated appearance, and her inability to concentrate. The nurse found that she was indeed a child of an alcoholic mother and that while the mother was pregnant with Shelia, an older sister was taken out of the home and put into a foster home.

It turned out that both parents were alcoholic. Shelia and her older sister took care of themselves. If they made it to school, it was because they dressed and fed themselves each morning. At a parent conference, her mother showed up greatly intoxicated. During the conference she kept repeating, "I love her. She's my honey. She's so sweet." Occasionally, she would grab Shelia and hug her. Her mother acted as if she felt very guilty. She told me she knew Shelia was nervous and small for her size but she didn't know if the child's condition had anything to do with the fact that she drank when she was pregnant.

I made a visit to Shelia's house to talk to her parents about her nervousness and her inability to concentrate. The parents knew I was coming, but the father met me at the front door and wouldn't let me come in. He said the mother had been called away. It was clear that the father had been drinking, and I feel sure the mother was passed out inside. Shelia appeared at the door wearing dirty and torn pajamas and a housecoat. The cinderblock house reeked with the smell of kerosene fuel that was used for heat. A lot of Shelia's nervousness is biological and comes from her mother's drinking while she was in the womb. But a lot of it comes from the kind of home she still lives in, too. I'm afraid she's going to have big problems because of this in first grade.

—Patti Young, kindergarten teacher

Health and Safety Hazards

Some children from alcoholic homes have serious health and safety problems in addition to psychological difficulties. Basically, alcoholic homes are psychologically unsafe and highly stressful. Stress has many physical side effects that impair children's health. These problems are best observed and addressed in schools, where kids spend most of their weekday time. Chronic stress and poor health interfere with academic performance and functional social relationships. Occasionally poor health has a biological basis that will remain a permanent part of the child's makeup, as in the opening case of

Shelia. But more commonly, problems manifested in school are an outgrowth of unstable family conditions stemming from alcoholism.

Clinical reports and research studies agree that children of alcoholic parents have a greater number and variety of health problems, including psychosomatic illnesses and compulsive disorders, than children from non-drinking families. One of the reasons children miss so much school is that the quarreling, violence, and disruption caused by alcoholism is so upsetting that they actually become physically sick. Children of alcoholic mothers who drink during pregnancy also run the risk of being born with fetal alcohol syndrome.

Fetal Alcohol Syndrome

Fetal alcohol syndrome (FAS) is a condition that results from maternal consumption of alcohol during pregnancy. FAS was discovered in 1973, but it is not known how alcohol causes this syndrome or how much alcohol must be consumed before FAS will occur. Babies with FAS are usually quite small at birth and slow to develop physically. Central nervous system damage causes irritability, hyperactivity, and retardation in intellectual development. FAS children may have heart defects, disturbed sleep patterns, unusually small heads, and facial abnormalities. These abnormal features include abundant hair; short distance between the inner and outer portion of the eye; an extra portion of skin over the thinner portion of the eye; a flat crease that extends between the bottom of the nose and the upper lips; narrow eye openings; flat nasal bridge; thin upper lip; short, upturned nose; and small chin (Holzman 1983).

Research has shown that long-term behavioral effects are still present during the preschool and elementary school years (Landesman-Dwyer, Ragozin & Little 1979). Although FAS children never fully recover from their disorder, they can improve in motor functioning, attention, relations with siblings and peers, temper, phobias, intellectual performance, and psycholinguistic abilities (Steinhausen, Gobel & Nestler 1984). No change, however, has been observed in their level of hyperactivity. It is clear from these findings and the case of Shelia that this birth defect continues to handicap children's academic performance throughout their school years.

Psychosomatic Complaints

Because they encounter an inordinate amount of stresses and strains at home, children of alcoholics often store their feelings and anxieties in the confines of their bodies and, as a consequence, experience more health problems.

They complain more often of headaches, difficulty sleeping, fatigue, nausea, stomachaches, and eating problems (Cork 1969; Nylander 1960; Steinhausen et al. 1982). Although they are more likely to seek treatment for these ailments, there is generally no physical origin for their psychosomatic maladies. Wives and daughters of alcoholics are more prone to complain of psychosomatic problems, to seek treatment for them, and to receive specific diagnosis than sons and husbands of alcoholics and females in nondrinking homes (Biek 1981; Roberts & Brent 1982).

Children of alcoholics often develop nervous conditions in reaction to an alcoholic environment that can be psychologically and physically unsafe. Kids who fear for their own safety or for that of another parent or sibling have shot nerves. Fingernail biting is the most noticeable sign of anxiety. Trembling, headaches, nervous tics, insomnia, and upset stomachs are also symptomatic. Lynn said she got especially nervous at night. That was when her father drank the most and when he and her mother argued and brutally fought. Lynn had a nervous stomach and shook so uncontrollably at times that she could barely hold a pencil in school. When she did complete assignments, Lynn trembled so much that her teachers could not read the scribbling. But she loved school and saw it as a sanctuary from her unhappy homelife. "My counselor helped me a lot with my nerves," Lynn explained. "She gave me stuff to read about alcoholism and we talked alot." Lynn's counselor also referred the child to a COA group, where I met her. Many of her nervous habits began to disappear as she took an active part in her own recovery.

Children whose parents are in recovery do not show the same pattern of psychosomatic problems. Studies in which parents were being treated for alcoholism found no significant differences between health problems, personality disturbances, or school problems of their offspring and those from nonalcoholic homes (MacLachlan, Walderman & Thomas 1973; Rimmer 1982). Children of recovered alcoholics have no greater incidences of allergies, anemia, asthma, frequent colds or coughs, and overweight and underweight problems than children from nonalcoholic homes (Moos & Billings 1982). In contrast, children of relapsed alcoholics have more psychosomatic problems than children from nonalcoholic homes.

Compulsive Disorders

Other health hazards taking their toll among children of alcoholics are addictions that do great harm physically as well as psychologically. As they progress through childhood, COAs have difficulty discarding their needs for perfection, compulsion, and control that they used in an effort to manage all that is controllable in a chaotic home (O'Gorman & Oliver-Diaz 1987). Having provided many years of comfort, these needs become an integral part of their adult personalities. Untreated in childhood, these compulsive dependency needs can be serious sources of stress in adolescence and adulthood, when they are converted into addictions. COAs often attempt to assuage the anxiety through alcohol or other drugs, work, food, sex, and other compulsive behaviors. They are at high risk for becoming alcoholics, workaholics, compulsive gamblers, compulsive spenders, or sex and drug addicts. Eating disorders are also common.

Eating Disorders

Overeating is the chief eating disorder, followed by bulimia (binging and purging), and anorexia (starvation, laxative usage, and stringent exercise). Like all compulsive behaviors, overeating begins in early childhood and becomes full-blown in adulthood. The box on page 50 presents an interview with Emma, forty-two, who talks of her compulsive eating problem and how, through hypnosis, she traced it to the fifth grade.

Type A Children and Work Addiction

Many COAs are hurried children—youngsters forced to grow up too fast. They acquire adult responsibilities as well as the stressful and tense side effects that accompany grownup problems (Elkind 1981). Many of the pressures from taking on the hardships of alcoholic parents—such as calling in sick to a drunken father's employer or making sure monthly bills get paid so utilities are not disconnected—can produce severe childhood stress and burnout. COAs who assume their roles of family hero and parent to a younger sibling (cooking, dressing, washing clothes, and overseeing household chores) or to a parent (becoming Mom's confidant and helping her solve her problems of the bottle or becoming her protector by keeping a violent father from assaulting her night after night) must become little grownups with adulthood's worries and burdens. Ultimately, they miss childhood altogether.

Hurried children often have what medical scientists call Type A personalities that, because of being overly stressed and burdened, lead to physical health problems. The Type A behavior pattern is associated with coronary artery and heart disease, the origins of which have been traced to childhood (Visintainer & Matthews 1987). Type A children are descriptive of those COAs who, through the family hero role, become compulsive

Compulsive Eating

My brother and I are both compulsive eaters. I went through a year of treatment at the Center for Behavioral Medicine in a group for compulsive eaters. In my private sessions with a therapist, we talked about my father's alcoholism. I had never realized until recently that I suffered from low self-esteem and that the eating is tied into that as well.

It's one of those things where if you eat the first peanut M & M, you're sure that the nineteenth will taste even better. When I eat, I feel comforted. It's calming to some degree. And then I feel guilty and I eat some more. Compulsive eating is just like drugs or drinking or anything else. The therapist told me that I didn't express as much anger about my father as people generally do. I guess the pushing down of feelings is one reason I stuff food into my mouth. And I think I'm constantly trying to fill up that emptiness with food. I used to go on diets and starve and lose twenty-five pounds, and that's how I'd keep my weight down.

My therapist hypnotized me and did a regression to the point where I started overeating. And it was the strangest occurrence because all of a sudden I remembered being in the fifth grade. Mrs. Autry's 5C was our room. I remember we were the last class to eat, and they'd bring these huge trays of homemade yeast rolls and they'd put the butter on with paint brushes. If they had three pans left, the cafeteria workers would put them on the table and tell us to go to it. The boys were always the ones to gobble down the rolls, except I would enter the contest and remember winning one day with a total of fourteen rolls on top of all the lunch I had already eaten. I had been a good basketball player in the fifth grade. Although I was very small, I was fast and very wily. All of a sudden, I was as round as the basketball. I can remember my elementary school principal—who was also the basketball coach—saying, "Emma, if you eat one more roll, I'm going to use you for the ball." I traced my overeating back to that point. That's when I remember starting to overeat.

But in the last three years since I started back to work and my last child started kindergarten, the thoughts of denying myself and dieting just make me sick! So I've tried every magic potion. I've been to every weight loss program there is in town. When I was going through therapy, I thought, "Damn, I'm not an alcoholic. I'm compulsive when I drink just like I am compulsive when I eat or talk or used to be when I smoked. I've got a compulsive personality."

> I have read that children of alcoholics are compulsive in some area. I bite my nails. I remember first biting my nails when (again in the fifth grade) my mother had been diagnosed with a fatal blood disease. I was in grandmother's kitchen when my mother had gone to the hospital, and I knew she was very ill and it seemed like the compulsive behavior had started around that point. Biting the fingernails came first, then the eating came along. In the process of therapy for my eating, my fingernails grew. Just like a lot of people cope with stress by drinking and smoking, I cope by eating.
>
> If anybody had asked me growing up if I'd ever drink, I'd have said, "Absolutely, positively not!" [Because of my father's alcoholism]. But I do. Although I wish I were just like my mother, I have a whole lot of my father in me, which I don't like.
>
> —Emma, age forty-two

overachievers and eventually workaholics (Robinson 1989) (see the box on page 52). They attempt to control, suppress fatigue, are impatient, strive for competition and achievement, and have a sense of time urgency and perfectionism.

This compulsive need to achieve is linked to such cardiovascular risk factors as fluctuations in blood pressure and heart rate. Type A characteristics have been observed among school children as young as five years of age, and these traits endured over a five-year period (Visintainer & Matthews 1987).

The numbers of Type A children who come from chemically dependent families are unknown. The similarities, however, between behavior patterns of Type A kids and the compulsive overachievement behaviors of many COAs are striking. The Matthews Youth Test for Health (MYTH) was developed with the help of classroom teachers for research purposes (Matthews & Angulo 1980) (see figure 3–1). Teachers and other interested practitioners can use the MYTH to distinguish Type A from Type B school-age children (youngsters who do not exhibit Type A traits). The child is rated on how characteristic each of seventeen items is on a scale from 1 (extremely uncharacteristic) to 5 (extremely characteristic). Possible MYTH scores range from 17 (extreme Type B) to 85 (extreme Type A).

Childhood is threatened with extinction as youngsters are pressured to achieve, succeed, and please (Elkind 1981). The period of childhood, compared to adulthood, is the shortest time in the lifespan and some children of alcoholics burn out before they live through this brief period.

Work Addiction

Weekends were difficult for me as a young adult because, as a child, that's when the crises with my father would erupt. Any time there was quiet, it was the calm before the storm, and the rapid-fire jolt of my father's inebriated outbursts would hit me like a jackhammer. Waking up on Saturday mornings or holidays with nothing to do made me panic stricken. I felt out of control and that something terrible could happen during those idle hours. It was difficult for me to be flexible and live moment to moment. I learned to cope by packing my weekends full so that I knew exactly what would happen next and how to prepare for it. Although staying busy seemed to alleviate a lot of stress, it left no time for spontaneous, relaxing moments, no time for play, and no time for smelling the roses and living in the now.

Schoolwork helped me feel good about myself and later the work world gave me the same sense of what I thought was fulfillment. It provided an escape so that I didn't have to deal with many feelings buried since childhood. It kept me disconnected from people and intimate relationships and gave me something with which to connect and with which to be intimate. Work also gave me a sense of total control of my life. I had found my drug of choice. I transformed my long hours of college study into long hours of work: weeknights, weekends, and holidays. I was hooked.

Like an alcoholic, I felt restless and became irritable when I went more than a few days away from my desk. Even when lounging on a tropical beach, all my thoughts revolved around my next project. Hardly a vacation passed that a stuffed briefcase of work didn't accompany me as part of my luggage. When family and friends complained about my overworking, I hid my work by sneaking it into my suitcase. While others swam and played in the surf, I toiled over a makeshift desk back in the cottage. I hid my work as my father had hidden his bottle. As a recovering adult child of an alcoholic I came to realize that, like most adult COAs, I was repeating my father's compulsive dependency. Unrecognized in a different form, I had merely switched addictions.

—Bryan Robinson

Adapted from *Work Addiction: Hidden Legacy of Adult Children of Alcoholics,* by Bryan Robinson, © 1989, Health Communications. Used with permission.

The Matthews Youth Test for Health

1. When this child plays games, he or she is competitive.
2. This child works quickly and energetically rather than slowly and deliberately.
3. When this child has to wait for others, he or she becomes impatient.
4. This child does things in a hurry.
*5. It takes a lot to get the child angry at his or her peers.
6. This child interrupts others.
7. This child is a leader in various activities.
8. This child gets irritated easily.
9. He or she seems to perform better than usual when competing against others.
10. This child likes to argue or debate.
*11. This child is patient when working with children slower than he or she is.
12. When working or playing, this child tries to do better than other children.
*13. This child can sit still long.
14. It is important to this child to win, rather than to have fun in games or schoolwork.
15. Other children look to this child for leadership.
16. This child is competitive.
17. This child tends to get into fights.

Reprinted from K.A. Matthews and J. Angulo. (1980). Measurement of the Type A Behavior Pattern in Children: Assessment of Children's Competitiveness, Impatience-Anger, and Aggression. *Child Development, 51,* 466–475. © The Society for Research in Child Development, Inc. Used with permission   *The scale is reversed for these items.

Figure 3–1. The Matthews Youth Test for Health

Physical and Sexual Abuse

Concern for the safety of children in alcoholic households is an important consideration in and out of school. Violence in an alcoholic home can become so heightened that it is unleashed on the child, causing physical injury and school absenteeism. Children often stay home to conceal welts, bruises, or other signs of abuse. The twelve-year-old girl who drew the picture in figure 3–2, said she "couldn't go to school for three days" because of the huge welts caused by her drunken mother's abuse. Risks of sexual abuse also run high in alcoholic families. After school large numbers of COAs are safety risks because they are home alone or left unsupervised with an inebriated parent.

Ginger tried to resist the sexual advances of her drunken father. Finally he threatened to leave his wife and family unless the mother instructed their thirteen-year-old daughter to engage in sexual activity with him. Fearful of being abandoned, the mother and child succumbed to his sexual demands. During the next four years, Ginger replaced her mother as her father's sexual outlet.

Figure 3–2. This twelve-year-old girl relived the time her alcoholic mother beat her with a flyswatter and a belt. The child says her mother's pet word for her when she has been drinking is "bitch."

Authorities estimate that two or three million children are victims of physical and sexual abuse each year. These estimates are low because many professionals never report cases or abused children are often afraid or ashamed to talk. Child abuse ranges from physical and sexual assault to neglect and failure to provide protection. About two thousand children die annually as a result of their circumstances. In retrospect, my sister and I were children of neglect when we were left alone in the empty streets after the Friday night movies at such a young age and at such a late hour. Occasionally, strange men (who must have been more sober "drinking buddies") would come for us and say our father had sent them. We were always frightened of these men because we didn't know if they were telling the truth or if they would hurt us. Every time we stepped into a car with one of these strangers, we wondered if we were being kidnapped.

Alcohol abuse is generally found among 50 to 80 percent of homes reporting physical and sexual abuse or neglect (Black 1987; Famularo, Stone, Barnum & Wharton 1986). Children of alcoholics report greater frequency of family violence than children from abstaining families. Physical violence includes abusive behaviors by and between parents and toward the children. Many children, like the child who wrote the letter in figure 3–3, witness one parent abusing another.

Dear Daddy,
I do not like you when you are drinking. Sometimes you push and slapp my mom. I hate you when you are drinking!

Figure 3–3. Evidence of family violence and abuse appear in this child's letter to his father.

A study of 409 adult children of alcoholics revealed that 95 percent described greater frequency of both parents being violent in general and 56 percent said their parents were violent while drinking (Black et al. 1986). Fathers were ten times more likely to be abusive. Children of alcoholics also described themselves and their siblings as performing violent acts more often than comparison groups. A total of 18.5 percent said they had been sexually abused as children either by fondling or oral sex. Daughters of alcoholics were two times more likely to be incest victims.

I suspected sexual abuse of eight-year-old Marla, whose dress and behaviors were sexually seductive and provocative. Dressed like an eighteen-year-old, Marla boasted, "All the boys at school [Marla is in third grade] want to go with me. My daddy says the reason I dress nice is because I want to attract the boys and make them want me." Although her father said Marla dresses in high style to attract the boys, Marla argued that she just likes to dress nice. When her father gets drunk and throws things and yells, Marla lays in bed and hugs her oversized teddy bear. She said her father gets crazy when he drinks and hits her mom and slams the phone down on her mother's fingers when she tries to call the police.

Marla has been told to call the police when her father gets violent, but she says she could never do that because she loves him too much. According to Marla, a next-door neighbor shared my concerns: "This lady next door says that if my daddy ever touches me in places that I should tell her. Or that if he wants me to touch him somewhere I should tell her too. Yuk, I wouldn't want to do that. But he'd probably whip me if I didn't do what he said."

Documented physical abuse, sexual overtones in Marla's dress and behaviors, and sexual themes in her discussions about her father raised my suspicions. These signs are among twenty indicators of child sexual abuse (Sgroi 1982, 40–41):

1. Overly compliant behavior
2. Acting-out, aggressive behavior
3. Pseudomature behavior
4. Hints about sexual activity
5. Persistent and inappropriate sexual play with peers or toys or with themselves, or sexually aggressive behavior with peers
6. Detailed and age-inappropriate understanding of sexual behavior (especially by young children)
7. Arriving early at school and leaving late, with few, if any, absences
8. Poor peer relationships or inability to make friends
9. Lack of trust, particularly with significant others

10. Nonparticipation in school and social activities
11. Inability to concentrate in school
12. Sudden drop in school performance
13. Extraordinary fears of males (in cases of male perpetrator and female victim)
14. Seductive behavior with males (in cases of male perpetrator and female victim)
15. Running away from home
16. Sleep disturbances
17. Regressive behavior
18. Withdrawal
19. Clinical depression
20. Suicidal feelings

Children of alcoholics become alcoholics or marry alcoholics or both; sexually abused children have kids whom they sexually assault or they marry abusers; and physically abused children become adult child abusers or marry batterers (Weatherford 1988). Youngsters who grow up under all three conditions are prone to repeat the cycle by living out a combination of sequences, unless practitioners intervene (Black 1986).

All fifty states have mandatory reporting laws of suspected or known physical and sexual abuse cases (Slavenas 1988). If you observe patterns of abuse, neglect, or harm, you can review the reporting policies and procedures in your respective school and state and file reports in accordance with them. You can obtain the specific laws that apply to you from your state's Child Protective Agency. Although you should ensure confidentiality in conversations with children from alcoholic families, the one exception would be in cases of physical or sexual abuse. Children should be encouraged to tell you in such instances, and you *must* always report it.

Latchkey Children of Alcoholic Parents

In addition to the hardship of everyday living in chemically dependent homes, many COAs are neglected by their parents (Nylander 1960). They have the added burden of before- and after-school responsibilities of caring for themselves, a younger sibling, and sometimes a drinking parent. All these factors combined can jeopardize safety, increase stress level, and interfere with school performance.

I asked Nina how things went during the Thanksgiving holidays.

"Not so good," she replied. "My momma and uncle yelled at me because the turkey didn't turn out right." Asked to explain, she said, "I cooked the turkey too long and it was too dry, so they fussed at me. I just went into my room and closed the door and hit my bed and cried."

I responded, "That's a pretty big job for a ten-year-old."

She looked at me as if I were half crazy. "I always cook Thanksgiving dinner, cause my momma's too drunk!"

Not only does Nina cook all the meals, she also looks after her six-year-old sister and gets her off to school every morning. She cleans the house, does the laundry, and any other chores that are necessary for her survival. Nina's mother is not a working mother: she is an alcoholic mother. Technically, Nina is a latchkey child by default (Robinson 1988d).

Latchkey kids are underage children who care for themselves on a regular basis before and after school, on weekends, and during summer vacations and holidays while their parents work (see Robinson, Rowland & Coleman 1986). There are roughly the same number of latchkey kids as there are children of alcoholics under age eighteen: seven million. Latchkey youngsters have received far greater attention and help in coping with their self-care arrangements than the millions of children like Nina, who are latchkey kids by default. Public school extended-day programs, neighborhood "block mothers," after-school hotlines, and "survival skills" training are just a few examples. Being a latchkey child is not necessarily detrimental when proper preparations have been made.

But because they are not officially classified as latchkey children, many kids who go home each day to an alcoholic parent do not get the adequate preparation they need for self-care. Those who have worked with children of alcoholics for any length of time know countless children who are technically latchkey kids, even though a drinking parent is home. The parent may be so physically and psychologically unavailable that the child is literally unsupervised. Such is the case of fourteen-year-old Fran and her eight-year-old sister, who are frequently left alone by addicted parents at all hours of the night. Fran, who had become the parent of the whole family, had the look of a child who carried the world on her shoulders. She spoke openly about her parents' use of cocaine and alcohol:

> It makes me sick to my stomach when they get high. They smile and ask me if I want some too. I feel like they don't really love me because they'll let me do anything I want. I can go anywhere and do anything and stay as long as I want to. But I don't because there wouldn't be anybody to take care of my sister.

Margaret Cork (1969), in her pioneer work, interviewed numerous children younger than age ten who were concerned about their alcoholic parents' inability to care for them: "Mom doesn't look after us. I have to be the mother myself" (p. 31). The older kids of fifteen and sixteen years of age were concerned because they had to take over parental responsibilities for younger siblings: "I feel like I have to be mother because Mom's too wrapped up in herself" (p. 31).

These children also face the challenge of latchkey arrangements. Above and beyond the many problems encountered through alcoholism, children of alcoholics may be at high risk for added psychological or physical hurt that plague some latchkey kids: accidents, fears of intruders, stress from emergencies that cannot be handled, sexual abuse, feelings of confinement, and isolation. Research suggests that during infancy and early childhood, children of alcoholics have more accidents and serious illnesses than children from nondrinking homes, presumably because of parental absence and neglect (Chafetz, Blane & Hill 1971).

One report revealed that COAs, from preschoolers to teenagers, had 60 percent more injuries, were five times more likely to report emotional problems, and were two and one-half times more likely to be classified as severely ill or disabled than children from abstaining homes (Woodside 1986). A combination of factors can put children at risk when left alone or with a drinking parent. Armed with the requested information in the box on page 60, the degree of risk to which individual children are exposed can be measured.

Younger children of alcoholics (roughly twelve and under) who must care for themselves are at greater risk than older ones. They are emotionally and intellectually more immature and thus lack the ability to assume responsibility for their own safety and welfare. They need close adult supervision before and after school, while upper elementary and junior high school children still need supervision from a sober parent but can handle more responsibility for being on their own.

The places where children of alcoholics live can make a difference in whether they are vulnerable to physical or psychological harm. City children on their own in high-crime areas may be at greater risk than those who live in relatively safe, crime-free settings in rural or suburban areas. Unsupervised urban youngsters generally need closer supervision and tighter rules than do children in small towns or rural areas.

Time alone is a major factor in children's adjustment. Children who spend unusually long hours alone or caring for an alcoholic parent are more likely to have greater adjustment problems. The longer they are alone the longer they must endure the potential dangers of being with an adult out of control. Also the greater are their chances of having accidents or expressing fears, especially after nightfall. Longer hours are also more likely to produce boredom and loneliness.

Some children are alone at home and some are supervised by an older brother or sister while the alcoholic parent is passed out in another room. Others are on their own but stop by a friend's house where no adults are pre-

The Latchkey Risk Quotient (LRQ)
for Children of Alcoholics

Listed below are a number of factors that, when combined, can place children of alcoholics in high-risk categories when home alone or with a drinking parent. Read each factor and decide the degree to which it pertains to a child. Circle the number that best describes the child's situation.

1. **Age of child**

1	2	3	4	5
14 and over	12–13	10–11	7–9	6 and under

2. **Location that Best Typifies Where the Child Lives**

1	2	3	4	5
rural area	suburbia	small town	city (pop. under 300,000)	city (pop. over 300,000)

3. **Length of Time Left Alone or with Drinking Parent Each Day**

1	2	3	4	5
One hour	two hours	three hours	four hours	five hours or more

4. **Degree of Nonalcoholic Supervision after School Each Day**

1	2	3	4	5
supervised by sober parent *in absentia* (daily phone calls and clear set of rules)	checks in with a next-door neighbor	supervised at home by underage sibling	unsupervised at friend's house	unsupervised, hanging out in neighborhood

Add the four numbers that you circled under each category to compute the LRQ: **Age + Location + Amount of Time Left Alone + Degree of Nonalcoholic Supervision.** The higher the score, the higher the risk for a child when left alone or with an alcoholic parent. A score from 4 to 9 is a low-risk score. Low-risk children have few or none of the combinations that would cause them to be hurt from self-care. A score from 10 to 14 is a moderate-risk score. Moderate-risk children are those who have some, but not all, combinations to place them at risk. A score of 15 to 20 is a high-risk score that contains many or all of the factors that place children at risk. This simple test is a thumbnail screen for risk levels. A higher score could indicate greater risks of accidents, fear or stress levels, getting into trouble, or physical or psychological harm.

sent or "hang out" at a local hamburger joint or video arcade. Some children are supervised *in absentia* by a sober, working parent through telephone calls, while others have no communication with nondrinking adults at all. These diverse arrangements make a difference in children's adjustment. Children who "hang out" at a friend's house (where no adults are home) or on the street are at higher risk of getting into trouble than kids who promptly report home and remain there alone. Kids who are supervised in absentia by sober parents adjust in similar ways to other children who are supervised by nonalcoholic parents at home during after-school hours (Steinberg 1986).

In addition to providing children of chemically dependent parents the necessary skills for surviving alcoholism, we can also give them the self-care skills they need when proper supervision is not available. The following points will provide the same preparation that latchkey kids need to function more effectively on their own (Robinson, Rowland & Coleman 1989).

Children must understand why it is necessary for them to stay on their own, how long it will be before the nondrinking parent will get home, how that parent will check on them, and the safety rules that will be enforced.

Important phone numbers such as the office number of the nondrinking parent, the 911 emergency number, and an at-home neighbor's number should be taped to the telephone or on the wall near the phone.

Children should be taught basic first aid and have a special location for a first-aid kit.

Children should have safety rules including such basics as: don't climb on furniture, don't play with matches, don't use knives or kitchen appliances without the sober parent present.

Nonalcoholic parents should have children call and check in each day when they get home from school.

Children should be encouraged to talk about how they feel about being alone or with the drinking parent. A pet may be a good "friend" for companionship and also give children a sense of security.

When nondrinking parents will be getting home late from work, they can call their children and let them know when to expect them.

Children should know not to let strangers in the house for any reason.

Children should have a set of housekeys and a key chain and should always keep the keys out of sight. If children wear keys on yarn necklaces, the necklaces should be worn inside their shirts. Visible keys are more easily lost and "mark" children who will be alone. Children should always know what to do if their keys are lost.

Children should be prepared for various phone calls by having pretend phone conversations. Children should never tell a caller they are alone. Children should say their parents are busy but will return the call later.

Children should know their full home addresses and telephone numbers in case they have to be given in emergency situations.

Children should be instructed on what to do in case of fire. Holding practice fire drills will teach them where the exits are and how to use the 911 number. A smoke detector should be installed and children should know to leave the house if it sounds.

Trusted neighbors who know there is an alcohol problem can be informed that children will be staying home without adequate supervision so the neighbors can "watch out" for small children.

Family meetings can be held to decide matters such as house rules, any simple chores to be done, how much television can be watched, whether friends may come over and under what conditions.

Children need instruction on basic procedures to follow in adverse or unexpected conditions, such as when the drinking parent becomes violent or out of control or when bad weather or power outages occur.

Children can get a break from self-care in the alcoholic home while simultaneously doing positive things for themselves by participating in after-school activities they enjoy, such as Scouts, sports, YMCA programs, and so forth.

Safe and healthy snacks, placed on low shelves or tables and in plastic or paper containers, can be provided for children.

Children do better when they are praised and trusted for undertaking self-care responsibilities. They need to hear it and they need special quality time with the nondrinking parent in which they are the sole focus of attention.

Nina is likely to grow into the kind of adult that everyone envies: responsible, achievement-oriented, able to take charge of any situation and handle it successfully. At least that's how she will appear to the outside world. Inside, she will no doubt continue to feel like the little girl who never does anything quite right, while holding herself up to standards of perfection without mercy, harshly judging herself for the most minute flaws. Convinced that she can never allow herself to depend on anyone, Nina will inevitably carry a sense of isolation into most of her adult relationships. Sadly, she might end up spending many nights crying in her bed, pounding her pillow over far more important things than dried-out turkey (Robinson, 1988d).

Tips for Practitioners

There are several points you can keep in mind in regard to the health and safety of children of alcoholics. You need to know when to consult with another resource person and when to recommend referral to another community agency, how to build on the child's strengths, important points to emphasize for children at risk in self-care situations, and how to help relieve childhood stress.

Know When to Consult and Refer

You can consult with the school nurse when physical, psychosomatic, or medical symptoms appear. It is important to know when the symptoms are constitutional, as they were with Shelia, or environmental, as they are with most children of alcoholics. Medical staff can be helpful resources in determining the appropriate approach. FAS children who are obviously developmentally delayed can be referred to the school psychologist or social worker for testing. Special curricula can be developed out of their assessments. It may be more appropriate to refer other children to a counselor for a special COA group or for individual counseling. You also must be prepared to intervene in cases where children show symptoms of physical or sexual abuse. The appropriate steps in reporting should be followed according to the respective laws in your state.

Emphasize Strengths

Capitalize on the children's strengths. Although Shelia had attention and concentration problems, her teacher stressed the child's excellent social skills and put her into situations where she was able to interact and to give moral support to other children.

Implement Self-Care Curricula

Determine those children who are in situations where they must ultimately care for themselves. This might include latchkey arrangements or situations in which children are left alone for fifteen minutes while a parent runs errands. You can help children who are vulnerable to crisis acquire self-reliance skills and ensure that they can cope safely on their own. Traffic safety, precautions with strangers, handling emergencies, accident prevention, and entering a safe house are topics that can be included as part of a health unit on safety. While all children benefit from such instruction, children of alcoholics would automatically learn (even though alcohol is never mentioned) whom to call in case of an emergency, accident, or if they get abandoned at the mall or movie by a drinking parent or need a safe place to get away from a violent, abusive, intoxicated parent.

Community helpers can be brought in and many of the points discussed earlier in this chapter can be included for children who are unprepared for self-care (see Robinson, Rowland & Coleman 1986; 1989). Children who have self-confidence in their abilities to care for themselves when alone are more likely to concentrate and perform better in school rather than dwell on their apprehensions. School counselors can help teachers plan special lessons on self-care and encourage children to talk about being alone. This way children learn that other children share many of their same feelings of fear or loneliness.

Help Relieve Stress

You can play a big role in children's lives by helping them keep the "child" in their childhood. Practicing stress-relief exercises will help all youngsters. Take a breather from learning each day and teach them how to relieve tension by practicing relaxation exercises. Accompanied by soft music, lead children through guided imagery and meditation. Emphasize the importance of physical exercise and good nutrition for stress reduction. Encourage children to practice these suggestions at home.

Many books on the market for adult children of alcoholics recommend healing the child within or getting in touch with the inner child (for example, Whitfield 1987). Practitioners can help kids by ensuring that they have this opportunity while they are still young, unlike many grown COAs who were deprived of their childhoods and in recovery must mourn that loss. Try practicing the following guidelines daily and sharing them with parents of all children.

- Avoid hurrying children. Let them grow and develop at their own unique pace, according to their unique developmental timetables.
- Encourage children to play and do things children do. Some of our fondest memories are of our childhood experiences.
- Do not forcefeed learning. Have reasonable expectations based on what children are capable of performing at their respective ages.
- Let children have a daily, flexible schedule in school and at home with free time built in for choosing from activities that match their interests.
- Protect children from the harsh pressures of the adult world, without overprotecting them, and give them time to play, learn, and fantasize.
- Try not to pass on needless stress and worry to children. Give them opportunities to talk about their own worries and stresses. Adults can save theirs for the therapist's couch.
- Guide children toward wise decision making by introducing limited choices that match their emotional maturity.
- Reward children for their triumphs and successes, no matter how small. Let them know you love them and are proud of them for who they are, not what you want them to be.
- Start the day on a positive note with pleasant words and calm routines.
- Plan special times together each week as a family (without television), and listen to what your children have to say.
- Do not burden kids with adult responsibilities of raising a sibling, keeping house, and the emotional worry of being a parent at age ten or twelve.

4
Academic and Behavioral Concerns

Depending on the severity of parental alcoholism, and other variables, children of alcoholics suffer a wide range of physical, psychological and emotional characteristics which impact on all aspects of their educational experience . . . attendance, classroom behavior, academic performance, peer group relationships, involvement in extracurricular activities, and interaction with those in authority.
—Ellen Morehouse and Claire Scola, *Children of Alcoholics: Meeting the needs of the young COA in a school setting*

Case 4–1

Ted, a student in my first grade classroom, had all the symptoms of a child living in active alcoholism. He showed signs of flagrant parental neglect. He bragged that he didn't have to do anything he didn't want to do at home or school. And he didn't. He was allowed to roam the neighborhood at will unsupervised, to stay up as late as he wanted to, and boasted that his mom even gave him a cigarette to smoke. He came to school in tattered and torn clothes. His unlaced and untied shoestrings usually dragged the floor. His shirts had holes in them, and his pants were missing pockets or belt loops. His face was often crusty, and he had body odor from not bathing and from wearing the same clothes day after day. One morning he showed me a severe burn across his chest that he said came from a kerosene heater. The burn may leave permanent scars.

Ted was quarrelsome and uncooperative with classmates and teachers. Late-night television watching of adult themes on cable channels caused him to repeat sexually explicit language to other children and to touch little girls in sexually aggressive ways. Ted had poor relationships with his classmates. His foul language, combined with his offensive smell and roughhousing, caused the other children to dislike and reject him.

Behaviorally, Ted commanded my constant attention by stealing and lying. Although he had free lunch at school, he repeatedly stole snacks and lunch from the other children. One day I watched Ted, after he had eaten a full lunch, go into the book bags and coat pockets of several children. He stole and ate three apples, a sandwich, and three bags of carrots on top of his lunch. Show-and-tell toys and valuables (such as a digital watch) began to disappear from the classroom. I had given Ted some used clothing—sweat shirts and pants. It finally came to my attention that Ted was taking home other children's possessions and telling his mother that I had given him the toys just as I had given him the clothes. On different occasions, he took credit for other children's work and told classroom visitors that he painted a picture or wrote a story that had been done by another child. Ted's conduct was out of control not only in school but also in his neighborhood. Once while playing with matches he set a fire in the woods, and the fire department had to be summoned to fight the blaze.

Academically, Ted had difficulty concentrating and made failing grades. He had a short attention span and always seemed to be on the move when he wasn't sleeping. He often slept during lessons or just simply refused to do his work. At the end of the year, he started to show some improvement in reading but was behind the other children in most areas. He still, for example, couldn't associate number values with manipulative objects. He was retained in first grade.

—Judy Watson
First grade teacher

Academic and Behavioral Concerns

Problems with children of alcoholics naturally emerge in the classroom, where they spend a large portion of their time. Ted's teacher was smart enough to put two and two together and realize that lying, stealing, and poor study habits were not his real problems. Instead, they were symptoms of a deeper-rooted, more pervasive problem of family alcoholism. Ted had many of the academic and behavioral signs that concern and puzzle classroom teachers. Fortunately for Ted, he had a sensitive and caring teacher who communicated closely with his parents and provided him with every opportunity to learn. She was successful in getting the mother to work with Ted on his reading and, although he lacked mathematical ability, the child became a proficient reader.

Academic problems occur with older children for many of the same reasons but with the added pressure of the peer group which has a bigger influence. Aaron, for instance, had trouble with school—skipping and sleeping through classes and "cutting up." Slightly rebellious, but articulate and charismatic, with coal-black hair and dark eyes, the fifteen-year old is already two grades behind.

> What do you do when you know you need help with algebra but you don't want to ask for it because the other guys will think you're not cool? I mean if I don't understand a problem, the teacher will come over and spend all this time hovering over my desk and everybody else laughs at me. So I just don't even ask anymore.

The peer group is essential for all teenagers but for Aaron, whose father is an active alcoholic, being accepted and fitting in is even more important— even if it means flunking his grade. He'd rather fail than look "dumb" in front of his classmates.

A host of problems related to academic performance is associated with drinking parents (see box on page 70). The upheaval that typifies the alcoholic household interferes with concentration in and out of school. Psychosomatic disorders are often accompanied by behavioral disturbances. Sleepless nights, stress, and depression lead to daydreaming and sleeping during class. Children have trouble keeping up. School absenteeism, frequent changes of schools, and preoccupation with problems at home lead to low scores on standardized tests, bad grades, and ultimately grade failure.

Alcoholic Fathers and Academic Achievement

Academic achievement is lower for boys and girls from alcoholic homes than children from nonalcoholic homes. Ervin and her associates (1984) found that children raised by alcoholic fathers had average IQ scores seven points lower than a comparable group of children raised by nonalcoholic fathers.

Two studies compared sixteen sons of alcoholic fathers with twenty-five sons whose fathers were not alcoholic (Hegedus et al. 1984; Tarter et al. 1984). In the first study, sixteen-year-old boys were given a battery of intelligence tests. Results showed teenage sons of alcoholics performed more poorly on tests measuring attention, memory, perceptual-motor coordination, motor speed, spatial sequencing, and language capacity. They also performed less well on reading comprehension. In the second study the adolescent boys were given achievement tests. Although both groups were of average intelligence and in the same grade, sons of alcoholics scored two years below the sons of nonalcoholics on learning achievement. The researchers also discovered that the lower scores of COAs were linked to family instability and disruption but also to neuropsychological capacity—a hereditary function of the brain that could suggest a possible neurobiological basis for the vulnerability to alcoholism (Hegedus et al. 1984). I will discuss the

Academic Problems of Children of Alcoholics

- Lower mental ability for boys[1]
- Lower verbal proficiency and lower reading comprehension[2,3,4]
- Lower academic achievement for children of alcoholic fathers[4,5,6] and children of alcoholic mothers[7]
- Lower scores on IQ tests[5,17,18,19]
- Deficits in perceptual-motor ability, memory, and language processing[4]
- Attend more schools than children from nondrinking homes[2,3]
- Repeat more grades than children from sober homes[2,3,8,20]
- Higher school absenteeism than children of nonalcoholics[9,10,11,12,13]
- Inability to concentrate and short attention span[4,8,13,14,15]
- Restlessness and impulsivity[2,15]
- More likely to be referred to school counselor or psychologist[2,3,16]
- More likely to be expelled and less likely to graduate from high school among low-income children of alcoholic parents[12,16]

Sources: 1. Kern et al. 1981; 2. Knop et al. 1985; 3. Schulsinger et al. 1986; 4. Tarter et al. 1984; 5. Ervin et al. 1984; 6. Hegedus et al. 1984; 7. Marcus 1986; 8. Cork 1969; 9. Haberman 1966; 10. Kammeier 1971; 11. Rimmer 1982; 12. Robins et al. 1977; 13. Wilson & Orford 1978; 14. Fine 1976; 15. Nylander 1960; 16. Miller & Jang 1977; 17. Aronson et al. 1985; 18. Gabrielli & Mednick 1983; 19. Steinhausen et al. 1982; 20. Shaywitz, Cohen & Shaywitz 1980.

high risk of children of alcoholics for developing alcoholism in a later chapter.

Two research investigations followed 134 sons of alcoholic fathers for twenty years and compared them to seventy sons of nonalcoholic fathers in Denmark (Knop et al. 1985; Schulsinger et al. 1986). Schoolteachers rated sons of alcoholics as more restless and impulsive and poorer in verbal proficiency than sons of nonalcoholics. Performance on neuropsychological tests also indicated that sons of alcoholics had poorer impulse control. Sons of alcoholics had reading difficulties and were referred to school psychologists for these problems more often than the comparison group. Based on the social history of sons of alcoholics, the investigators found that they attended more schools, repeated more grades, and had unhappier childhoods in unstable homes.

Alcoholic Mothers and Academic Achievement

Adrienne Marcus (1986) conducted one of the major studies showing that children of alcoholic mothers also have problems in academic achievement. She compared forty elementary school children of alcoholic mothers with forty children of nonalcoholic mothers. Children of alcoholic mothers were more often placed in some type of special education class and scored lower on mathematics, reading recognition, and reading comprehension subtests of academic achievement. These lower scores in some cases may be caused by broken homes (65 percent of the COAs were from single mother households) and turmoil in the home environment, which interferes with learning or contributes to a negative home learning environment. But significantly more alcoholic mothers drank during the term of pregnancy so that the presence of fetal alcohol syndrome among some COAs could be a contributing factor, as it can be in all studies with alcoholic mothers. Early academic failure and special education placement by third grade were also noted in another investigation of heavy-drinking mothers (Shaywitz, Cohen & Shaywitz 1980). Other studies also show that children of alcoholic mothers have lower IQ scores than children of nonalcoholics (Aronson, Kyllerman, Sabel, Sandin & Olegard 1985; Steinhausen, Nestler & Huth 1982).

Sex of Child and Academic Achievement

There is evidence that the academic achievement of boys is more severely affected by parental alcoholism than girls, both in terms of their lack of resilience (Werner 1986) and poor academic performance (Kern et al. 1981; Schulsinger et al. 1986). Sons of alcoholics, compared to sons of nonalcoholics, are at higher risk for repeated school grades and are more likely to be referred to a school psychologist for academic difficulties (Schulsinger et al. 1986). Kern and his associates (1981) compared the mental ability test scores of twenty children of alcoholics (ages eight to thirteen) with twenty children of nonalcoholics. Although girls from alcoholic homes were not affected, boys from drinking homes scored lower on mental ability than boys from nonalcoholic homes. The researchers speculated that depressed mental ability in male children may be an outcome of their perceived inability to control their destiny in the area of intellectual performance.

Research in the area of separation and divorce shows that young boys have a harder adjustment time than girls and this is pronounced in school work and cognitive tests (Skeen & McKenry 1980; Flake-Hobson, Robinson & Skeen 1983). Interference with school performance, thus, may be a factor not only of alcoholic parents but also of family turmoil or even family splits. Chafetz, Blane & Hill (1971), for example, found no differences in school achievement between one hundred children of alcoholics and one hundred children of nonalcoholics on the basis of parental alcoholism alone. They did find, however, among the one hundred children from nondrinking homes, that school problems increased as a consequence of parental separation and were more prevalent among boys than girls.

Poverty and Academic Achievement

A twenty-year, long-term study of 147 low-income children of alcoholics revealed that, compared to 112 control children of abstainers, the outlook for academic achievement was not optimistic (Miller & Jang 1977). Children of alcoholic parents were less likely to graduate from high school. More children of alcoholic parents dropped out because of early marriage or pregnancy, because they joined the military or became institutionalized, or because they were expelled. It is important to note, however, that all 149 children in the sample were from low-income families that were already beset by serious social problems.

Other studies of children from low-income families also conclude that poverty conditions, combined with parental alcoholism, place elementary school children at higher risk for being expelled, failing their grades, truancy, and dropping out of school before graduating from high school (Robins et al. 1977). Researchers in another study examined the records of one hundred children from alcoholic households (average ages ten and eleven) and compared them to those of one hundred children from sober homes (Chafetz et al. 1971). All children were enrolled in a child guidance clinic, were mostly from low income families, and had emotional problems. Alcoholic families consisted mostly of single mothers and had much less income than the nonalcoholic, mostly two-parent families. Findings revealed that during adolescence, children of alcoholic parents had greater school difficulties and police or court problems than children from nondrinking homes.

It would be incorrect to assume that mere exposure to alcoholic parents will lead to horrendous school failure. A lot has to do with how early kids are exposed to alcoholism, presence of divorce or separation, other debilitating conditions (such as poverty and emotional stability) and how resilient kids are. Resilient children score higher on aptitude and achievement tests and are more achievement-oriented than children who develop behavioral problems before eighteen years of age (Werner 1986). School performance, as you saw with psychological adjustment, also depends upon the family environment, social support system, and coping behaviors (Clair & Genest 1987). Some children of alcoholics appear relatively invulnerable to the stressors and ill effects of having an alcoholic parent, while others are clearly more dysfunctional.

Reasons for Poor Achievement

For some children school is a hiding place, a place of safety and comfort. They like school because it is the one place they can retreat from their unstable home life. As a result, these kids thrive in the classroom. Smart teachers and other school personnel will capitalize on children's motivation and build self-confidence that will equip them with other coping skills. In contrast, there are those children who perceive school as another stress factor in their tormented lives. Fear of teachers, fear of failure, and fear that other students will not like them increases the anxiety and stress and lowers children's performance abilities.

Actress Suzanne Somers (1988), who confessed that her thoughts were never far away from the problems of home, describes the school fears and bad grades that accompanied her father's alcoholism:

> Instead of school being a place to escape the trauma of my home life, it became another kind of prison. I was dumb and stupid in school. I hid from my dad at home, and I hid from my teacher at school. I always tried to sit at the back of the room out of Sister Cecile's eyesight. I would panic when she called my name. I was never paying attention. The kids in my class made fun of me. I wasn't smart and I was skinny. (p. 32)

Children of alcoholics do poorly in school for many reasons. Typically, parents are so consumed with their own problems that those of their kids take a back seat. Even if a child does well in school, it is often without the support and praise of a parent. For the majority of kids in Margaret Cork's (1969) sample, school held little sense of adventure or achievement. When children did poorly in school, they were castigated or belittled by their parents and when they did well, they received little recognition at home. Despite the yelling and screaming at home, I managed to make fairly good grades in school. One term I made all "A's" except for a "B" in science. My parents' response was, "Why didn't you make an 'A' in science?" Nothing was mentioned about the seven "A's." The letter in figure 4–1 was written by a fourth-grade girl on treatment night just after her alcoholic father became enraged and slapped her for failing a test at school.

It is difficult for children to study or keep their mind on homework in a home where chaos is the norm. In alcoholic homes, children must learn to concentrate through a Mt. St. Helen's eruption! The unpredictability and inconsistency of alcoholic households that I described in chapter 2 have a direct bearing on children's school performance. The constant upheaval at home makes it practically impossible for children to get their homework done. A third grade child with whom I worked said her father had taken off all the doors in their house so that there was no place she could be alone or

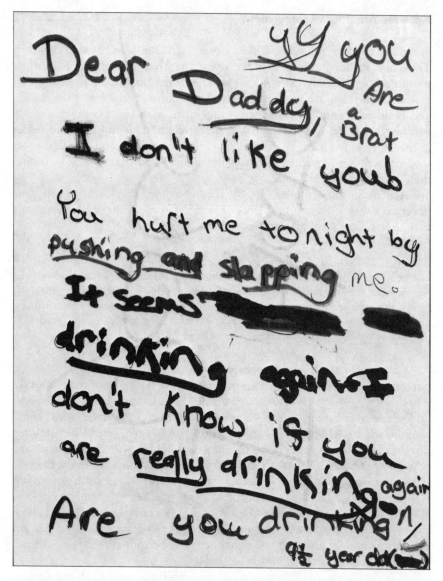

Figure 4–1. A letter written by a nine-year-old girl to her alcoholic father, who had slapped her for failing a test in school.

be quiet. Anxiety interfered with her solitude and concentration and it overtook her interest in everything.

Although my parents were sticklers about good grades and homework, they did little to provide a supportive environment at home. Despite the constant noise and dissention, I was expected to do well in school. How I achieved that was my problem. Rarely an evening went by that I could concentrate and study because of the screaming and yelling. Many times I was chastised for not having my homework by teachers who, although unaware of my home situation, had my best interests at heart.

Even when there were few rare quiet moments at home in which I could study, I usually spent that time recuperating from the stress and preparing myself for the next bout. Often alcoholism zaps 90 percent of children's energies and they may have only 10 percent to give in the classroom. Children become so preoccupied with maintaining calm and sanity at home that they may never think of school, much less homework, after the bell rings. All their energies revolve around the alcoholic parent and trying to control and stabilize their roller coaster existence.

Research indicates that difficulty concentrating on schoolwork is a common complaint of children with alcoholic parents (Cork 1969; Fine 1976; Tarter et al. 1984; Wilson & Orford 1978). Poor concentration and low attention span, when not linked with FAS, stem from lack of sleep or stress and worry about what happened the night before or what is happening at home in their absence. During my childhood, a day never went by that I did not wonder in the middle of a lesson if everything would still be in one piece when I got off the school bus in the afternoon.

As a consequence of their disrupted family conditions, children of alcoholism usually attend more schools than children from sober homes (Knop et al. 1985; Schulsinger et al. 1986). Their families may be transients because of evictions, job changes, and other family disruptions that are used to keep the drinking problem a secret (Priest 1985). Because of sleepless nights and bouts of parental alcoholism, higher rates of school absenteeism are found among children from drinking homes (Haberman 1966; Kammeier 1971). Children also stay home from school to protect the nonalcoholic parent, usually the mother, from the alcoholic parent (Wilson & Orford 1978). School absenteeism makes it difficult for children to keep up with their assignments and often leads to poor grades. Many of these children come to school despite sleepless nights and end up sleeping or daydreaming through class.

I spent a lot of my classroom hours daydreaming and fantasizing about living in a peaceful house where everybody loved and cooperated with one another and laughed and planned fun things to do. I spent a lot of time dreaming of traveling to faraway lands and having exciting adventures. I imagined that I explored the temples of India and Egypt, walked the pasture land of Scotland and Ireland, and swam in the Mediterranean Sea. By the time I was through with my fantasies, I had missed most of the lessons. But it was my way of psychologically relieving myself of the horrible reality of the night before and the terrible dread of what I would face in the night to come. Meanwhile, my grades suffered and no one, least of all my teachers, knew why.

Suzanne Somers (1988) described her bewildering school experience of trying to stay awake in class:

> I woke up with a start. I didn't know where I was. Then I realized that everyone in class was laughing at me. Sister Cecile was standing over my desk. "Miss Mahoney, what *is* the capital of Montana?" I couldn't think. How long had I been sleeping? "Maybe we should talk to the principal about why you can't stay awake in class. Don't your parents make sure you go to bed on time?" she questioned . . . How could I tell her that we were up all night with screaming and yelling and hitting? How could I tell her I finally cried myself to sleep at 5 A.M.? How could I tell her how nervous I was? How could I tell her this was a normal part of my life; that most nights were like this? (p. 31)

Suicide

All COAs need educational intervention. The few that need intensive therapy or confinement to correctional facilities are the ones who act out, rather than conceal, their pain and frustration. They direct it either against society in the form of delinquent acts or conduct and developmental disorders or against themselves in the form of suicide.

Almost one-fifth of the adolescents who attempt suicide come from homes where one or both parents have drinking problems (Hafen & Frandsen 1986). Patrick McKenry and his colleagues at Ohio State University conducted a series of studies that suggest that children of alcoholics are at high risk for suicide attempts (McKenry & Tishler 1987; McKenry, Tishler & Kelley 1983; Tishler & McKenry 1982). The researchers studied ninety-two adolescents between the ages of twelve and eighteen who entered the Children's Hospital Emergency Room in Columbus, Ohio. Half the adolescent patients had attempted suicide and the other half were admitted to the hospital for minor nonsuicidal injuries.

Parents of suicidal adolescents used more alcohol and drugs and used them more often than parents of nonsuicidal adolescents. Suicidal adolescents routinely used more alcohol, depressants, marijuana, and stimulants than the nonsuicidal group. Drugs, in fact, were used in the suicide attempt by thirty-nine of the forty-six adolescents. During clinical evaluations, 24 percent of the suicidal adolescents reported that at least one parent had a serious drug or alcohol problem and one-third of them actually used drugs belonging to their mothers or fathers in their suicide attempts. Parents of the suicide attempters, compared to parents of nonattempters, were coping more poorly, were more depressed, more anxious, and had more suicidal thoughts and lower self-esteem—many of the same symptoms shared by active alcoholics.

This research confirms earlier reports that some teenagers reacted to parental alcoholism with suicide attempts, acting out, psychiatric problems, and difficulty with the legal system (Kearney & Taylor 1969). Other evidence suggests that adult men (average age fifty-six) who grew up in alcoholic homes where they had been abused as children had a higher incidence of serious suicide attempts, suicidal drinking, an increased level of anxiety, more legal difficulties, domestic violence, and violence against authority figures than a group of men without a history of child abuse (Kroll, Stock & James 1985). More recently, out of a sample of fifty thirty-year-old adult children of alcoholics, 44 percent had deliberately tried to hurt or kill themselves in adulthood (Weatherford 1988).

Conduct and Developmental Disturbances

A strong body of research suggests that some COAs who fit the scapegoat role develop a variety of delinquent and behavioral disturbances. As I have emphasized before, only a small portion of the seven million kids of alcoholics are so severely disturbed that their behaviors warrant attention from the justice or mental health systems. Still COAs are overrepresented in these institutions. Approximately 20 percent of the caseloads of juvenile courts and child guidance clinics are children from alcoholic homes (Ackerman 1983).

Cases in which the behavior patterns become so disruptive that they require professional intervention are ordinarily based on information from therapists, mothers, and classroom teachers. Children of alcoholics between ages eight and eighteen admitted to a mental health clinic were more disturbed in their behavior patterns than children from abstaining homes also attending the mental health center (Fine et al. 1976). Compared with children from nondrinking families, COAs were less able to pay attention, less responsive to environmental stimulation, and more prone to emotional upset. As a rule, they were more anxious and fearful children, they had trouble managing their excitement or mood, and they tended to be more dependent. They were more socially aggressive and domineering toward other children and often annoyed and provoked their peers into hitting or in other ways attacking them. They were also more socially and emotionally detached from the happenings around them and preoccupied with inner thoughts. As with autistic children, the COAs showed extreme sensitivity to noises, bright lights, heat or cold, and shut out visual and auditory stimuli by covering their eyes and ears.

Research also suggests that violence in alcoholic fathers was linked to

developmental disorders in boys and girls (Wilson & Orford 1978). Boys—
but not girls—with alcoholic fathers showed a greater number of developmental disorders than a control group of children. More symptoms of developmental disorders existed among COAs with violent fathers.

Mothers' reports of their offspring unearthed eight behavioral symptoms
that distinguished COAs from other children. COAs were more likely to
stutter, wet the bed after age six, fight with peers, get in trouble in the
neighborhood, isolate themselves from peers, and have temper tantrums, unreasonable fears, and trouble in school (Haberman 1966). Direct observations of 229 COAs, along with mothers' reports and teacher judgments, indicated a greater prevalence of emotional disturbances among the COAs than
a comparison group of 163 nonCOAs. Bedwetting, hysterical symptoms, and
speech disorders were more typical of the COAs than nonCOAs (Nylander
1960). Classroom teachers' comparisons of boys with alcoholic fathers and
nonalcoholic fathers revealed that sons of male alcoholics tended to have the
same passive-aggressive personality traits as their fathers (Aronson & Gilbert
1963).

Other studies confirm that COAs, compared to children of nondrinking
parents, have an assortment of conduct disorders (Merikangas, Weissman,
Prusoff, Pauls & Leckman 1985; Steinhausen et al. 1984). They are more
hyperactive (Aronson et al. 1985; Bell & Cohen 1981), have more temper
tantrums and problems paying attention (Steinhausen et al. 1981), engage in
more avoidant coping behaviors such as smoking, drinking, and eating (Clair
& Genest 1987) and are more often involved in fights and impulsive behaviors at school (Schulsinger et al. 1986).

Children from active alcoholic homes have twice the number of behavior
problems than those from nondrinking families (Rimmer 1982). The greatest
problem was disobedience, followed by stealing at home and discipline problems at school. Truancy and fighting were also common problems. Other
problems, although less common, were playing with matches, stealing, cheat-
ing at school, being expelled or suspended from school, and lying.

Sometimes COAs tell lies because they are embarrassed that their parents
drink or they just try to make things look like they wish they could be. Ted,
in the earlier case, often took credit for other children's work because he felt
his was inferior. Shelia's kindergarten teacher said the child constantly lied
about her alcoholic parents by constructing a fantasy world at school:

> She lived in a fantasy world. I noticed this especially when we started having
> show and tell at the first of the year. She came up with some strange concoc-
> tions of where her mother was going to take her and it was always Disney-
> land or Disney World. Then I noticed a pattern. If the child ahead of Shelia
> happened to say something about their parents taking them to Disney
> World, then Shelia would get up in front of the group and say that her mom
> was also taking her to Disney World. She would describe in great detail how

---

Common Conduct Disturbances Reported among a Small Portion of Children of Alcoholics

Socially aggressive behaviors
Isolation from peers
Fighting with peers
Quarrelsomeness and uncooperativeness
Delinquency
Disruptive, disobedient, and oppositional behaviors
Stealing
Lying
Truancy
Substance abuse
Temper tantrums
Hyperactivity

---

they were going to get there and when they were going to go. One time during show and tell Shelia picked up something that belonged to another child and told the class about it. Then the child who owned the object said, "But that's mine!" Shelia suddenly snapped out of her dream world and seemed very embarrassed.

It is difficult to know how much of delinquent and behavioral problems are caused by divorce, rather than alcoholism. But analysis of this body of work revealed that, once the influence of one-parent families is considered, parental alcoholism does not increase the risk for delinquency beyond that attributable to divorce (West & Prinz 1987).

Children with behavioral disturbances are signaling to those around them that something is wrong. Behind the angry, hostile, and aggressive mask lies a frightened little child. At sixteen, Rick had become the family scapecoat. He had pulled away from his one-parent family by running away, fighting at school, and using alcohol and other drugs. The first night I met him, he wanted me to know he was a cool dude and tough enough to make it on his own. Through hostility and arrogance, he assured me that he didn't want to be in the COA program and would rather be with his friends getting high and listening to music. On his first night in the group, we unrolled a huge parachute and played with it in a large circle. Rick became absorbed into the activity, squealing with laughter and delight each time we made it ascend and descend and offering various suggestions on ways we could make the parachute "behave." His inner child emerged in all its glory. Much to our surprise, Rick thrived in the program taking advantage of all its offerings.

Figure 4–2. **Many children vent their anger about their alcoholic parents at teachers and others outside the home.**

He actively pursued the creative writing and art each week, and wrote the poem expressing his feelings about his grandmother in the opening case in chapter 2. Gradually, he began to lose most of his tough exterior. He clung to parts of the role, though, because he still needed them to survive.

Tips for Practitioners

Teachers, counselors, and school administrators are in a better position than most practitioners to help kids whose parents drink because of their greater daily contact. While they cannot and should not be therapists, school personnel can follow many helpful practices that ultimately can make a difference in youngsters' lives. A speaker at the 1988 National Association for Children of Alcoholics Conference shared through tears that he had been a lost and shy twelve-year-old troublemaker when an angel turned his life around. That angel was his classroom teacher, who introduced him to Alateen. Today that man is a recovering child of an alcoholic and a leader in the field of chemical dependency. Many behavior problem children like this man still await the concerned practitioner's touch.

Look beneath the Symptoms

Some children of alcoholics may need greater opportunities for success in school so that their performance will be commensurate with their potential. Look beneath the daydreaming, inability to concentrate, or sleeping during class and sympathetically address the reasons behind these and other symptoms. Once you have gained the ability to look past the symptoms and identify family alcoholism as the problem, you will begin to see significant changes in the attitudes and behaviors of both you and the child.

Give Extra Attention

You can help highly stressed kids by setting aside a special block of time toward the end of each day for homework completion so that they do not fall behind in their assignments (Brenner 1984). Some COAs may need extra attention completing in-class assignments. One way of providing this attention is to set aside a few minutes out of the day for the teacher, a counselor, a parent volunteer, or another child to work closely with children who have difficulty completing in-class and homework assignments. This can also be a time for the child to build rapport with this special person who functions as a supportive listener. Extra attention makes children feel someone cares and gives them a chance to talk about disturbing thoughts or feelings that could be interfering with school performance. Boys from alcoholic homes in particular may need individual attention, since they appear to be more vulnerable to the negative effects of parental alcoholism. Depressed mental ability in boys may be an outcome of their perceived inability to master their destiny in the area of intellectual performance (Kern et al. 1981). By keeping a pulse on family transitions such as divorce or new stepfamilies, you will be more successful in helping children through these added conflicts.

Catch Children Being Good

Make a point to praise children for classroom successes and goals that are achieved—good work, good grades, good behaviors. They need the strokes they may not be getting at home. Exercises that allow children to learn that they can gain a sense of mastery over their environment can instill feelings of competence and self-esteem.

Be Supportive of Parents

Make a concerted effort to remain objective and supportive of parents and to provide an informal atmosphere in which parents can share their problems and solutions about children. It is important that parents always feel that they can discuss their problems about their children with school personnel. You can often help parents share information about alcoholism without prying by saying, "Molly's mind hasn't been on her schoolwork lately. She seems to be daydreaming a lot. Is there anything that I should know about?" That way you have opened the door for parents to bring up any personal problems without making accusations or putting anyone on the defensive. It is important to remember that alcoholic parents are in a crisis situation and may not be able to parent as well as they would like. Contrary to their outward behaviors, all chemically dependent parents love their children, but the disease of alcoholism gets in the way of expressions of love. Be sure to treat both the dependent and codependent parents with equal respect and concern. Never side with the codependent parent against the alcoholic parent or the child against alcoholic parents. Blame and taking sides are counterproductive and contrary to the concept of alcoholism as a disease. Such strategies actually reinforce the battle lines to which children are accustomed in dysfunctional families and further divide the family. Although it may be difficult, you must remember that parents suffering from alcoholism need empathy and understanding too, as they are often in a bitter struggle to overcome their illness.

5
Identifying Preschool Children
of Alcoholics

> While there is a substantial number of problematic children from alcoholic homes, the majority of these children simply do not draw enough attention to themselves to even be identified as being in need of special attention. They are a neglected population. If they are busy and look good, they will be ignored.
> —Claudia Black, *It Will Never Happen to Me!*

Case 5–1

Everything I remember about my childhood is bad. My parents were really heavy into drugs, like LSD during the 1960s and later alcohol. They were so chemically dependent that they spent all their money on dope and alcohol and ended up broke. My mother beat on me from the time I was four years old. I remember my mother lying in her bedroom and staring up at the ceiling and that's all she'd do all day long.

When I was four years old in nursery school, I wanted to make the babies cry for some unknown reason. I would go into the infant room and pull the babies' hair. I didn't know why I wanted to hear them cry. I remember my mother used to pull my hair when she'd get high. She'd yank it for no reason. Now that I'm grown, I know I was angry with her for doing that to me. It was the only way I knew how to cry out for help. I was trying to show in an outside way the pain I was having on the inside. But nobody listened. I can still see the preschool teacher right in my face, nose-to-nose and all the little kids surrounding her, and she was yelling at me. And I can still see her face. I was getting real upset because I had to go to the bathroom but the teacher wouldn't let me. She spanked me with a paddle as hard as she could, and the whole time I was using the bathroom while she was doing that. I'll never forget that as long as I live. And I'll never forget that preschool. I still remember the nightmares I had about that awful place!

—Deidre

Identifying Preschool Children of Alcoholics

Deidre is one of the millions of invisible (Bosma 1972), forgotten (Cork 1969), and ignored (Black 1982) children of alcoholics who live a life of silent suffering (MacDonald & Blume 1986). Most of these kids, who pass before our eyes everyday, remain unseen unless they make waves or cause problems. Even when they cause problems, practitioners often focus on the symptoms rather than underlying causes, as illustrated by Deidre's preschool teacher, who punished and humiliated the child for pulling hair. The last few chapters dealt with psychological, health, academic, and behavioral problems that, while appearing at elementary age, are already brewing long before in the preschool years.

The Need for Early Identification

The neglect of COAs is more pronounced among preschool children than any other age. The identification, treatment, and research with this age group is practically nonexistent. Instead, professionals tend to postpone identification and treatment until about age eight or nine when kids are old enough to take a test or tell us something is wrong. That is too late. The implication of the blatant neglect of preschoolers is that they cannot be seriously affected if they are preliterate. Child development research, however, shows that this is a fallacy, since the preschool years are the most important ones in the lifespan for establishing the bedrock for adulthood.

Most authorities concede that schools are the best places to identify and treat children of alcoholics because school systems have direct access to all children over the span of their youth (Ackerman 1983; Deutsch 1982; DiCicco, Davis & Orenstein 1984; McElligatt 1986; Morehouse & Scola 1986). While schools should continue to play a primary role in this process, identification efforts must start earlier in the preschool years. Postponement of identification and treatment until the first or second grade is ill-advised, given the clinical observations that denial systems and family roles are already firmly entrenched by age nine (Black 1987). Preschool intervention can interrupt the disease cycle of alcoholism before dysfunctional patterns are firmly in place.

Barriers to Early Identification

Many of the same good reasons that more COAs are not identified in elementary schools also explain the lack of detection in the early years. Most practitioners have not been trained in alcohol education and do not know enough about alcoholism to spot its effects. They may not know how to ask about substance abuse or feel uncomfortable about intruding into the family's personal business. They may be immobilized by their own fears of traumatizing the child, angering the parent, or stirring up trouble (McElligatt 1986).

Despite these barriers, early intervention is possible today more than ever before with most preschoolers in some type of group care and with increasing public school support for three- and four-year-old classrooms. While children are accessible, however, it is much more difficult to identify children younger than age six than it is elementary school youngsters. COAs are not easy to spot because they have no common distinguishing markings. Children with Down's syndrome, autism, or even those who have been physically abused can be easily identified almost immediately because of certain common physical attributes.

Standardized procedures for identifying children of alcoholics have been developed for school-age children (see the next chapter). The Children of Alcoholics Screening Test (CAST) (Jones 1983), for example, and other standardized measures are designed for children age nine or older. But these tests are inappropriate for preschool youngsters because children must be old enough to read and write to complete the forms. Because preschool children and preliterate kids are automatically excluded from the standardized approach, identifying them is much more difficult.

One of the most effective techniques of identifying older elementary children, self-referral, is also developmentally inappropriate for preschoolers, because they cannot verbalize how they feel or what they think about alcoholism as older kids can. Because they are preliterate, they cannot write their feelings, respond to a survey, or take a test. Moreover, their art ability, lacking fewer elements of detail than school-age kids, has not developed enough to be used as a confident diagnostic medium.

Still, identification is possible in the preschool years, although it is totally contingent upon the subjective impressions of the caregiver. There are four areas of the preschool child's life that practitioners can examine to determine if stress and possible chemical abuse are present in the home: (1) daily routines, (2) play observations, (3) emotional adjustment, and (4) parental

Figure 5–1. This five-year-old's sadness about her mother's drinking is more difficult to interpret from her drawing, lacking fewer elements of detail, than the anger expressed by the seven-year-old COA in figure 5–2.

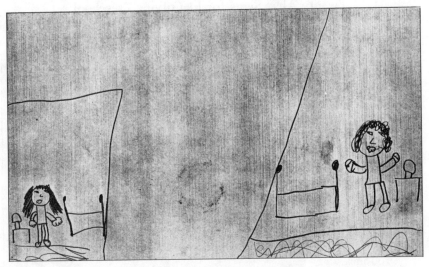

Figure 5–2. **When her alcoholic mother (right) gets angry and throws things, this second-grade girl goes to her room and gets mad too.**

relationships. Examining these four areas unearths the alert signs outlined in the box on page 88.

Monitoring Daily Routines

Developing habits for sleeping, toileting, eating, and adjusting to routines are important milestones in the life of preschoolers. Persistent trouble in these areas is symptomatic of deeper problems that could be alcohol-related. Preschoolers who are off developmental schedule in physical-motor, cognitive, language, or social-emotional areas also may have alcohol-related difficulties.

Sleeping Difficulties

By their first birthday, healthy infants have spent over half their lives asleep. During the first two months, they sleep about seventeen hours a day, but by three months, this time has dropped to fourteen hours. By six months most babies sleep through the night. A lot of sleep is normal during the first

Twenty Alert Signs for Identifying Preschool Children of Alcoholics

1. Sleeping difficulties

2. Persistent fatigue or lethargy

3. Relapses in toileting habits

4. Extreme eating behaviors

5. Problems in adjusting to transitions and changes in routines

6. Developmental delays

7. Recurring alcoholic themes in dramatic play

8. Isolated play

9. Lack of sustained attention

10. Hyperactivity

11. Abrupt and uncharacteristic behavior changes

12. Frequent fussiness and fretfulness

13. Frequent temper tantrums or attacks on other children

14. Regressive behaviors such as thumbsucking or "baby talk."

15. Excessive fear of unfamiliar people or new situations

16. Persistent clinging and exaggerated fear of separation

17. Insecure attachment behaviors

18. Parental authoritarianism and unrealistic expectations

19. Parental indifference and frequent preschool absences

20. Signs of neglect or physical and sexual abuse

twelve months. But as children approach one year of age, they require less and less sleep. After one year of age, persistent fatigue or lethargy and the desire to oversleep is a sign of a physical problem or emotional depression that could be related to family alcoholism.

By age two, toddlers are expected to adjust their sleeping habits to those of the family and most children do so with little difficulty. Sleep patterns are an excellent indicator of how well preschool youngsters are adjusting and how well other things are going in their lives. Just as adults have difficulty sleeping when something is bothersome, erratic sleep patterns indicate problems among preschoolers. The first signs of nightmares normally appear in toddlerhood, and some bad dreams typically accompany the child's newfound ability for symbolic representation. Still, recurrence of bad dreams, disrupted or erratic sleep patterns, or refusal or fear of sleeping at naptime all are indicative of potential alcohol-related problems.

Toileting Habits

Although toilet training is developmental and unique for each child, most children are both bowel- and bladder-trained by twenty-seven months on the average. Most children sleep through the night without bedwetting by thirty-three months. Soiling and wetting accidents are common occurrences, even after they are well in control of their toileting needs. Accidents also occur, however, when children become unusually upset or experience trauma. Regressive toileting habits are natural responses when preschool children get overly excited, become ill, experience a break in daily routines, or become fearful or worried about something. Family alcohol problems can lead to repetitive lapses in toileting habits—either frequent bedwetting or soiling pants after toilet training has been achieved.

Eating Practices

By twelve months of age, most babies are eating three meals a day. Loss of appetite or refusal to eat new foods are normal behaviors in toddlerhood as children grow taller and leaner. But starvation, compulsive eating, eating rituals, or preoccupation with food are not normal throughout the preschool years. We know that a compulsive eating disorder is a clear symptom of adult children of alcoholics. These disorders can originate in the eating habits that are established in the first year of life. Overprotective or overanxious mothers, for example, often feed their babies every time they cry, and they sometimes overfeed infants as a substitute for love they are unable to give. Food for some children becomes a substitute for the love they never received from alcoholic parents. Overfed children can develop compulsive food habits and become obese children. Some overweight children develop adult-sized fat cells by two years of age. These excessive fat cells are difficult to remove by weight loss in adulthood, so obese babies tend to be obese adults (Flake-Hobson, Robinson & Skeen 1983).

On the other extreme, continued loss of appetite, finicky eaters, and malnourishment are signs of problems. Children of alcoholic families may reflect their worry and depression through loss of appetite, much like adults do. Children who are being neglected and are not getting proper meals at home may show it by their gauntness. Thin children who eat as if their stomachs are bottomless or who constantly take food from other children may suffer from alcoholic neglect.

Handling Transitions

All preschool children need the consistency and predictability of everyday routines, whether at home or in the preschool classroom. Secure children from stable homes can handle occasional changes in daily routines. Children from insecure alcoholic homes, however, may show signs of upset when the order of the day is altered. In particular, caregivers will notice that insecure children have difficulty adjusting to transition times in the day care preschool curriculum. As one activity terminates and flows into another, children of alcoholics may have difficulty following the flow and may perseverate in the terminated activity or become anxious or aggressive as the change takes place. An unexpected event in the day that causes a change in normal routines also can be emotionally upsetting to these children.

Developmental Delays

Developmental norms can be useful yardsticks for practitioners to detect problems in development. Serious developmental delays, noted by the use of norms, could signal alcohol-related difficulties. Children who are far behind the norm on language or motor skills alert caregivers to a possible developmental problem. Children who have fetal alcohol syndrome suffer from developmental lags in several areas, including physical and intellectual delays and perceptual-motor disturbances.

It is important for practitioners to remember that because norms are only averages, the ages at which individual children acquire skills will vary. Generally, it is only the sequence of skills that remains the same. Individual children, for example, do not begin crawling, sitting alone, or walking right on schedule according to the norms because they all have unique, biological clocks that regulate the same skills at different rates. Still, norms are useful tools that skilled caregivers and medical practitioners can use to spot developmental delays that could be associated with parental alcoholism. Preschool teachers, in cooperation with parents, can refer children with severe developmental delays for appropriate treatment.

Play Observations

Play serves not only as a workshop for developing social skills but also as an important aid to emotional development. Through play, children deal with reality in a nonthreatening way. Play helps children deal with fears aroused by trauma such as alcoholism. The play of young children is a revealing mirror into their thoughts and feelings. Through play observation, practitioners learn many of the secrets of child development.

Dramatic Play

Preschoolers enjoy a type of activity called dramatic play, in which they act out scenes they observe from everyday life. Preschool classrooms generally have an area especially designated as the housekeeping corner or dramatic play area. Props such as dress-up clothes, empty soup cans and cereal boxes, and dolls are usually on hand to help stimulate dramatic play. They act out their joys and frustrations and, as they pretend, they will even repeat scenarios they have observed at home. Adults can gain a sense of trouble when children use props as bottles or beer cans and imitate drinking parents or when they perform acts of spousal hostility in the housekeeping area.

Some alcoholic treatment programs place beer cans, wine bottles, beer glasses, liquor bottles, shot glasses, and an Alcoholics Anonymous Big Book in the play area for children from chemically dependent families to play out their feelings. Recurring themes in the play of preschool children of alcoholics are violence, anger, guilt, and fear (Hammond 1985). Fears of being left and parents' fighting are commonly played out in the preschool classroom. The fear of emotional and physical safety of four-year-old Brad was apparent when he picked up an empty beer can off the drama shelf, made pouring motions into the glass, and asked the therapist to drink it:

> *Brad:* "It's poison."
> *Therapist:* "Oh, no! I'm getting sick."
> *Brad:* "I'll call the doctor."
> *Therapist:* "Thanks."
> *Brad:* "The doctor says you're better."
> *Therapist:* "Oh, good." (Hammond 1985, 12)

The ability to create and resolve the consequences in such scenarios gives preschool children of alcoholic parents an enormous sense of control over their fears and worries.

Stages of Play

Between the ages of two and five, preschool children typically play alone less and become more socialized in their play (Parten 1932). Children from alcoholic homes will have more difficulty progressing through these stages and can be observed in more isolated types of play (unoccupied, onlooker, solitary, and parallel) than social types (associative and cooperative).

In *unoccupied play,* children are not playing but are occupied with anything that happens to be of fleeting interest to them. During *onlooker play,* children spend time watching others play, often asking questions, giving suggestions to other children but rarely entering into play. The child plays alone and independently with toys in *solitary play,* sometimes within speaking distance of others. Between eighteen and twenty-four months, children begin *parallel play,* in which they play independently but alongside one another, frequently engaging in disputes over the same toy. Children play with peers who are engaged in similar activities in *associative play,* which ordinarily appears between three and four years of age. Sharing, borrowing, and lending play materials are typical. The most socialized play is *cooperative play,* in which children play in groups organized for the purpose of making some material product or attaining some common goal. Typical of five- and six-year-olds, children play cooperatively, assigning each other roles and acting in accordance with those designated roles. Five-year-olds who still spend most of their play time as onlookers or in solitary or parallel play should be cause for concern.

Sustained Attention and Hyperactivity

Children who are unable to sustain attention when playing with toys and who flit from one activity to another are cause for concern. Hyperactivity among preschoolers is a chief symptom of parental alcoholism and a frequent side effect of fetal alcohol syndrome. It is characterized by difficulty paying attention and concentrating, high levels of motor activity, poor impulse control, and attention-seeking behavior. Ordinarily, preschool children have short attention spans, have a need to be active, and have difficulty sitting for long periods of time. The amount of time preschoolers spend paying attention to an activity increases gradually. Signs of potential family alcoholism are reflected in preschool youngsters who cannot sit through short group story or music times; children who cannot plan and complete activities they begin; and children who do not have the patience or enthusiasm to work on a classroom project that requires them to carry attention over several days.

Abrupt Changes in Play

Sudden change in behavior can be indicative of alcoholism in the lives of school-age children. Similar abrupt changes can be observed in preschool youngsters where alcohol is a problem. An outgoing child, for example, who withdraws into a shell or a shy child who suddenly starts to act out could be troubled. The dramatic switch in Jacob, who overnight became apprehensive of exploring the playroom, and the abrupt appearance of Deidre's hair-pulling episodes are two extreme changes in behavior that indicate fear and frustration with alcoholic parents.

Of equal concern is the child who suddenly begins to lodge attacks on other children or classroom pets during playtime. Caregivers should be alert to children, like five-year-old Lenney, who demonstrate an inordinate amount of dramatized violence in their play or who do not exhibit a broad range of play behaviors. Lenney had an array of activities to choose from in his preschool: transportation toys, blocks, art activities, dress-up and house-keeping, and so forth. But in lieu of these activities he perseverated in walking about the classroom with a stick that one minute became his machine gun and the next a machete to cut and slaughter. One day, with the preschool teachers out of sight, Lenney took the class hamster from the cage and squeezed it to death.

Limited range of play need not be violently obtrusive to warrant the practitioner's attention. Children who become suddenly preoccupied with one particular toy or activity and who play with that toy in the same ritualistic way day in and day out are cause for concern. Marcy, for example, got in the habit of holding and rocking her doll and repeating, "Mommy loves you."

Assessing Emotional Adjustment

The reactions of preschool children to a variety of situations can be an emotional barometer of the stability and security of their family lives. Observations of children's moods, their emotional control, their regressive behaviors, and the degree to which they handle separation anxiety can give practitioners possible clues to family alcoholism.

Moody Children

All children have their unique temperaments. Even as infants, some children are labeled as "easy," while others are called "difficult." "Difficult" babies are described as irregular in biological functions, negative and withdrawn toward new people and situations, unable to adapt to change easily, and intense, mostly negative in mood. "Easy" babies are characterized by regularity of such biological functions as hunger, sleep, and eliminating, a positive approach to new people and situations, easy adaptation to new situations or changes in routines, and mild, mostly positive moods (Thomas & Chess 1980).

Some children by nature are temperamentally more difficult than others. Still, contrasting temperaments can be used to spot preschool children from alcoholic homes. In one study, infant temperament was a major distinguishing factor between babies (of alcoholic parents) who did and did not develop serious coping problems by age eighteen (Werner 1986). Babies with easy temperaments who were rated as "cuddly and affectionate" by their care-

Dear Daddy
I hope You get
help for Your
drinking problem
Would You pleas
Stop drinking?

4 yr. old female

(dictated to mother)

© 1986 The Randolph Clinic. Used with permission.

Figure 5–3. Having an alcoholic parent can be emotionally trying for preschoolers, as this letter dictated by a four-year-old girl indicates.

givers during the first year of life were two times more likely to be resilient children than those who later developed learning and behavior problems.

Temperamental children who are fussy, cross, or fretful much of the time are exhibiting their feelings that something is wrong. Irritability, nervousness, and erratic behaviors can be signs of fetal alcohol syndrome. Regardless of biological predisposition, children who remain stuck in depressed, mostly negative moods are evidencing emotional distress, as are children who have flat affect and whose emotions never change. Frequent mood swings from happiness to anger or vice versa also indicate problems that could originate from the stress of alcoholism in the home.

Temper Tantrums

Healthy preschoolers, like healthy adults, have a range of emotions toward others—from love to rage. Temper tantrums are normal emotional outlets for toddlers who are still learning to balance adult boundaries with autonomy and inner control of their feelings. Brief aggressive conflicts over toys are also common in toddlers' play. Ordinarily, temper outbursts decline after two years of age and disappear by age four (Flake-Hobson, Robinson & Skeen 1983). Preschool youngsters who persist with frequent temper tantrums after this age or who have difficulty controlling their emotions need special attention. Aggressive acts directed at other youngsters are also alert signs indicative of children of alcoholic parents.

Regressive Behaviors

Caregivers should be alert to children who show regressive behaviors such as bedwetting, baby talk, or thumbsucking. While some relapses typically occur as children acquire new developmental abilities in other areas, prolonged and exaggerated regression is a sign of emotional maladjustment. Thumbsucking, for example, is normal to some degree and for some children it replaces the familiar security blanket by providing comfort during moments of hurt and fear. But obsessive thumbsucking among young children and continued thumbsucking past age five are signs of emotional insecurity that could stem from alcohol abuse in the home.

Separation Anxiety

Toddlers often display anxiety in the absence of those closest to them. Separation anxiety reaches a peak at eighteen months, diminishes gradually, and levels off by age three, usually disappearing in the preschool years (Weinraub & Lewis 1977). It is normal for preschoolers to cling to, follow, and remain near their parents and familiar caregivers as they adjust to such new situations as the preschool classroom.

Children who have established secure anchors with their parents experience less anxiety when separated from their parents or caregivers. In contrast, preschoolers who fret for long periods of time in the parent's absence, follow and cling to the caregiver for an inordinate amount of time, and become visibly upset when the caregiver leaves the room are displaying unhealthy adjustment problems. The same is true for preschoolers who are constantly afraid of strangers and new situations. Generally, their maladjusted behaviors stem from an insecure upbringing—one that could be linked to alcoholism.

Insecure Attachments

Child development research shows that the type of attachment patterns established in the first twelve months of the child's life remain stable over childhood (Flake-Hobson, Robinson & Skeen 1983). Children of alcoholics who received a great deal of attention from their primary caregivers during the first year of life were less likely than those who received little attention to develop serious coping problems by eighteen years of age (Werner 1986). Preschoolers with an active alcoholic parent who is inconsistent, often inaccessible, and generally unresponsive to the child's needs early in life will develop insecure attachments. By one year of age children of alcoholics who have developed insecure attachments become uncertain that their caregivers will be there when they need them. Signs of insecure children are visible by eighteen months of age when toddlers are anxious and emotionally distressed even on the mother's knee. Unlike secure children, insecure preschoolers are upset when their mothers leave and remain fretful for longer periods of time, and have difficulty getting involved in play.

Attachment patterns at twelve months are associated with personality traits two, three, and six years later (Ainsworth et al. 1978). Insecurely attached children of alcoholic parents, compared to securely attached youngsters, are more uncooperative, negative, more quarrelsome, easily frustrated, and aggressive toward adults and peers in preschool and elementary schools. Insecure children tend to have difficulty forming close relationships with others and are often disliked by classmates and teachers.

Observations of Parents

Practitioners can gain information by observing the interactions of parents with their children and noting their attitudes and parenting practices and how interested and involved they are in their child's development. Parents' interactions with the preschool and cooperation with the administrator and caregivers also can provide clues to family alcoholism.

Child-Rearing Practices

Children may be at risk when their parents are unusually harsh, impatient, or highly critical. Practitioners can pay particular attention to authoritarian parents who displace their anger and frustration onto their preschoolers. Authoritarian parents were first described by Diana Baumrind (1967) from her observations of parenting practices and their relationship to the personalities of three- and four-year-old nursery school children. Authoritarian parents, Baumrind noticed, use power and firm disciplinary controls without reason or explanation. Disapproval, physical punishment, and fear techniques are routinely administered. Authoritarian parents are generally more detached, less approving, and less affectionate in relationships with children. Their harsh and controlled practices lead children to develop behaviors governed by external controls of guilt or fear of being punished.

Clearly, scientists in the chemical addiction field have shown that alcoholic mothers (Krauthamer 1979) and alcoholic fathers (Udayakumar et al. 1984) tend to use authoritarian parenting styles. Research in the field of child development indicates that children of authoritarian parents have many of the same characteristics as children of alcoholic parents. They are usually more withdrawn and hostile, easily upset, moody, unhappy, mistrustful, apprehensive in times of stress, and less competent in peer relationships than other children (Baumrind 1967).

Child Development Knowledge and Attitudes

Children are at risk when their parents have unrealistic child-rearing attitudes or expectations for them. An alcoholic parent with little understanding of normal child development might, for instance, view naughty behavior as the child's deliberate attempt to "get them." Or they might take it personally when a child spills food or breaks a prized vase. They may expect their child to respond in far more mature ways than is developmentally possible.

Misunderstanding of children's developmental milestones, such as when they should begin walking, talking, or become toilet-trained, and an attempt by parents to rush these developmental steps also puts preschoolers at risk. Practitioners should be alerted when parents place unreasonable demands on children or depend on them to meet certain emotional needs for which they are not capable. Either the alcoholic parent or the codependent parent may expect the preschool child to act as a source of reassurance, comfort, and love for them—a huge responsibility for a small child.

Parental Indifference

A drinking problem also may exist when parents refuse to show an interest or become involved in the child's development. Parents who cannot be reached by telephone, refuse to respond to notes, or do not show up for conferences also have high-risk children. Parents who repeatedly fail to pick up their children after preschool or who are persistently late may have a drinking problem (Morehouse & Scola 1986). Children who are frequently absent from preschool, especially on Monday mornings or after holidays, may be home with a parent who is nursing a hangover.

Parental Abuse and Neglect

Signs of parental abuse and neglect are the best indicators for identifying children of alcoholic parents, because 90 percent of the time alcohol is involved in incidents of abuse. Practitioners should look for unusual cuts, welts, bruises, or burns on the child's body. Bruises or wounds in various stages of healing indicate that the injuries occurred at different times and may have been inflicted on a regular basis. Injuries that occur on multiple planes of the body or that leave a mark that looks like a hand or tool should also be considered nonaccidental. Physical abuse can be suspected if injuries show up a day or so after a holiday or long weekend, since bruises take a day or so to appear (Meddin & Rosen 1986). A child who cowers when the preschool teacher raises her hand to catch the attention of the class may be a child who expects to be abused.

Neglect is apparent when children have poor hygiene, wear soiled or tattered clothing, wear winter clothes in warm weather and summer clothes in subdegree temperatures, and are always famished. Neglect in which preschool children are routinely left home alone for long periods of time without adult supervision puts them in situations that they are developmentally unprepared to handle. Some preschoolers are latchkey children, in effect, even though a drinking parent is at home with them. The parent may be so wed to booze that the child is literally unsupervised. Such is the case of five-year-old Mark, who gets off his school bus and stays at home for two hours, unsupervised by an alcoholic father, until his mother gets home from work. There is no such thing as a preschool latchkey child; there is only the preschool neglected child (Robinson, Rowland & Coleman 1986).

Tips for Practitioners

None of the alert signs discussed in this chapter should be used singularly to identify preschool children from alcoholic homes. When used in concert, however, these symptoms form patterns indicative of alcohol-related problems in young children. Early identification can lead to primary intervention that can interrupt the disease cycle before it is implanted and before it takes its toll on the child physically, cognitively, emotionally, and socially.

Dealing with Denial

Once identified, you will find that preschoolers are easier to reach in some ways than older kids (Black 1987). A four-year-old will accept the family disease idea easier than older kids because the denial and the barriers have not had as much time to form. Younger school-age children (age six to nine) also are much more willing to express their feelings honestly and talk about alcohol than older kids. Claudia Black (1982) found that children age nine and older were much harder to reach. As parents and older children dismiss what young siblings say as unimportant or as inaccurate, children begin to learn in the preschool years that they cannot trust their own realities: "The way I see it is not how it is" (Black 1987).

Validating Preschoolers' Perceptions

One of the most significant contributions you can make when family alcoholism has been confirmed is to accept preschoolers' perceptions of what they see as accurate. Without doing anything with the information, you can simply validate what children say they see. This validation helps youngsters define the situation and learn to trust, rather than deny, their own instincts and realities, thus betraying the disease of alcoholism.

Although they are a challenge in treatment, older children are much easier to identify because they have acquired more of the dysfunctional behaviors as well as the prerequisite developmental skills—reading, writing, test taking, art ability, and verbal articulation—that aid in identification. I will address these issues in the next chapter.

6
Identifying School-Age and Adolescent Children of Alcoholics

Early identification and education can be crucial in ameliorating and preventing future alcoholism and problems for children. Fortunately, practical and simple ways exist for health practitioners, educators, and other school personnel to serve as resources for help.
—Migs Woodside, "Children of Alcoholics: Breaking the Cycle," *Journal of School Health.*

Case 6–1

One day my mother was drinking and forgot to pick me up from elementary school. I knew she didn't really forget. She was just too messed up. The teacher took me home. I remember being really angry because the teacher believed my mother who said, "Well, I didn't forget. I was going to be there." I was so mad because nobody believed me. I don't know whether children tell those things. I didn't, and I never told about my mother beating on me like that. But when my grandmother came to visit one time, she said, "Sara, you asked me when I spent the night, 'Grandmommie, are you not scared in this house? I am!'" That was the only thing that I ever said that made my grandmother wonder what was happening.

When I was six, my mother beat me over the head with a frying pan. That was the day they took her off to the institution, and I lived with my grandmother ever since. Having grown up with my grandmother, now that I'm twenty-one I don't even know my mother today. My father would visit occasionally but he finally died of drugs and alcohol at the age of forty-one. The worst thing for me was that he led such a tortured, empty life and how sad he was. I feel relieved in a sense that I never have to worry about him again.

I'm majoring in child and family development because I want to make some kind of different impression about teachers than I had because it was such a nightmare. I had to take care of my little brother and nurture him.

I even had to cook his meals. To this day I feel like I want to take care of everybody. I never thought I'd want to be anything else but a preschool teacher. I want to be somebody who makes a difference. I see some of the parents come into the day care center and ignore their kids and say, "Come on, let's go to the car." Then they walk ten feet in front of the child without even giving them time. I grew up with something like that, and I understand those kids who are going through those things.

—Sara, age twenty-one

Identifying School-Age and Adolescent Children of Alcoholics

Sara is among an estimated 95 percent of children of alcoholics who pass through elementary schools and are never identified or treated. Sara's grandmother was the only adult around her who was astute enough to pick up clues that she was being abused by her alcoholic mother. Estimates are that only 5 percent of the seven million school-age children of alcoholics are identified and treated (NIAAA 1981). Classroom teachers are astounded to learn that one in five of the kids in their classrooms are COAs. That means in a classroom with twenty-five students, five are COAs. "No, that's impossible," is the general retort from teachers when hearing this news for the first time. But armed with new facts about COAs and upon closer scrutiny, most teachers come back and confess, "I would never have believed it, but it's true!"

Research indicates that COAs are generally undetected by many practitioners, not just classroom teachers. One study found that none of the kids identified as COAs by a formal screening test (a total of one-fourth) had ever been diagnosed as COAs by counselors or social workers and none of them had been referred by teachers or had been self-referrals (Pilat & Jones 1985).

Roadblocks to Identification of Older Children

Some of the same problems in identifying preschool youngsters also hinder the identification process with school-age children and adolescents. Lack of alcohol education and the practitioner's own attitude toward alcohol can make a big difference. Many practitioners have denial systems of their own that prevent them from dealing with alcoholism among children with whom they work (Whitfield 1980). Some practitioners feel incompetent to deal with alcoholism, while others are afraid of causing trouble. They may be apprehensive and unknowledgeable of what to do with the information once children are identified. Still others fear parental reprisals, lack of administrative support, and even loss of their jobs. Or they may have seen drinking problems so often that they have become desensitized to their effects:

> They [may] no longer identify it as a distinctive condition requiring specific intervention strategies. Many caregivers cling to the belief that only by "curing" the parent can we really help the child, rather than viewing the child as a primary client who requires help whether or not his or her parent is willing to accept help. (DiCicco, Davis & Orenstein 1984, 1)

One problem that hampers practitioners' identification efforts of older children more than preschoolers is the denial system. As Sara's case illustrates, school-age children have already developed enough denial not to bring up the topic even if it is troubling them. Entertainer Suzanne Somers (1988) described how her problems in fourth grade were misunderstood by teachers:

> No teacher ever asked me if there was something wrong. They just assumed I was one of those lazy students. I'm not even sure if they *had* asked what I would have said. I was already, at nine years old, used to covering up; pretending that life inside our house was as pretty as the outside. (p. 31).

According to Claudia Black (1987), 80 percent of COAs look good, which is a chief reason they have gone unnoticed. Their survivor roles help them cope through the tough times until they are grownups. Then, just as they start to sigh from the relief of being out of the alcoholic home, their symptoms ambush them, jolting them back into turmoil. At twenty-one years of age, Sara had to seek counseling to cope with her emotional barriers and difficulties with intimacy that she had devised as a child to "make me independent and determined to stand on my own two feet, to be absolutely different from my parents."

Another problem is that there are few reliable methods for identifying COAs. The lack of precise tools leaves a great deal to the subjective interpretation of practitioners who may be ambivalent about their roles. Once teachers, counselors, and social workers feel comfortable enough to openly discuss alcohol and its accompanying problems, a climate of acceptance can be created and many roadblocks to identification removed. As practitioners reveal that it is normal for children of alcoholics to feel troubled and confused, more youngsters will come forward, identify themselves, and break the family secret (McElligatt 1986).

Importance of Identification

Because practitioners encounter COAs routinely and often unawarely, the identification of COAs takes on monumental importance. Intervening with a nine-year old child can even be a step toward primary prevention of another

Figure 6–1. This nine-year-old girl said she felt different because she was the child of an alcoholic. Once identified and receiving help, COAs realize they are not different and are not alone.

adult alcoholic. Identification breaks the denial system frequently operating in schools and opens the door for a multitude of services to children. It allows classroom teachers to match their expectations, goals, and interpersonal behaviors with knowledge of the alcoholic environment in which certain kids live. It also enables practitioners to establish support systems for COAs outside the classroom. Practitioners can refer COAs for such services as individual counseling, and they can create special COA groups that convene regularly in the schools.

Some children are easily identifiable because their parents are patients in alcoholic treatment centers or attend Alcoholics Anonymous. Because of their parents' recovery, these children may already be involved in some type of recovery program of their own—a COA group in treatment centers, for example, or Alateen. But these children are more the exception than the rule. Most COAs are not that easily identified and are not getting the help they need.

To close this gap, numerous ways have been devised to spot school-age kids and adolescents from alcoholic homes. As with preschoolers, the practitioner's informal observational assessment is an important method. But two additional procedures can be used with older children that make identification more objective and precise: formal standardized procedures and the child's self-identification.

Identification through Practitioner Observations

Although older COAs are not easily identified, practitioners actually have a better chance of spotting them than younger children because more concrete signs have had time to develop. Observing parents and looking for extreme behaviors also provide telltale signs. There are at least twenty behavioral and psychological signs that practitioners can look for that are best observed in school classrooms. Many of these signs were discussed in earlier chapters.

Behaviorally versus Psychologically Oriented

Some children's symptoms may appear behaviorally and thus are easily detected, while others may manifest more psychological and thus more subtle symptoms of family alcoholism. Some children may manifest both. Behaviorally oriented children are more easily detected because they manifest their feelings outwardly where practitioners can observe the signs. They are often the classroom behavior problems and have difficulty getting along with their peers. Or on the other extreme, they may isolate themselves in the background from teachers and classmates.

Sometimes COAs are victims of physical abuse or neglect, which has a whole set of its own symptoms. The child who arrives at school early and leaves late, for example, may dread being at home. By the same token children always in a rush to get home at the end of a school day may be concerned about the welfare of an alcoholic parent in their absence. Health care and school performance are sporadic. School grades and concentration nosedive. Tardiness increases, and homework is incomplete. Tidy children suddenly attend school unclean or unkempt, wear dirty clothing, or dress inappropriately for the weather. Children who never have lunch or lunch money or who take food from other children may be showing signs of alcoholic neglect. Children who refrain from activities where they must undress (such as costume plays or physical education) are often fearful of revealing bruises or other identifying marks of abuse. Cowering in the presence of adults is sometimes another sign of physical abuse.

COAs are frequently the kids who miss a lot of school, usually Mondays because of parental weekend drinking. They may use drugs themselves, overeat, overachieve, frequently complain of headaches or stomachaches, or say

Twenty Behavioral and Psychological Signs of Children of Alcoholics in School Settings

Behavioral Signs

1. Difficulty concentrating

2. Persistent absenteeism

3. Poor grades and/or failure to turn in homework

4. Low scores on standardized IQ and achievement tests

5. Sudden behavior changes (quiet and moody or acting out)

6. Signs of neglect or physical and sexual abuse

7. Compulsive behaviors (overeating, overachieving, smoking, chemical abuse)

8. Shy and withdrawn from other children

9. Quarrelsome and uncooperative with teachers and classmates

10. Constant health problems (headaches, stomach-aches)

Psychological Signs

1. Low self-esteem
2. Anxiety
3. Easily embarrassed
4. Suppressed anger
5. Perceive problems as beyond their control
6. Poor coping skills
7. Prone to depression
8. Unreasonably fearful
9. Sad and unhappy
10. Difficulty adjusting to changes in routines

they just do not feel well. They may have difficulty concentrating, staying on task, and sitting still. Some may be overactive, always fidgeting, or on the move. Others may daydream or sleep through classroom lessons. They score poorly on standardized tests, and may have poor grades for no apparent reason. They may show abrupt behavior changes, from shy to outgoing or vice versa. Or, like preschoolers, school-age children may suddenly regress into thumbsucking, bedwetting, or "baby talk." Sudden changes in behaviors during alcohol education activities—the ears of a typically distracted child may suddenly perk up during a discussion—or absences from school during these activities are associated with children of alcoholics (Deutsch 1982).

The more psychologically oriented COAs are those who may not manifest any outward signs that something is wrong. Their misery is internalized. They may be tops in the class—"a natural-born leader," the best and most popular student. They make the best grades and are sticklers for getting their work in on time—sometimes even before it is due. Because the signs are more subtle for psychologically oriented kids, practitioners must look more closely at these children to see their problems. Underneath their quiet success and achievement may be an obsessive drive to excel at everything and a compulsive need for approval, deepseated unhappiness and a sense of poor self-worth—children who browbeat themselves into perfectionism and refuse to allow themselves to make mistakes. They are overly serious, have trouble having fun, and judge themselves unmercifully. A closer look might show that these children have great difficulty when they are not in control of their lives and their greatest fear is loss of control. Unusual changes in daily routines may make them anxious or upset. This is not to say that all successful children are COAs, but many are family heroes who have successfully disguised their misery to fool even the most astute professional.

Parental behaviors such as repeatedly missing appointments, calling the school at odd hours for irrelevant reasons, or consistently failing to pick children up on time are dependable signs of alcoholic neglect. Children's failure to return permission slips, absence slips, and other parental communications is also a clue. Robert Ackerman (1983) suggests that parental report card signatures may develop a certain pattern that can cue practitioners to alcohol problems:

> A familiar pattern for children of alcoholics may be that one parent signs the report card on the occasions it is returned on time, and that the other parent signs the card when it is returned late. Although this may be a minor point, it can serve as a clue when other patterns are present that might suggest alcoholism. The nonalcoholic parent may sign the report card whether both parents have seen it or not. However, if the alcoholic parent was too inebriated to look at or understand the report card, the nonalcoholic may decide to wait for him or her to see it. (p. 101)

Looking for Extremes

It may sound contradictory that COAs can be both withdrawn and aggressive or both superachieving and incompetent, or that they either seem reluctant to leave the classroom at the end of the day or rush home immediately when school is dismissed. That pretty much covers the range of behavior. But it is the extreme behaviors you must look for. It doesn't sound contradictory to

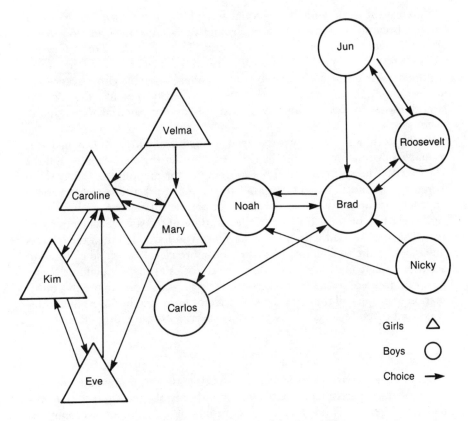

Figure 6–2. Example of a Sociogram

be concerned over someone who is too fat or too thin. It is generally accepted that either extreme body weight is indicative of an eating disorder that can be dangerous (obesity and anorexia, respectively). Analogously, COAs can be total failures or superachievers. But either avenue brings heartbreak, unhappiness, and lack of self-esteem.

One way for you to look for extremes is to conduct a *sociogram*—a map of the relationships within a classroom or other specific group. Simply ask the children to write down the names of two other children in the group with whom they would like to work on a group project. Once you have assured the children of confidentiality of their selections, take this information and plot it into graph form. An example of a sociogram is shown in figure 6–2.

Symbols are used to designate sex of child, and lines and arrows show direction of choices. Children like Caroline and Brad who receive a large number of choices are called *stars.* These are the class members all the other children want to be with. Stars could resemble either mascots or heroes—chosen because they are fun to be around or because they are considered group leaders and are efficient at their jobs. Those children like Velma and Nicky who receive no choices are called *isolates*. They are the children often on the outside of the social group. Isolates could resemble either scapegoats or lost children—unselected because the children do not like them or are afraid of them or because the children simply do not pay much attention to them.

This technique was not developed to identify COAs. Still, it provides valuable information on who the children consider the class isolates and the class stars. The sociogram is more meaningful for pinpointing COAs when you use it in tandem with other data—for example, practitioner observation, anecdotal recordings, and examination of permanent folders. The information in the box on page 106 and the descriptions of the survival roles in chapter 1 can also be used with these data. Once you have identified the isolates and stars by the sociogram, you can look more closely at these children to see if the isolate matches any of the characteristics of the lost child or scapegoat or if those of the hero or mascot fit the class star. You can use this information to group children who are suspected or known to be COAs in various ways and to build social skills and self-esteem as suggested in chapter 1.

Seeking Balance

Once extreme behaviors are identified—whether they be aggression, compulsive behaviors, persistent absenteeism, or withdrawal—the key to recovery is balance. The goal is not to rid heroes totally of their drive to accomplish. Instead, you can help them become more well rounded through balanced play and leisure. Similarly, the lost child needs some time alone, but this alone time can be balanced with some social companionship. You do not want the mascots to lose their sense of humor, just to know that life has its serious moments as well. And you would not want the scapegoats to become non-assertive and wimpish. Their balance comes by standing up for their rights without depriving others of theirs.

Caution in Practitioner Observations

Identifying COAs can be tricky business. The risk in identifying and describing a special group of children is labeling and stereotyping them through generalizations. Labeling children of alcoholics can have harmful effects on their self-image as well as cause school personnel to develop unfavorable attitudes, expectations, and responses toward them. It would be misleading for you to think that all COAs turn out the same way. There are many interacting factors that lead to diverse possible outcomes. COAs grow and pass through the same developmental stages as all kids. Aside from certain common developmental principles that govern everyone and from having an alcoholic parent, COAs are a heterogeneous population.

While COAs need special attention, you must avoid labeling them in a way that would cause others to behave differently toward them. COAs are not emotionally disturbed or mentally handicapped as a population. One message COAs need is that while they are special, as are all children, they are not that different from other kids. As a child, I thought my situation was so unique that my thinking segregated me from other children and made me feel so different I started to act that way. COAs I've worked with come into treatment believing they are different or something is wrong with them. They are always relieved to know they are not alone and that many children share their pain and suffering.

Ironically, special programs for COAs that help them feel "not so different" single them out as a group and set them apart, leaving them open for negative stereotypes. A worker mused on his first night in an outpatient group of COAs, "Funny, these kids don't look like children of alcoholics!" With a wave of books flooding the market drawing generalizations about ACOAs and COAs, it is easy to make sweeping conclusions.

The popular and scientific press have been criticized for making generalizations about COAs from anecdotal data on children whose parents are in treatment or who are otherwise atypical (DiCicco, Davis & Orenstein 1984; El-Guebaly & Offord 1977; Goodman 1987; Woodside 1982). Most research investigations that show COAs have difficulty functioning were undertaken by clinicians who studied COAs with problems. These studies were usually conducted with children involved in treatment centers or support groups. Other sampling biases make it difficult to generalize all research findings to the whole population of children of alcoholics (see, for example, West & Prinz 1987). Factors such as family size, pyschopathology of parents, severity of alcoholism, divorce, and socioeconomic status can make a difference in how children turn out. Researchers still do not understand how these many factors, individually or combined with parental alcoholism, can influence children's development.

Recent evidence suggests that COAs from the general population not involved in treatment do not have the same coping problems as COAs undergoing therapy. While COAs from the general population were equally as well adjusted as children from nondrinking homes, COAs in treatment had more coping problems in self-regard, intimacy, self-acceptance, feeling reactivity, and inner-directedness (Barnard & Spoentgen 1987). Additional research indicates that COAs recruited for study from the general university student population also scored similarly to nonCOAs on self-concept, anxiety, and knowledge about the effects of alcoholism on children (Robinson 1988c). These studies further indicate that COAs are not a homogeneous group characterized by a host of psychological problems. While some have interpersonal and intrapersonal problems, others appear to recoil from the effects of living in alcoholism.

As you begin to identify COAs from a set of published characteristics, you can avoid labeling and stereotyping these children by using this knowledge in conjunction with other information. The key is to remember that generalizations are guidelines and only guidelines and that, as an individual, each child is a creative wonder of the universe.

Identification through Standardized Procedures

Regardless of the procedure used, children of alcoholics should never be publicly identified. The best starting point in the identification process is with alcohol awareness programs that are provided to all children. During these sessions, children with alcohol-related problems can be identified anonnymously, through teacher observations, tests, or self-referral, for further specialized help. Once identified, these youngsters can receive safe and confidential help individually and in groups.

The most confident way to confirm the identity of COAs is through a standardized test that has been subjected to rigorous scientific scrutiny. Data from these measures yield the most objective and self-assured results. A major drawback of standardized procedures, however, is that children must be old enough to read and write in order to complete the forms. As I discussed in chapter 5, preschool children and preliterate kids are automatically excluded from this approach. Still, standardized procedures for kids ages nine and older have been developed and have demonstrated beneficial results.

The Children of Alcoholics Screening Test

One of the most popular measures for identifying COAs is the Children of Alcoholics Screening Test (CAST) (Jones 1983). It is an objective instrument that does not depend upon the practitioner's judgment, which could cloud the conclusions. The CAST makes it possible to identify at-risk children who are living with or who have lived with alcoholic parents. The instrument can be used by practitioners who need to identify at-risk children for inclusion in intervention programs. The CAST can also be used by the courts to determine if alcohol is involved in child abuse and custody cases. As figure 6–3 shows, the CAST is a thirty-item inventory that measures children's attitudes, feelings, perceptions, and experiences related to their parents' drinking.

The CAST can be administered to children nine years of age and older, individually or in group settings. The "yes" answers are added to yield the total score, which can range from 0 to 30. A score from 0 to 1 indicates children of nonalcoholics; 2 to 5 indicates children of problem drinkers. These

CAST

Please check (✔) the answer below that best describes your feelings, behavior, and experiences related to a parent's alcohol use. Take your time and be as accurate as possible. Answer all thirty questions by checking either "Yes" or "No."

Sex: Male_____ Female_____ Age:____

Yes	No	Questions
____	____	1. Have you ever thought that one of your parents had a drinking problem?
____	____	2. Have you ever lost sleep because of a parent's drinking?
____	____	3. Did you ever encourage one of your parents to quit drinking?
____	____	4. Did you ever feel alone, scared, nervous, angry, or frustrated because a parent was not able to stop drinking?
____	____	5. Did you ever argue or fight with a parent when he or she was drinking?
____	____	6. Did you ever threaten to run away from home because of a parent's drinking?
____	____	7. Has a parent ever yelled at or hit you or other family members when drinking?
____	____	8. Have you ever heard your parents fight when one of them was drunk?
____	____	9. Did you ever protect another family member from a parent who was drinking?
____	____	10. Did you ever feel like hiding or emptying a parent's bottle of liquor?
____	____	11. Do many of your thoughts revolve around a problem drinking parent or difficulties that arise because of his or her drinking?
____	____	12. Did you ever wish that a parent would stop drinking?
____	____	13. Did you ever feel responsible for and guilty about a parent's drinking?
____	____	14. Did you ever fear that your parents would get divorced due to alcohol misuse?
____	____	15. Have you ever withdrawn from and avoided outside activities and friends because of embarrassment and shame over a parent's drinking problem?
____	____	16. Did you ever feel caught in the middle of an argument or fight between a problem drinking parent and your other parent?
____	____	17. Did you ever feel that you made a parent drink alcohol?
____	____	18. Have you ever felt that a problem drinking parent did not really love you?
____	____	19. Did you ever resent a parent's drinking?
____	____	20. Have you ever worried about a parent's health because of his or her alcohol use?
____	____	21. Have you ever been blamed for a parent's drinking?
____	____	22. Did you ever think your father was an alcoholic?
____	____	23. Did you ever wish your home could be more like the homes of your friends who did not have a parent with a drinking problem?
____	____	24. Did a parent ever make promises to you that he or she did not keep because of drinking?
____	____	25. Did you ever think your mother was an alcoholic?
____	____	26. Did you ever wish that you could talk to someone who could understand and help the alcohol-related problems in your family?
____	____	27. Did you ever fight with your brothers and sisters about a parent's drinking?
____	____	28. Did you ever stay away from home to avoid the drinking parent or your other parent's reaction to the drinking?
____	____	29. Have you ever felt sick, cried, or had a "knot" in your stomach after worrying about a parent's drinking?
____	____	30. Did you ever take over any chores and duties at home that were usually done by a parent before he or she developed a drinking problem?

____ TOTAL NUMBER OF "YES" ANSWERS.

© 1983 John Jones. Used with permission of Camelot Unlimited, Publisher

Figure 6–3. Children of Alcoholics Screening Test

children have experienced problems caused by at least one parent's drinking behavior. These are children of either problem drinkers or possible alcoholics. A score of 6 or more is indicative of children of alcoholics. These parents can be in the early, middle, or late stages of alcoholism.

Research has shown that the CAST has withstood scientific scrutiny and and has yielded impressive reliability and validity (Pilat & Jones 1985). In one study, for instance, the cutoff score of 6 or more accurately identified 100 percent of a group of COAs who had been clinically diagnosed by psychiatrists, counselors, and psychologists.

Survey and Interview Responses

Another objective means for identifying adolescent COAs is by their responses on surveys and interviews. DiCicco, Davis, and Orenstein (1984) say that it is impossible to identify COAs by having them describe their parent's drinking. Alcoholics cannot be diagnosed by how much they drink. It takes multiple criteria to diagnose alcoholism—a process that becomes too complicated for kids to accurately perform. Plus, the denial system would interfere with the child's objectivity of parental drinking.

Lena DiCicco and her associates (1984) suggest that a more efficient approach aims questions to children on how they have been affected by or react to parental drinking. By focusing on the child's reaction, it is possible to raise the issue of alcoholism in an unobtrusive way that promotes more reliable disclosure. A case in which a child is afraid, mad, confused, or embarrassed by his or her parent's drinking and wishes for the parent to stop, should be considered alcoholic, simply because of the negative effects it has on the offspring. The child's perception in this case is the more critical variable in producing behavioral and self-image problems.

For eight years, the Cambridge and Somerville Program for Alcoholism Rehabilitation (CASPAR) has used a single question on a survey form to identify COAs. That item is known as the Children from Alcoholic Family (CAF) item:

Have you ever wished that either one or both of your parents would drink less?
1. Parents don't drink at all
2. Yes
3. No

DiCicco and her associates (1984) found that statistically the CAF is reliable and valid as an identifier of COAs. There is considerable stability over time in the way teenagers answer the CAF item which suggests that their "wish" is a relatively enduring characteristic. Other data confirm that the

CAF item coincides with clinical judgments. Among seventy-one respondents who said "yes" to the CAF item, for example, 83 percent also were identified by the clinical staff as COAs. Correlations also have been drawn between the CAF item and COA reports of frequency of parental drinking. Among respondents who say "yes" on the CAF, 61.5 percent also report "fairly regular" paternal drinking and that they are concerned about this drinking.

Another more detailed screening interview permits the identification of adolescents adversely affected by a problem drinking parent (Biek 1981). The brief interview questions, shown in figure 6–4, are appropriate for use with teenagers in a variety of settings but are especially recommended as a routine part of the evaluation process for all adolescents attending primary health care settings. This screening test fosters early identification, referral, and intervention to treat families in which there is alcohol abuse, thus promoting healthier psychosocial development. Teens with high scores on the screening interview had twice as many somatic complaints and health questions as those who gave no indication of having a drinking parent. Teens of alcoholics complained more of such problems as shortness of breath, stomachaches, headaches, sleep problems, and tiredness. Early identification and intervention of alcohol-related problems help medical personnel to place vague, somatic complaints in a more meaningful perspective. This identification and intervention potentially could also lower the chances of teenagers with high scores becoming problem drinkers since, as offspring of alcoholics, they would be at higher than average risk.

Self-Identification

Perhaps the most successful method of identification is self-referral by the child. This approach puts the assurance of psychological safety and anonymity in children's hands. Those youngsters who come forth and join groups on their own are motivated to learn more about COA issues and ready to work on the problem. They also end up with close-knit relationships that support and carry them through their ordeal. Steps in the self-identification process are simple, easy to use, nonthreatening, and highly effective (see figure 6–5).

The Self-Identification Process

Counselors Betty Newlon and William Furrow (1986) found that classroom guidance activities combined with small-group counseling offers a way to reach COAs. They began the steps in their identification process by giving two guidance lessons on alcoholism and the family in the classroom. Sessions were comprised of films, lectures, handouts, and group discussion to cover the differences between alcoholic and responsible drinking, alcoholism as a

1. Do you know any teenager who has ever had some difficulty because of either parent's drinking?

YES   NO

2. Have you known either of your parents to ever take a drink? (This item to rule out possible abstainers' children, for whom the following questions would be irrelevant.)

YES   NO

Following a "No" response to item 2, exit the interview

3. Has the drinking of either parent ever created problems between him/her and the other parent or near relative? ("Yes," meaning recently or "Yes" meaning long ago?)

YES   NO

4. Do friends or relatives think either of your parents has a drinking problem?

YES   SOMETIMES   NO

5. Do you ever worry because of either parent's drinking?

YES   SOMETIMES   NO

6. At any time in your life, have you ever felt hurt, scared, or angry because of either parent's drinking?

YES   SOMETIMES   NO

7. Has your parent's drinking ever made things more difficult for you in any way?

YES   SOMETIMES   NO

Following all "No" responses to items 3–7, exit the interview.

Following any "Yes" or "Sometimes" responses, the interview is continued with the open ended question.

8. How has the drinking of your parent affected you?

   a.

   b.

   c.

   d.

9. At any time in your life has your own drinking caused any trouble or concern for you?

Scoring: Questions 3 through 7 are scored as follows:
   "Yes" = 3 points; "Sometimes" = 2 points; "No" = 1 point

The possible range of scores is 5 to 15 points:
   Low Score: 5 points with no "Yes" or "Sometimes" responses
   Medium Score: 6 points with 1 "Sometimes" and 4 "No" responses
                    7 points with 2 "Sometimes" and 3 "No" responses
   High Score: 8–15 points with 1 "Sometimes" and 1 "Yes" response OR 2 or more "Yes" responses

From Biek 1981. Used with permission.

Figure 6–4. Screening Interview for Identifying Teenagers with Problem Drinking Parents

1. Conduct alcohol education awareness classes.
2. Introduce the concept of an ongoing group for those who have drug or alcohol problems in their homes.
3. Disseminate self-referral forms.
4. Hold screening interviews with all children who indicate interest in the COA group.
5. Select the number of children based on prioritized criteria that best fit your unique situation.

Figure 6–5. Steps in the Self-Identification Process

family illness, and the characteristics of COAs. At the conclusion of the two sessions, children were given a self-evaluation form on which they could indicate interest in attending a small group in which alcoholism was discussed on a more personal level. A brief screening interview was conducted with each child who expressed a desire to participate in groups. Those who disclosed that they had an alcoholic parent were automatically eligible for the group. Selection of the remaining children was done by teachers who were asked to choose out of the list of volunteers those who might be having difficulty at home. Of the eighty children who participated in the classroom guidance lessons, eleven were successfully identified as COAs.

Similar self-referral steps used by the Cleveland County School System in North Carolina are expedient and highly successful. At the end of the alcohol education program for fifth and sixth graders, school personnel introduce the idea of an ongoing small group. Children are informed that a group will be started for those who think one or both parents might have a drinking problem. Counselors ask them to complete a simple form like the one in figure 6–6. Once forms are collected, counselors hold individual screening interviews with each child who indicates an interest in participating in the group. Children considered to be in the most trouble and those in the sixth grade (because this will be their last chance for help before going on to junior high school) are given priority slots in the group. The final group size usually totals between twenty and twenty-five students.

Legal Considerations

Alcoholic parents love their children, and they do not want them to be stigmatized. An active alcoholic parent is not going to say, "Yes, teach my kids about the problems they are having because of my drinking." The denial is too strong. You should check the laws of your respective state, as some states require written parental consent for children to participate in groups.

Sometimes we all need someone to talk with, especially if we don't understand what's going on. If you think that a parent, grandparent, sister, brother, or someone else that you care about has a drinking or drug problem, and you would like to join a group of kids just like you, fill out the form and return it to the office. Your guidance counselor [the name of the appropriate person could be substituted here] will get in touch with you about the group.

Name _____ Grade _____

Teacher_____

Yes, I'm interested in the group _____

No, I'm not interested, but thanks _____

Cleveland County Community Organization for Drug Abuse Prevention. Used with permission by Vicky V. White, Program Director.

Figure 6–6. Sample Self-Referral Form

Programs in those states can send home permission slips requesting parental permission for children to participate in groups to improve self-esteem and to learn about drug and alcohol prevention. This approach gets around stigmatizing anyone concerned and has a high success rate of getting children into programs that meet their needs.

Identifying Practitioners Who Are COAs

COAs are everywhere. They cut across all geographic, racial, socioeconomic, age, and gender lines. They enter all professions too. But a higher concentration of COAs are found among helping professionals than any other occupational group. Many of them carry a conscious or unconscious desire to save the world. My experience as a COA sparked a desire to help others in some way. As an idealistic undergraduate psychology student, I always refrained, "I just want to make the world a better place for others." But as I pursued work in psychology, counseling, and child and family development, I never consciously knew why. Now I know that by helping others, I would better understand and help myself. Sara, in the opening case, was a college student of mine who, like many adult COAs (ACOAs) enter the human services field to make life for unfortunate children better than hers had been.

A study by Pilat and Jones (1985) included the administration of the CAST to practitioners enrolled in a family alcoholism treatment course. Of the forty-seven family therapy students, 25.5 percent were ACOAs; of the eighty-one experienced therapists, 28.4 percent were ACOAs; and of the twenty-six health professionals, 46.2 percent were ACOAs. The findings indicate a high incidence of alcohol addiction among practitioners and suggest that many therapists' interests in the field of alcoholism stem from early exposure to the family disease.

Barbara Wood (1982) suggests that many, if not most, of these ACOA helpers are family heroes: "Tempered, tested, and often still troubled by their own experience with an alcoholic parent, they have made the restoration of dependent families a life-long mission: They have turned pro." (p. 2).

Barriers to Practitioner Effectiveness

Being an ACOA in the helping professions is not necessarily a bad thing. In fact, ACOAs bring to their work a wonderful capacity for empathy and desire to help others. But these positive aspects also can be accompanied by negative factors that can actually impede the practitioner's work. Physician Charles Whitfield (1980) believes one of the reasons that more COAs are not identified and helped or that help, when it is given, is misdirected at the symptom is because many practitioners have the same condition of enabling or codependence as the very people they want to help: "The helpers themselves are denying, covering up, and perpetuating the disease of alcoholism in an enabling or co-alcoholic fashion. If this is true, then it is a basic and serious treatment issue for the children of alcoholics" (p. 88). The analogy of an elephant in the living room describes the denial and avoidance of alcohol addiction (Hastings & Typpo 1984). Everyone—parents, teachers, counselors, the clergy, social workers, caregivers—tiptoes around the elephant (alcoholism), pretending it does not exist. So it continues, unidentified and undiscussed, while the child remains quietly confused and afraid.

Another barrier to effectiveness is the practitioner's lack of self-inventory and the "will to restore," which manifests itself in an impatient "rush to recovery":

> In the adult child whose heroic role armor has not been pierced by self-analysis, supervision, or psychotherapy, this will to restore usually operates as a compulsive, destructive force. Fueled, in large measure, by fear and flagging self-esteem, it may actually interfere with the process of recovery. (Wood 1987, 145)

It is important that ACOA practitioners inventory their past and present to determine if and how the past influences present interactions with clients. Practitioners may find themselves drawn to certain kids who mirror their own childhoods. Or a particular child or parent may exhume negative memories for the practitioner.

The associated negative feelings may cause practitioners to dislike or be unusually harsh with that client. A volunteer in a COA program who was an ACOA herself had to leave the group because hearing and seeing the kids brought back too many ugly images of her own childhood, which interfered with her effectiveness with the children. At the end of the evening she frequently left tearfully or depressed from some of the children's stories about their home life. She realized she still had unresolved feelings and issues surrounding her own alcoholic upbringing. Once practitioners openly confront the existence or absence of their own COA issues, their effectiveness in identifying and treating children will be greatly enhanced.

Self-inventory for Practitioners

If you are a helping practitioner, chances are you have been affected by growing up with an alcoholic parent or in a dysfunctional family. Through a series of inventories you can assess your personal relationship with alcohol as a child growing up, as an ACOA, and as an adult drinker. You can take the CAST yourself and compute your score to see if you are a child of an alcoholic. Next, you can take the ACOA test (appendix 6A) to determine the number of ACOA items that apply to you. Last, you can take the test published by the National Council on Alcoholism to assess your own drinking activities and potential signs of alcoholism (appendix 6B).

The annotated book list in chapter 10 provides further readings if you find you are an adult child of an alcoholic parent or that you or a family member have some of the symptoms of alcoholism.

Appendix 6A

The ACOA Quotient

Here are the thirty-six items developed by the authors which they feel will result in differing responses from COAs and nonCOAs.

1. I have difficulty in establishing a close personal relationship.
2. I am quite upset whenever I am criticized or "put down."
3. I enjoy trying new experiences.
4. Ventilating anger is a healthy release.
5. It takes a lot for me to change my mind.
6. I disdain the material things of life.
7. I look forward to a hard job I can really sink my teeth into, and want credit for doing it well.
8. High grades in school do not mean a person is smart.
9. I usually repeat a story pretty much the same way I heard it.
10. I would rather work alone on a project.

10. I would rather work alone on a project.
11. I like meeting new people.
12. I look forward to holidays with great delight.
13. It is very important to me that I am liked by those around me.
14. Most really important people had to do something unethical to get there.
15. I have difficulty letting go of casual or transient relationships.
16. I am a real perfectionist.
17. I feel somewhat embarrassed when dancing in public.
18. I find constructive criticism helpful.
19. I think it very important to have a title that reflects the importance of the position that a person holds.
20. I become uneasy in the presence of an angry person.
21. I form close relationships easily.
22. I am unable to ask for what I want or would like to have from others.
23. I would rather be self-employed than have a boss.
24. I don't count my chickens until they are hatched.
25. I feel much better when I know exactly what to expect in any given situation.
26. I feel personally attacked when my work is criticized.
27. I begin to worry when things seem to be going right.
28. My love relationships never seem to last very long.
29. I have a need for approval.
30. I sometimes exaggerate and overreact to situations.
31. I have trouble taking orders, especially from people who don't know as much as I do.
32. I can remember when I have felt embarrassed because I was unfairly criticized in front of others.
33. I usually go along with the majority rather than make an issue.
34 It bothers me when even just one person in the crowd is angry with me.
35. I can usually see the merits of both sides of an argument.
36. I sometimes embellish a story to make it more interesting for the listener.

Eight items (1, 2, 22, 27, 29, 32, 33, and 34) are sharply more true of COAs than non-COAs.

Used with permission from *Changes Magazine,* published by Health Communications, Pompano Beach, Florida.

Appendix 6B

What Are the Signs of Alcoholism?

Here is a self-test to help you review the role alcohol is playing in your life. These questions incorporate many of the common symptoms of alcoholism.

This test is intended to help you determine if you or someone you know needs to find out more about alcoholism.

YES NO

☐   ☐   1. Do you occasionally drink heavily after a disappointment, a quarrel, or when the boss gives you a hard time?

☐   ☐   2. When you have trouble or feel under pressure, do you always drink more heavily than usual?

☐   ☐   3. Have you noticed that you are able to handle more liquor than you did when you were first drinking?

☐   ☐   4. Did you ever wake up on the "morning after" and discover that you could not remember part of the evening before, even though your friends tell you that you did not "pass out"?

☐   ☐   5. When drinking with other people, do you try to have a few extra drinks when others will not know it?

☐   ☐   6. Are there certain occasions when you feel uncomfortable if alcohol is not available?

☐   ☐   7. Have you recently noticed that when you begin drinking you are in more of a hurry to get the first drink than you used to be?

☐   ☐   8. Do you sometimes feel a little guilty about your drinking?

☐   ☐   9. Are you secretly irritated when your family or friends discuss your drinking?

☐   ☐   10. Have you recently noticed an increase in the frequency of your memory "blackouts"?

☐   ☐   11. Do you often find that you wish to continue drinking after your friends say they have had enough?

☐   ☐   12. Do you usually have a reason for the occasions when you drink heavily?

☐   ☐   13. When you are sober, do you often regret things you have done or said while drinking?

☐   ☐   14. Have you tried switching brands or following different plans for controlling your drinking?

☐   ☐   15. Have you often failed to keep the promises you have made to yourself about controlling or cutting down on your drinking?

☐   ☐   16. Have you ever tried to control your drinking by making a change in jobs, or moving to a new location?

YES NO

☐ ☐ 17. Do you try to avoid family or close friends while you are drinking?

☐ ☐ 18. Are you having an increasing number of financial and work problems?

☐ ☐ 19. Do more people seem to be treating you unfairly without good reason?

☐ ☐ 20. Do you eat very little or irregularly when you are drinking?

☐ ☐ 21. Do you sometimes have the "shakes" in the morning and find that it helps to have a little drink?

☐ ☐ 22. Have you recently noticed that you cannot drink as much as you once did?

☐ ☐ 23. Do you sometimes stay drunk for several days at a time?

☐ ☐ 24. Do you sometimes feel very depressed and wonder whether life is worth living?

☐ ☐ 25. Sometimes after periods of drinking, do you see or hear things that aren't there?

☐ ☐ 26. Do you get terribly frightened after you have been drinking heavily?

Any "yes" answer indicates a probable symptom of alcoholism.

"Yes" answers to several of the questions indicate the following stages of alcoholism:

Questions 1–8—Early stage.

Questions 9–21—Middle stage.

Questions 22–26—The beginning of final stage.

To find out more, contact the National Council on Alcoholism in your area.

Reproduced with permission of the National Council on Alcoholism.

7
Effective Programs for Children of Alcoholics

There still is a widespread misconception that children of alcoholics recover by osmosis . . . that if we can get Mom and/or Dad sober and the other parent in Al-Anon that the kids will "come along."
—*Cathleen Brooks*, "Listening to the Children," *Professional Counselor Magazine*

Case 7–1

Pauline was shrewd, and at only twelve years of age, had convinced herself that she could control the drinking of her parents—both of whom were alcoholic. When she came to the treatment center, she had already developed a sophisticated system of manipulating and controlling her mom and dad's drinking. When they went out to eat, she made sure the restaurants they frequented did not serve alcoholic beverages. That way she didn't have to worry about her parents getting out of hand and embarrassing her or getting too drunk to drive her and her younger sister home.

When shopping, she encouraged her parents to spend as much money as possible so there would be none left over to buy booze. When drinking friends called, Pauline deliberately "forgot" to give her parents telephone messages so they wouldn't get mixed up with company that would encourage their drinking. Pauline was constantly emptying liquor bottles and disposing of unopened beer, hoping her parents would not notice and punish her.

Constantly conniving and creating ways to prevent her parents from drinking, Pauline had become consumed with the alcoholism and her life revolved around it. Her preoccupation with trying to control the disease was heartbreaking because inevitably, no matter what she did, Pauline admitted that her parents somehow got their beer and wine. The child started to blame and feel bad about herself because she could not accomplish her goal. All the while, she was missing out on the most important period of her life—childhood.

Untreated, Pauline's compulsive need to control would ultimately insinuate itself into school, work, and friendships. In adulthood it would interfere with trust and intimate relationships with people for whom she cares. In the weekly program sessions she attended, we tried to help her see the consequences of her actions and to help her learn to refocus her energies on taking care of herself. The six-week curriculum was just the beginning of a path of recovery in which she learned to let her parents be responsible for their drinking while she gave up that burden in lieu of fun, play, and being good to herself, while still caring about and loving her parents.

Effective Programs for Children of Alcoholics

Once on a radio show I was asked, "What's the point in trying to help kids whose parents are alcoholic if they have to go right back home and live in it?" This is an important question and one that lurks in the minds of many who are unfamiliar with the disease of alcoholism. The answer that we professionals give is even more significant. Children must have a distinct and separate treatment program of their own regardless of whether the parent is recovering from alcoholism. Children like Pauline who live in active alcoholism can learn that they cannot control or cure the disease and that ultimately their best recourse is to take care of themselves. They learn it is okay and even advisable not to get into a car with an intoxicated parent, for example. They also learn that it is good practice to carry correct change to call a relative or neighbor in case they get abandoned by a drinking parent.

Underlying the radio commentator's question was the myth that the welfare of the child hinges on the parent's actions. When alcoholic parents get treatment, their kids will automatically recover; or conversely, if parents do not get help, then it is hopeless for their children. Today, we know that children can recover regardless of their parents' behaviors and, as a result, programs for children of alcoholics have begun to appear in school systems and in treatment centers that historically treated only the alcoholic and the codependent parents.

Psychoeducational Programs

Most children of alcoholics, like Pauline, do not need intensive therapy. They need education, the most powerful weapon against alcoholism. Educating children about the disease removes the mystique surrounding it and provides them with a language and context for understanding and expressing their personal experiences with it. Knowledge also equips them with an intellectual mastery that will help them solve problems and cope with parental alcoholism in their future lives (Bingham & Bargar 1985). Professionals and potential caregivers can be educated on simple, easy, low-cost, and effective ways to help this huge and generally neglected population of kids. Considering their numbers, children from alcoholic families can be found in all kinds of programs and service organizations. Rather than creating new bureaucracies, the helping professions can implement psychoeducational programs through systems already in place: public schools, colleges and universities, and treatment centers.

The School System

Classroom teachers and counselors are not in the business of alcohol rehabilitation, but it is incumbent upon schools to ensure that all children's educational opportunities are met. The fact that parental alcoholism severely interferes with children's learning is rationale enough for schools to play a big role in helping children of alcoholics. Schools are the most logical resource to educate children about alcohol use and abuse. Teachers and other school personnel are already in key positions to identify and help children of alcoholics. Because of their contact with children on a regular basis, school personnel can establish an ongoing relationship of security and trust that is prerequisite to working with children of alcoholics. Teachers can lighten the child's load and give kids one special person who understands and listens. In the rare instances when families ask schools for help, teachers, counselors, administrators, and others can refer them to appropriate treatment.

The Phoenix Union High School District in Arizona is an exemplary program on chemical awareness and its positive outcomes (Watkins 1988). The program provides comprehensive prevention intervention for students from K-16 who are harmfully involved with their own chemical use, affected by a family member's use, or experiencing problems unrelated to chemical use but considered at risk. The Phoenix program is a systematic effort to identify, refer, and support students having problems that interfere with their education and life development. All staff are given in-service training on chemical dependency. Alcohol and substance abuse education for students is provided through assemblies, course curricula, and class presentations. Children of alcoholics, students involved with chemicals, and other troubled students are identified through referrals from peers, teachers, staff, families, community agencies (such as social services or police), and self-referral. Special group facilitators are trained to lead student support groups. In-house student support groups meet weekly and are scheduled throughout the school day. Four groups, designed with diverse needs of students in mind, meet separately: to maintain a chemically free lifestyle; to get help when having problems resulting from substance abuse; to get support when concerned about the chemical abuse of a family member or friend; and to receive support for other problems not related to chemical dependency. Groups meet once a week and are scheduled during a teacher's preparation period.

Results of the program have been dramatic. A survey of 335 students revealed that 73 percent were able to find new positive ways to deal with problems and to communicate and express feelings in a positive way. Fully 61 percent of the students using alcohol and other drugs decreased or stopped as a result of the support group. Feelings of self-worth improved for 71 percent of the students. Improvements were also noted in general attitude toward school (50 percent), school attendance (35 percent), and overall schoolwork (31 percent).

Higher Education

College and university campuses are also prime settings for psychoeducational programs for future practitioners and adult children of alcoholics. Courses on substance abuse and family dynamics can be added to curricula. Special lectures on children and alcoholism can be added to such existing courses as child development, sociology, psychology, nursing, and family studies. Special psychoeducational groups for students with alcoholic parents, established by university staff through campus counseling centers, have achieved success. A five-week collegiate group at a major university helped sons and daughters of alcoholics understand the roles they had assumed in the family and other useful information in the event alcoholism becomes a possibility in their lives (Donovan 1981). An eight-week educational support group on another university campus improved the psychological functioning of students with alcoholic parents (Barnard & Spoentgen 1987).

Treatment Centers

Psychoeducational programs for children are also important components in treatment centers in which the primary aim is the dependent and codependent parent. Survey results from treatment agencies during the eighties indicate that children of alcoholics still remain on the periphery of the treatment process. When they do receive services, it is generally in the form of individual counseling (Regan, Connors, O'Farrell & Wyatt 1983).

Although few treatment programs still exist nationwide for COAs, the numbers of programs are increasing. The impetus for this gain is a resolution passed by the National Association for Children of Alcoholics in 1987, requesting that all chemical dependency treatment programs establish a component especially for children of dependent parents. As greater numbers and variety of programs appear on the horizon, they should have the common denominator of appropriate goals, plus a built-in system of evaluation.

Establishing Program Goals

Program planners must understand that children's programs should contain appropriate goals for treatment to be meaningful. Intervention programs have a number of messages that are important to convey to children. Numerous curriculum packages have been marketed especially for children of alcoholics for implementation in schools or in treatment centers simultaneously as parents receive treatment (see chapter 10 for examples of program curricula). Most of these curricula have several key points in common. The key points, shown in the box below, are important goals that should be part of any psychoeducational program for children of alcoholics. Most programs incorporate these ten key points in a variety of ways around designated central themes—one for each week in the program cycle.

Key Points for Children of Alcoholics Programs

1. Alcoholism is a disease.
2. Everybody gets hurt in the alcoholic family, including the children.
3. Children whose parents drink too much are not alone.
4. Children do not cause, cannot control, and cannot cure their parent's alcoholism.
5. There are many good ways that children can take care of themselves when parents drink so that they feel better about themselves.
6. It is healing for children to identify and express their feelings about parental drinking.
7. It is okay for kids to talk about parental drinking to a friend or within the safety of a group.
8. Kids of alcoholics are at high-risk of substance abuse themselves.
9. It is important for children to identify and use trusted support systems outside the family.
10. There are many practical ways of problem solving and coping with parental alcoholism.

Alcoholism Is a Disease

Children need to understand that alcoholism is a disease the drinking parent cannot control. Frequently, children equate their parent's drinking with not being loved. Robert Bly (1987) said, "Every child of an alcoholic receives the knowledge that the bottle is more important to the parent than he or she is" (p. 96). Kids need to know their parents love them even though the disease symptoms may make them think otherwise. As children begin to understand the disease concept, the stigma of alcoholism can be removed and they feel safer talking about it. They also acquire a language and context in which to verbalize their thoughts and feelings, and learn that parents can and do recover from the illness.

Everybody Gets Hurt

Kids must know that alcoholism affects all family members in negative ways. Individual family members devise roles (such as hero, lost child, scapegoat, mascot) to cope with and survive the disease. These roles cover up poor self-esteem, anxiety, depression, and a host of other feelings. They also prevent children from expressing their true emotions and getting close to others. By stressing that alcoholism influences everyone in the family, kids begin to realize, if they are not already aware, that indeed, they too have been hurt.

Children Are Not Alone

A major relief for children whose parents drink too much is to learn that they are not alone. They discover there are many other children just like them—seven million to be exact, nationwide. The importance of group work is that children learn firsthand they are not so different after all and that other kids, who have had similar experiences living in alcoholism, also think and feel the same way about a lot of things. Young children are usually surprised to hear that famous people—such as Chuck Norris, Brooke Shields, or Suzanne Somers—also grew up in alcoholic homes. Such discussions send children the message that they are not isolated, different, or crazy and that their reactions to parental alcoholism are normal.

Cause, Control, Cure

Quality COA intervention programs address the issues of cause, control, and cure. Children often feel their parent's drinking is, directly or indirectly, their fault. They need to know they are not responsible for their parent's drinking, and no matter what they do and how hard they try, they cannot control or cure their parent's alcoholism. Because it is an illness, they cannot change it anymore than they can change the course of heart disease or cancer. Unyielding attempts to control parental alcoholism only lead to self-defeat and poor self-worth. Children can learn, however, that there are other things in their own lives they *can* successfully manage, mainly themselves, that will make them feel better and help them recover from the disease.

Taking Care of Self

Although powerless over their parents' drinking, children need to know they deserve help for themselves and that preoccupation with trying to stop or alter the course of parental drinking leads to frustration, anger, and numerous emotional side effects. Children need help in letting go of serious adult problems and embracing the carefree world of childhood. They must learn how to take care of themselves when a parent is drinking and whom to call or where to go for help when they need it. Children need to recognize their own good points and develop their strengths by learning to feel good about themselves, thereby separating parental alcoholism from self-concept. Practitioners can implement many self-esteem exercises to help COAs in this area. Research substantiates that self-regard and capacity for intimacy with others improve after short-term educational intervention with COAs (Barnard & Spoentgen 1987).

Identifying and Expressing Feelings

Children learn that many emotions are common reactions when parents drink too much. They find that identifying the ones they have and expressing them in appropriate ways make them feel better inside and about themselves in general. Using creative media for the expression of emotions—art, music, puppets, role play, clay, etc.—is a nonthreatening way for children to share their feelings. Once expressed, the creative medium serves as a springboard for a discussion on feelings. It is important to point out that feelings are neither good nor bad. All feelings are appropriate. Even hate (a common report from COAs) can be a genuine feeling and a natural reaction to the disease. There are, however, appropriate and inappropriate ways of expressing these feelings. Anger expressed as violence against another person, for instance, is always forbidden even though children may observe this at home. An appropriate release of anger would be talking about it, telling the person at whom you are angry, strenuous exercise, drawing a picture of the anger and talking about it, role playing it, or hitting a pillow or a solid surface with plastic bats.

Talking about Parental Drinking

Denial, especially among older kids and adolescent youth, can be a difficult barrier to break. Because children have an emotional need to disbelieve alcohol educators, it is common for them to deny that their parents have a drinking problem. Even when they know deep down, they sometimes try to hide the truth from others.

At age twelve, Seth's defenses were firmly in place. A soft-spoken, blond child, he denied his mother and father were alcoholic, that he had beaten his drug-addicted mother and put her in the hospital, or that anything was wrong at all. He remained close-mouthed and body-tight in group and listened intently to the other children's stories as if their problems were totally alien to him. When his father relapsed and got drunk on his fortieth birthday, Seth, with a smile and a shrug of his shoulders, said simply, "I don't care. It doesn't bother me. I just ignore it. I slept in the car on the way back from the bar." Seth's ambivalence toward his dad's drinking is reflected in a letter the child wrote during a group exercise:

> Dear Dad: I don't like when you drink. It's o.k. on birthdays. I know you don't like to but you do sometimes. I don't really care too much. I just ignore you. I am glad you have stoped [sic].

From one sentence to the next, Seth vascillates from not liking his father's drinking to feeling okay about it, to not really caring at all, to feeling glad his dad has stopped. Outwardly, Seth is struggling with denial of his true feelings of being upset, scared, and disappointed when his dad drinks. Our goal in the program was to create a safe setting for Seth to exhume his real feelings and deal with them in a constructive way.

Children need to know it is okay to talk about parents' drinking to a trusted friend or in the confines of a safe group. Creating a safe setting for children to talk about alcoholism takes time. Children gradually begin to feel safe once they know practitioners are sincere and care and conversations will remain confidential within the group and will not be repeated to parents. It is crucial that practitioners never minimize or deny the child's perceptions of his or her experience with alcoholism.

High Risk for Addiction

The nature of the disease of addiction is that it can carry over into many areas of one's life. COAs are at high risk for becoming alcoholics, workaholics, compulsive eaters, gamblers, spenders, and sex and drug addicts. Children of alcoholics are four times more likely to become chemically dependent than children from nondrinking homes. Children often fool themselves into thinking they are in full control and may even frequently repeat the old

©1986 The Randolph Clinic. Used with permission.

Figure 7–1. This picture was drawn by a ten-year-old girl during a six-week treatment program.

adage, "It will never happen to me." They may even boast, "I don't drink like my old man. I might do crack or weed. But I'll never be an alcoholic." Switching addictions is the way COAs often cope with parental alcoholism, unaware that all addictions are part and parcel of the same disease package. Children need to understand that these switches, too, are abuse and to learn to "just say no" for their own sakes to break the cycle.

Caution should be exercised in drawing the analogy of cancer to alcoholism when explaining the disease concept to younger children. Sometimes they express anxiety over "catching" the disease of alcoholism. These kids need reassurance and understanding that becoming addicted can be prevented by learning about alcohol and making wise decisions regarding its use.

Support Systems

The group experience is only the beginning of a child's journey into recovery. Children need to know about resources they can depend upon for support once they have completed a program. They need to know that supports exist all around them and that they can reach out to these support systems when they need help. Children need practical information about how to reach out as well as whom and where to reach out to—a friend, counselor, teacher, relative, neighbor, Alateen, etc.

Problem Solving and Coping

Children get help with problem solving and coping by devising advanced plans of action to a variety of situations. Dad stops off at a bar and after three or four hours of drinking, staggers back to the car to drive home. What should the child do? Mom forgets to pick the child up after the movie. A violent father has beaten Mom and threatens the child. Or the child just needs a quiet place to study. These are examples of the kinds of situations with which children are generally unprepared to cope. Children will have their own agendas about coping and problem solving. Practitioners must be prepared to listen and help derive options and solutions that will maximize the child's well-being. Through small group exercises, children can brainstorm ways to deal with troublesome situations, try to anticipate the consequences, then share and evaluate their plans (Schall 1986).

An excellent activity called "Wheel of Misfortune" involves cooperation and teamwork in solving the real-life problems found in alcoholic families (Moe & Pohlman 1988). The activity helps children come to see that they have choices and options in handling tough situations. After the facilitator divides the children into groups of three, each group selects a team name. Each team spins the wheel and lands on a letter of the alphabet, which corresponds to various scenarios, as illustrated by the following example:

> Bobby, Jeremy, and Lori, all nine, called their team "The Cool Cats." With a spin of the wheel they found Mom passed out on the living room rug. What to do? The suggestions flew back and forth—some silly, some outrageous, others ingenious. Bobby suggested that they go get a neighbor. Lori wanted to call 911. Jeremy said, "It's a good idea to try and wake Mom first." They finally agreed to do all three—try and revive Mom, call 911 for an ambulance, and then get a neighbor. They were met with cheers and clapping when they shared with the larger group. (Moe & Pohlman 1988, 48)[a]

[a]© 1988 *Kids Power: Healing Games for Children of Alcoholics* by Jerry Moe and Don Pohlman. Used with permission.

Through such exercises, children learn they can face and solve their problems relating to alcoholism and are capable of handling unexpected situations. Increased competence, in turn, will improve self-esteem and help children overcome feelings of helplessness.

Evaluation of Program Goals

Program evaluation is an important component to any COA program because it lets you know what works and what doesn't. It also tells you what to throw out or keep. Best of all, it gives you concrete feedback that your hard work has paid off and visual evidence that indeed kids are changing for the better as a result of your efforts. Politically, evaluative evidence is important to sell administrators and school personnel on your program.

There are many kinds of evaluation. Whatever type a program uses, the evaluation should match the goals. If program goals include teaching self-help skills, the evaluation component should measure the degree to which children have indeed acquired the ability to care for themselves. COA curricula need an objective evaluation process so that they can demonstrate clearly that program content does indeed affect kids and families. In years to come, as more programs appear on the market, proof will be necessary to make decisions about which ones work best.

I have repeatedly heard (and have even said myself), "I know it works because I can see the change in the kids" or "Susie is so much more self-confident now and can take care of herself." Still, these subjective impressions are not always enough to convince others. While it is important to see and value these types of changes, such observations, unfortunately, do not qualify as objective evaluation. Programs that ask children or parents open-ended questions at the end of the program (such as "Do you feel better about yourself?" or "Do you understand more about the disease of alcoholism?" _____ yes _____ no) are steps in the right direction. But critics would view these responses as mere subjective biases on the part of participants rather than actual proof of change.

The most realistic and rewarding approach to evaluation is to establish the program goals, decide how the five- or six-week curriculum will reach the goals, and finally, the degree to which the goals are achieved. Although COA programs help kids with self-esteem, anxiety, and other psychological processes, an evaluation component of the educational aspects of the program will give the most realistic and beneficial feedback. I do not mean to indicate that COA programs are not developing self-esteem or reducing anxiety or helping children solve problems. More than anything, programs plant seeds during their short intervention cycles so that children take the information and gradually internalize it in the course of their lives. The results of the program then may not be evident for months or even years later. It is self-defeating to expect to see dramatic changes on the short-term basis on which most programs operate.

The implication and hope is that kids will incorporate this new-found information into their daily lives and, over time, make significant changes in attitudes, behaviors, and feelings. Ultimately, through the psychoeducational process, these changes will result in improved self-esteem, reduced anxiety and guilt, a sense of competence and control, talking about feelings, and reaching out to trusted significant others as kids go about their daily lives.

Children of Alcoholics Information Test (COAT)

I developed the children's version of the COAT (Children of Alcoholics Information Test) as an evaluation instrument for children of alcoholics programs to gain a sense of the degree to which program curricula are actually working (see the box on next page). The COAT is based on the ten key points or goals. Regardless of their respective intervention strategies, short-term programs implementing the information in the box on page 129 can use the COAT for evaluation. Preliminary data from a pilot study of children of alcoholics in treatment indicate this instrument is a reliable and valid measurement of alcohol knowledge that can help children cope with parental alcoholism. After completing a six-week psychoeducational treatment program, children of alcoholics scored significantly higher on the post-tests than on the pre-tests (Robinson 1988b).

Administering the COAT

The children's version of this test was devised for use in psychoeducational programs for children of alcoholics to measure the extent to which children (ages nine and older) have gained useful information to help them cope with parental alcoholism. The test can be administered individually or in groups before and after the intervention program.

A reliability score can be computed to determine how carefully children respond to the questions. Five questions are repeated throughout the test. To determine the consistency with which children answer questions on the COAT, a percentage score can be computed by giving 20 points for the matching questions that are answered the same way.

Question	Question
2	8
3	12
5	19
6	22
10	25

Children's Version of the COAT

____Age   ____Sex   ____Date   ____Identification Number

Below are twenty-five sentences about children whose parents drink too much. Read each one and answer "yes," "no," or "don't know" beside each sentence. Put an X under "yes" if you agree with the statement, an X under "no" if you disagree, or an X under "don't know" if you are not sure of the answer.

Yes	No	Don't Know		
___	___	___	1.	Alcoholism is a disease.
___	___	___	2.	Alcoholism hurts everybody in the family, including the alcoholic's children.
___	___	___	3.	Sometimes I feel like I am the cause of my parent's drinking.
___	___	___	4.	I feel alone, like I'm the only person in the world with problems because their parent drinks too much.
___	___	___	5.	I can help my parent stop drinking by doing good in school and helping out around the house.
___	___	___	6.	Children should not talk to others outside the family about their parent's drinking.
___	___	___	7.	The best way to deal with my parent's drinking is to look on the bright side and pretend it isn't happening.
___	___	___	8.	When parents drink, it hurts the kids and everybody in the family.
___	___	___	9.	I know how to take care of myself if my parent drinks too much and gets angry and upset.
___	___	___	10.	Children whose parents drink too much sometimes pretend nothing's wrong when there really is, but this is their way of hiding their feelings.
___	___	___	11.	It is hard for me to get close to other people.
___	___	___	12.	Sometimes I feel like it is my fault that my parent drinks.
___	___	___	13.	Children will feel better inside when they get help even if their parent doesn't stop drinking.

Yes	No	Don't Know		
___	___	___	14.	There is a big chance that children of alcoholics will grow up to be alcoholics too if they are not careful.
___	___	___	15.	It is hard for me to talk about my feelings.
___	___	___	16.	Children with alcoholic parents all behave the same way.
___	___	___	17.	There are millions of other children like me whose parents drink too much.
___	___	___	18.	It is hard for children of alcoholics to like themselves.
___	___	___	19.	I can help my parent stop drinking if I try hard enough.
___	___	___	20.	Alcoholism can make children sad, mad, afraid, and confused.
___	___	___	21.	Children need to get help for themselves whether or not their parent stops drinking.
___	___	___	22.	Children should not talk to others outside the family about their parent's drinking.
___	___	___	23.	It helps to have someone to talk to about your problems.
___	___	___	24.	Going to Alateen and Al-Anon can help me deal with my parent's drinking.
___	___	___	25.	Sometimes children act like nothing's wrong when their parents drink, but it's just their way of keeping their feelings inside.

The higher the consistency score, the greater the confidence that can be placed in the children's answers. High scores indicate the child has read and responded consistently to the five pairs of questions, and presumably to the entire test. Scores of 60 percent or higher indicate the test results are meaningful and that answers to three out of five of the items were identical. Reliability scores of 40 percent or below raise questions about the consistency with which children answered the questions and reduce the likelihood that their scores are reliable. These lower test scores should not be used in a group pre- and post-test evaluation, since they indicate the child may not have been paying careful attention to the questions or the answers.

Number of Identical Responses	Percent
5	100
4	80
3	60
2	40
1	20

Scoring the COAT

Scores are derived by giving 4 points on the pre- and post-tests each time the child's answer matches the ideal scores (see table 7–1). The highest possible score is 100. The gain score or final score is calculated by subtracting pre- and post-scores. For example, a pre-test score of 50 subtracted from a post-test score of 90 gives a gain score of 40.

Table 7–1
COAT Score Sheet

Ideal Score	Pre-Test Score	Post-Test Score	Gain-Score
1. Yes	_____	_____	_____
2. Yes	_____	_____	_____
3. No	_____	_____	_____
4. No	_____	_____	_____
5. No	_____	_____	_____
6. No	_____	_____	_____
7. No	_____	_____	_____
8. Yes	_____	_____	_____
9. Yes	_____	_____	_____
10. Yes	_____	_____	_____
11. No	_____	_____	_____
12. No	_____	_____	_____
13. Yes	_____	_____	_____
14. Yes	_____	_____	_____
15. No	_____	_____	_____
16. No	_____	_____	_____
17. Yes	_____	_____	_____
18. Yes	_____	_____	_____
19. No	_____	_____	_____
20. Yes	_____	_____	_____
21. Yes	_____	_____	_____
22. No	_____	_____	_____
23. Yes	_____	_____	_____
24. Yes	_____	_____	_____
25. Yes	_____	_____	_____
Totals	_____	_____	_____

Tips for Practitioners

Effective psychoeducational programs hinge on establishing a climate of trust and safety. Children who have been deeply traumatized bring with them a natural resistance to intervention. Practitioners should not expect them to talk about what is bothering them right away. Whether in a weekly intervention program or during daily classroom routines, trust and safety are created by patience. Assuring confidentiality, providing nurturance, listening to children, and showing them you care without lecturing, prying, or pushing will earn their trust. Given time, practitioners and children can form a natural, gradual relationship built on mutual trust and respect.

Advocate for Children

Another way of showing compassion for children of alcoholics is being their advocate. Because of the nature of the disease, COAs do not have parents who advocate for them as parents of disabled or emotionally disturbed children. So their voices must come from practitioners who can speak for their rights and needs. Classroom teachers, counselors, and social workers working in schools, or practitioners already employed in chemical dependency treatment facilities can start a children's program using points discussed in this chapter and drawing upon the resources provided in chapter 10. In most instances it is possible to develop children's programs using current levels of facility resources.

Even if it is not possible to develop a children's program, you can speak out for children's rights by seizing opportunities to tell others in your respective fields about the needs of COAs. The National Association for Children of Alcoholics has been the biggest advocate for kids. It advocates for alcohol education through the public schools and for special children's programs in all facilities that treat chemical dependency. In 1988 the organization distributed posters with cartoon characters like Spider Man and the Incredible Hulk to every elementary school system in the United States. The posters address COA needs and have such captions as, "If your mom or dad drinks too much, you're not alone. There are millions of kids with alcoholic parents." You can check with school administrators to see if and how the posters are being used. If you find that your posters are not being used, see that they are appropriately displayed. If posters are unavailable in your school or if you are employed in a nonschool setting, you can obtain copies by writing to the national organization (see chapter 10 for the address).

Conduct Alcohol Education Programs

Counselors can work closely with other school personnel to help children adjust to parental alcoholism. School counselors can help teachers structure special lessons on family alcoholism, using the program goals presented in this chapter. Conducting in-service workshops for classroom teachers and administrators on the plight of children from alcoholic families can generate better understanding of the problems these kids face, and thereby enable teachers to help children better adjust to their tough situations. Establishing alcohol awareness days throughout the school where all children learn about drinking and its effects will reach COAs in a nonthreatening way and serve as a springboard to establishing special groups for children of alcoholism.

8
Treatment Strategies for Children of Alcoholics

Some therapists specialize in grief, anger, or anxiety, but how many work on joy and laughter? Children have shown me a magical connection between the head and heart. When the two come together, healing ensues.
— Rokelle Lerner, "Codependency: The Swirl of Energy Surrounded by Confusion"

Case 8–1

It was Rodney's first night at the treatment center and not unusual for him to be quieter than the other kids. Still, I was baffled by him. Something about his moves and gestures puzzled me, but I couldn't put my finger on exactly what it was at first. Rodney, a six-year-old handsome Italian child, was by no means mentally handicapped or autistic, but he appeared to be suffering from shell shock. He was emotionally disconnected from everything and everyone around him. On the playground he appeared to be carrying on conversations with himself or imaginary companions. As the game of kickball swirled around him, Rodney entertained himself in his own make-believe world with hand motions and inaudible verbalizations. No wonder. He already had been in three different first grades this school year. He didn't know the name of his current school. His family had been evicted six times because his alcoholic father hadn't paid the rent. He told me that when he lived in Seattle he came home from school one day and all the family belongings were on the front lawn, packed in huge black plastic bags.

Knowing his past and his need for a self-created fantasy world, the staff's goal was not to jerk that away from him. Many children often withdraw into their imaginations. Their mental creations become their survival tools because imagination is the one thing that is theirs—the one thing they can latch on to when all else around them is falling apart. Our approach was to gently keep Rodney in present time during kickball. "Okay, Rodney, this one's coming to you," or "Get ready Rodney, watch third base." Each time he was pulled back to reality from a self-created fantasy world. Rodney didn't know how to play kickball. I explained the rules to him and compared it to softball. I was stunned that the child didn't understand the concept of "outs," changing sides, or running bases. A half hour into the game, he tugged at my shirt sleeve and asked, "When are we going to play?" Shocked beyond belief, I thought I had misunderstood. "Pardon?" I asked. "When are we going to play?" he repeated. I looked down at his innocent face waiting for an answer and said the only natural thing, "We *are* playing, Rodney."

Rodney had never played before, and he didn't even recognize play when he saw it or was involved in it. Gradually, I began to understand what it was about him that caught my eye from the beginning. Play deprivation, clearly reflected in his demeanor, had negatively affected Rodney physically, cognitively, socially, and emotionally. He was clumsy and uncoordinated when he walked and ran. He lacked the cognitive concepts of play, the notion of rules, and how to play with others. He had poor social skills and didn't know how to interact with children his own age. I asked him if he had any playmates or friends to play with. He reflected on the question, and after a long pause he excitedly proclaimed, "My next-door neighbor's dog is my friend!"

Treatment Strategies for Children of Alcoholics

In some ways Rodney is unusual but in other ways he is typical of children of alcoholics. In fact, my experience with COAs has led me to conclude that we can add a fourth rule to Claudia Black's three rules of "don't talk," "don't feel," and "don't trust." The fourth rule that all COAs learn directly or indirectly is "don't play" or "don't have fun." The case of Rodney is an extreme example of a child of alcoholism so deprived of play that he was affected physically, cognitively, socially, and emotionally. We had to literally teach him step by step what play is and how to do it. Other children learn the rule perhaps to a lesser degree, but they internalize it just the same. Alcoholism is serious business and surviving it takes every ounce of energy for everyone in the family. None can be "wasted" or "frittered away" on something as trivial or frivolous as play. Play is only one of many strategies that practitioners can use in treating children of alcoholics.

Therapeutic Value of Play

Play is the work of young children. While all children need play opportunities, play is doubly important for COAs. According to Rokelle Lerner (1986),

"Connecting the head and the heart through humor and play can be just as healing as the work we do with anger, misery, and anxiety" (p. 114). Through interactive play, COAs learn to work out mutual problems and to internalize rules and roles of society's norms. Through play, COAs learn spontaneity and flexibility and to negotiate and interact with peers on an equal basis. Kids do not learn these important skills in an alcoholic home where it is "the parent up and the kids down" (Black 1987).

All COAs need to be taught to play and to have fun as part of their treatment program. It is through play that the free child emerges and kids learn to deal with their feelings. Children develop motor coordination and balance, competence in social interactions, and how to negotiate problems and work them out on their own. Roles and rules in childhood games provide children with opportunities to learn about similar roles and rules in adult society. Feelings of cooperation and competition are developed through play. Concepts such as justice and injustice, prejudice and equality, leading and following, and loyalty and disloyalty begin to take on real and personal meaning. Play also provides kids with sheer fun and diversion in an otherwise serious and traumatic life. Many types of play strategies can be integrated into treatment interventions.

Dramatic Play

As I discussed in chapter 5, dramatic play can be a vehicle for observing feelings and frustrations related to alcoholism, especially among preschool children who act out domestic scenes. An area in the room designated as the housekeeping corner or dramatic play area complete with props helps stimulate children to act out troublesome situations they have experienced at home. Many times these scenarios involve a drinking parent ordering everyone else around or episodes of spankings or spousal arguments. Adult guidance during dramatic play can help children sharpen their questions, clarify issues, and explore alternatives of action. By joining a domestic quarrel, for example, a practitioner can model successful ways of handling interpersonal conflict or dealing with fears by acting out a situation.

Stages of Play

Some young children like Rodney who were deprived of play at earlier ages may need to be taken through the stages of play that they missed. The goal may be to move the child into parallel play and then gradually into associative and eventually into cooperative play with other children. Although these stages are ordinarily reached by five or six, older school-age children who are having difficulty may need opportunities to retrace their steps through these stages.

Imaginary Playmates

Play does not always involve "real people." Sometimes young children invent imaginary playmates—especially when they have few real friends, have no siblings, or have problems such as family alcoholism that they need to work out alone. They get emotional satisfaction from carrying on lengthy conversations and sharing toys with these "unseen friends." Imaginary playmates help children reduce loneliness, cope with fears or unsatisfactory relationships such as violent, drinking parents, and find an outlet for anger and hostility. Most imaginary playmates appear between the ages of two-and-a-half and ten but disappear as children enter school, meet other friends to play with, or receive treatment for severe problems (Flake-Hobson, Robinson & Skeen 1983).

Board Games

School-age kids enjoy board games such as checkers or Monopoly. The use of board games designed as therapeutic tools is an excellent way to get important points across without preaching or lecturing. The most popular board game that I have used is called Just Say No, a Monopoly format that helps kids resist pressure to drug use. Although "just saying no" is not the solution to the problem, it does get youngsters to see they have choices. School-age children enjoy this game and want to play it over and over again. Several other good board games are available to emphasize different issues of children and alcoholism and are presented in chapter 10.

Noncompetitive Group Games

Group games such as hopscotch, Blindman's Bluff, chasing games, hide-and-seek, and Red Rover are popular games among school-age children. Adolescents from alcoholic homes generally like group games too because many of them missed these activities when they were younger. These games allow children to let off steam and pent-up energy as well as develop physical-motor capacities and build social skills.

Programs that stress competition and open comparison of children are setting kids up for failure and inadvertently sabotaging their recovery programs. An alternative approach is to emphasize noncompetitive games that kids enjoy playing where nobody wins and more important, nobody loses. It is important to avoid any games in which the self-worth of the child is at stake, because one of the points of COA programs is to build self-worth that has already been shattered. Games in which some children are chosen and others left out should also be avoided. Being excluded can only add to some children's personal history of isolation and rejection from the group. Many of us can remember the fear and humiliation of being the last one chosen for a team sport. Practitioners can prearrange teams for balance of abilities or can organize them around a numbering system. Children can count off by ones, twos, or threes or they can choose a number of which two group leaders are thinking. Those closest to the numbers are on the respective sides.

It is important that group games requiring teams, such as kickball or volleyball, de-emphasize winning and stress team spirit and fun of the game. COAs need to learn that both losing and winning are a part of life. But most of them have already learned how to lose. The focus of COA programs is to convey to kids that they are all winners. Noncompetitive games help children develop their free spirit of childhood and to feel a part of the group, while teaching mutual cooperation and working together without taking anything away from anyone. An excellent resource for noncompetitive games for all ages is *The New Games Book* and *More New Games*.

Psychodrama

One of the most effective techniques I have used with adolescents is letting them play out their feelings associated with alcoholism. I begin by using The Stamp Game (see chapter 10) or a similar method for helping children identify their feelings. I ask them to think about a specific instance when their parent was drinking and how they felt during that situation. Having cards that name specific feelings helps them identify their own emotions. Once identified, I ask them to enlist one of the group leaders or another group member to act out the scenario. Although this approach is extremely effective, practitioners must be prepared for the frequently accompanying powerful reactions of anger or tears. Group processing of the scenario follows. The role play often taps emotions of group members on the periphery who need a chance to share their reactions. Two group leaders with a small number of adolescents (a maximum of ten) is suggested so that one is always free to attend to emotional flare-ups.

Other types of psychodrama, such as the empty chair technique, are also effective. The group member sits facing an empty chair surrounded by a circle of supportive group members. The member in the middle of the circle pretends the alcoholic parent is sitting in the empty chair and carries on a conversation with the parent. Practitioners encourage the participant to get out unexpressed feelings toward the parent through words and actions: "What would you like to say to your mom/dad that you've never been able to say before?" This can include things the child would never actually say or do to the parent such as yelling or hitting the "parent" with a plastic bat. After the conversation, the whole group participates in processing the experience.

Creative Outlets

No treatment program for children of alcoholism is complete without regular use of creative activities. Most child-oriented programs use some type of creative outlet as an integral part of every session. Each week, for example, sessions might alternate between painting, clay, music, creative writing, movement, puppets, collage, woodworking, and so forth. These are just a few creative outlets that serve as vehicles for communicating any of the ten key points for children of alcoholics programs (discussed in the previous chapter). The possibilities are endless. Presenting the points through creative activities makes the process fun, interesting, nonthreatening, and relevant at the child's level. Creative activities not only provide outlets for an array of pent-up emotions—anger, sadness, fear, embarrassment, rage, loneliness—but also give children some say-so and sense of control over their lives.

One of the most successful activities that I have used with COAs is having them express the feelings they have when a parent drinks. With stations set up around the room (such as puppets, art materials, writing areas, dramatic play areas, and musical expression), I give them free time to move about the room expressing the feelings that come up. Younger children gravitate toward puppets and artwork, while older school-age children and adolescents will write letters, poems, songs, or plays or use psychodrama. The activity is always followed by a group discussion. Children share with the group their creative outcome (a song, a picture, a puppet vignette) to express how they feel when a parent drinks. For some children this is a difficult activity because their feelings have been denied and suppressed for so long. The identification of even one feeling is an accomplishment. Most youngsters approach the activity with interest and enthusiasm and feel more comfortable with something concrete in hand that helps them put into words how they feel. I have learned through my work with COAs that they are children of fear. They are afraid of what is happening at home and terrified that something awful is going to happen to them. Many of them cope by building walls around themselves. This activity helps them remove a few stones from the walls.

Bibliotherapy

Literature can have a dynamic effect on children and family members. *Bibliotherapy*—the use of books as a therapeutic tool for helping families adjust to difficult situations—is a valuable intervention strategy in alcohol education (Brisbane 1985; Fassler 1987; Manning 1987). An advantage of bibliotherapy is that it presents problems and possible solutions in a non-threatening way. Practitioners can use children's books that tell stories about

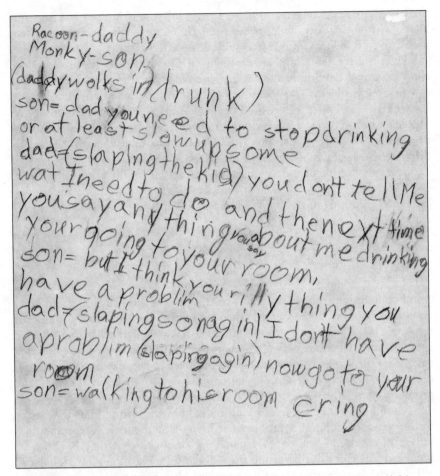

Figure 8–1. This seven-year-old boy wrote a play about a son and his alcoholic father.

a parent who drinks too much, how it makes the character feel, and how the characters deal with these feelings (see chapter 10 for a comprehensive list of children's books). Bibliotherapy helps COAs to identify, understand, and deal with their feelings about family alcoholism. And it helps them confront and overcome many of alcoholism's problems. Children's stories let kids know they are not alone in their heartache and pain. Storytelling offers typical lifelike situations and gives the reader the opportunity to experience a variety of possible actions vicariously without having to actually experience the consequences. Conversations between adults and children can be stimulated by books. When children see story characters experiencing their own problems and feelings, the fear of uniqueness diminishes.

Practitioners who implement bibliotherapy must be sensitive to the child's age and developmental level, the child's reading level, and any special reading problems (for example, of handicapped children) (Pardeck & Pardeck 1987). The stories should provide a fair and realistic picture of the problem with accurate information and not be moralistic, "preachy," condescending, or "pat" (Manning 1987). Successful bibliotherapy leads kids through three stages: (1) identification with the character or situation, (2) vicarious sharing of the feelings and motivations of the book's character, and (3) achievement of insight as readers internalize some of the coping behaviors exhibited in the book and apply them to their personal problems with alcohol (Jalongo 1983).

Filmed Vignettes

Another nonthreatening approach to treating COAs is through film and other audiovisuals. As in bibliotherapy, the viewer can identify with the character on screen in a protective group situation that is enhanced by a darkened room. Filmed vignettes help children express and deal with situations that emerge on the screen. Audiovisuals can be effective because they trigger children's reactions to experiences that are similar to those in the film and promote discussion.

Practitioners should exercise caution in showing strong films that strike at the heart of children's problems. Movies about alcoholism sometimes arouse in children some of the frightening emotions that they have felt at home before. Once during group time, for instance, Rodney sat stonefaced as other children chatted about the problems they were having with parental alcoholism. Not until the showing of the film "Soft Is the Heart of the Child" did his feelings erupt into a flood of words. During one scene where the father was drunk and behaving violently, Rodney blurted, "I hate it when people drink! I hate my dad when he gets drunk! We're not going back home until he gets well, either!" I reassuringly put my arm around him and let him vent his feelings. This release marked the beginning of Rodney's recovery.

As practitioners show filmed vignettes, it is crucial that they keep a constant visual survey on the children for signs of disturbance or erupting emotions. Younger children especially must be monitored during dramatic films that realistically portray active alcoholism. They will often slide toward grownups or crawl upon their laps for comforting. After the films, children are almost always eager to discuss what happened and to tell about similar experiences they have had.

Group Work

Group work offers several advantages over individual counseling and is the preferred strategy for treating children of alcoholics. Children learn through group experiences that they are not alone, and they can say and hear things that are mutually beneficial and growth productive. Group, more than individual experiences, increases the likelihood of breaking the silence and denial associated with family alcoholism. The therapeutic group process can provide the safety and protection that children need as they become aware of their feelings and begin to risk sharing them with others whom they trust (Bingham & Bargar 1985). Group work also gives kids the experience of healthy social interactions as well as building trust in social situations, an experience that many COAs are severely lacking. Group process also gives children opportunities for group validation and the building of confidence and esteem.

Positive peer group support helps children try out new approaches to old problems. The encouragement and empathy provided by peers lessens the child's resistance to making healthy changes. Ellen Morehouse (1986) notes that positive peer support often extends beyond the group, as when group members exchange phone numbers, become friends, and call each other when problems occur. She also cites empathetic confrontation as a special advantage of groups. Hearing one group member, for example, confront another group member with, "You can't keep blaming your poor grades on your mom's drinking. We discussed several weeks ago how you could stay after school to study," helps children rethink how responsible they are being for their own behaviors.

The short-term nature of most group intervention programs limits observable outcomes. Visible results may be few and far between, but the seeds of recovery have been planted. Children will continue to recover long after they have left the group. One of the final goals of the group is to help them connect with supports in their everyday worlds so that continuing recovery is assured. The group experience prepares older children for Alateen, a peer therapy group that helps children keep their own lives and personal development from being affected too deeply by the close association with an alcoholic parent or family member. Alateen attendance or encouragement to attend Alateen occurs in the final phase of most treatment programs. Some regions of the country also have Alatot, special groups for younger children of alcoholics. The box on page 152 distinguishes among the many other self-help groups that have evolved nationally for adult and young children of alcoholics to help them overcome their problems. Research confirms that self-help groups such as Alateen, ACOA, and Al-Anon are effective in helping participants with self-esteem, relationships, and other problem areas related to parental alcoholism (Cutter & Cutter 1987; Hughes 1977).

The Self-Help Cafeteria

What is the difference between Al-Anon and ACOA meetings? Or between ACA, ACOA, and COA groups? If you're asking these questions, so are a lot of other people.

Sorting your way through distinctions between groups for children of alcoholics can be confusing. Here is a brief synopsis of available options. Since we are yet young as a movement, it is difficult to include all of the subjective meanings or even each and every type of group available.

ACOA/Al-Anon

There are currently nine hundred of these groups registered. They are considered a special-interest group of Al-Anon. The focus is on the Twelve Steps and Twelve Traditions of Recovery, as well as the problem of alcoholism as it relates to adult children. The program offers structure and support, as it sticks close to the principles on which Al-Anon was founded. Al-Anon listings are in most urban directories.

ACA

The term ACA has many definitions. Meaning varies according to various groups as well as individuals. The only way to know is to ask. Some use the term broadly to differentiate between young and adult children. Some use it to refer to a particular type of meeting geared to issues and concerns of adult children.

ACA World Service

Approximately four hundred groups have chosen to register with the ACA World Service Offices out of Los Angeles. This is a Twelve-Step program striving to develop materials, literature, and guidelines that are geared to the needs of adult children. This organization is autonomous—that is, it is completely separate from Al-Anon and AA. Various intergroup representatives are located throughout and beyond the United States.

Independent ACOA and/or ACA Meetings

A bulk of nonregistered independent, self-help support meetings are within this category. Groups may choose to not register for a variety of reasons. Members may feel too new for the task of serving as a responsible, registered group. It usually takes some time to determine the direction and wishes of the group as individuals strive to unearth their own particular needs. A number of groups are not aware of the options regarding registration and various ways to organize. Some groups choose to deal with specific themes that do not fit into the structure and content of either Al-Anon or ACA guidelines.

Other groups may lean toward being more educational with respect to alcoholism or adult children issues. There are also therapy groups for adult children, and these are not usually listed as free meetings open to the public. They are found through listings of available services, often by word of mouth.

Coalitions

Several geographic areas have coalitions working to offer support to one another, educate newcomers, and formulate projects. These groups are frequently interested in bringing about change on a political/societal level. They are not generally listed as self-help groups, but may offer an atmosphere for personal sharing.

COA

While the term COA is sometimes used to include all young and adult children, it is important to know that groups and services for children are available. Many teenagers are successfully working in Alateen. There is an increasing number of children of alcoholics meetings geared toward adolescents. Therapists and organizations around the country are providing educational and therapeutic help for young children.

Some members of Alcoholics Anonymous describe that program as "a cafeteria—take what you like and leave the rest." This may also be a useful way to see how support groups can meet your needs.

Reprinted from "The Self-Help Cafeteria" by Debbie Hazelton, © 1987, *Changes Magazine*. Used with permission.

Treatment Tailored for Children

Adult programs masquerading as children's programs are inadequate substitutes. Programs that meet the developmental needs of children cannot be carbon copies of programs for grownups. Instead, they must be specifically designed with kids in mind. Programs tailored for children must be developmentally appropriate. Watered-down versions of adult programs run the risk of reinforcing the dysfunction of the alcoholic home where kids are expected to be little adults. Children must be treated as kids, and program content and expectations and goals must be aligned with their developmental abilities. The following guidelines will help practitioners ensure that treatment programs achieve appropriate tailoring for children.

Homogeneous Grouping

Ideally, children should not all be lumped together. Programs for four-year-olds will not appeal to ten-year-olds. Programs for ten-year-olds will not appeal to seventeen-year-olds. Successful programming is contingent on grouping children by their developmental abilities and interests so that fifteen-year-olds will not think the program is too babyish and six-year-olds can participate at their own level.

Ordinarily, grouping in programs with a psychoeducational focus should consider level of understanding for children to grasp the concepts that are presented. This can be achieved by using Piaget's stages of cognitive development deriving three developmental groups:

1. Preoperational—kindergarten and early elementary (five to seven years)
2. Concrete operational—school-age (eight-to-eleven years)
3. Formal operational—adolescence (twelve years and up)

These age ranges represent only one method out of many possibilities and should be used as merely a rule of thumb—not as hard-and-fast cutoff points. Practitioners should be flexible in placing kids in groups and consider additional factors such as the child's developmental maturity, interests, the child's social skills with peers, and program goals. Considering these factors, for example, some twelve-year-olds might be better placed in the school-age group, while others would fit better in the adolescent group.

Many programs cannot afford the luxury of three groups because of staff, equipment, and space shortages. Individual programs will have to work within their means to accommodate children in the most optimal way. That might mean limiting services and emphasizing quality programs to a specific age group rather than trying to accommodate all ages when resources do not permit. Programs may decide to have only two groups with larger age ranges of ages six to eleven, and twelve to eighteen or to restrict services to smaller age ranges of five to eight and nine to twelve.

Another consideration in grouping is placing siblings in the same treatment group. My experience has consistently shown recurring problems when different-age siblings are grouped together. Perceptions of parental alcoholism varies depending upon the child's age. This causes open disagreement over interpretation of specific family events. Joint sibling placement also interferes with older siblings' gaining full benefit of the group and encourages younger brothers and sisters to depend on them. Older children also tend to censure younger brothers or sisters through nonverbal cues or by breaking confidentiality and informing parents of specific information the child shared in the groups. Denial is thus perpetuated and intervention thwarted. Once age groupings have been decided upon, curricula can be geared to each group that will heighten interest and learning.

Developmentally Appropriate

At each developmental stage, youngsters confront different developmental challenges and have different abilities and interests. Nothing is more disturbing than to observe a program with well-intentioned goals and dedicated staff and see five- and six-year-olds arranged in a circle listening to a lecture about family roles in chemically dependent homes. Even worse is a rap group for six-year-olds where kids are expected to articulate their feelings. This approach goes against the natural developmental grain of the child. Children are not little adults. Programs for them cannot be run by personnel without appropriate experience with kids. Ideally, every children's program should hire a child development specialist on their staff to ensure developmentally appropriate practices.

Developmental Matching

While program content can be virtually the same regardless of age, the presentation of content should be matched to children's developmental levels. Five- and six-year-olds can express their feelings better through puppets, art, and play. Preschool and early elementary-age kids who are preliterate and still learning basic skills can be reached best through play, stories, dramatic play, and lots of movement. School-age children enjoy board games, group games, music, group projects, artwork, films, crafts, and some discussion. Fifteen-year-olds will benefit more from rap groups, interacting with peers through group exercises, role play, information dissemination from the group leader, and films and discussion.

Practitioners must have some understanding of child development in order to make an appropriate match between children's development and curriculum goals. The concept of alcoholism as a disease, for instance, can be communicated to all age groups. The specific method of conveying this idea, however, is dependent upon the child's developmental level. Preoperational children learn best through active exploration, interaction, and manipulation of their surroundings. Appealing to their magical thinking will

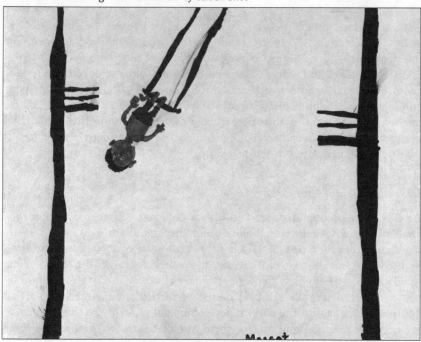

Figure 8–2. Creative activities such as artwork can be good treatment strategies for revealing children's thoughts and feelings, as when this seven-year-old boy drew his life in alcoholism as a trapezist, out of control and flying through space.

help them grasp the concept. One example is a puppet show, depicting interaction of family members and how the disease affects their behaviors. Children can take an active role using a puppet with the group leader acting as facilitator.

Concrete operational children also learn best through concrete experiences. Their logical thinking will give them a clearer understanding of the disease and can be presented in a variety of ways. "The Alcoholism Circle" teaches school-age children about the disease through a group game (Veenstra 1987):

> One person is asked to volunteer to be an alcoholic and be in the center of the circle. The children in the circle are asked to tightly hold hands and imagine they are "alcoholism" which is determined to keep this alcoholic trapped in the circle. Then the alcoholic tries to break out of the circle. (p. 29)

This game can be followed by a discussion of how this experience is similar to the disease of alcoholism and how children felt on both the inside and outside of the circle.

Adolescents are at the stage of formal reasoning and can (and usually prefer to) learn concepts in more adult-like fashion. Practitioners can give a brief overview of the disease concept of alcoholism and the accompanying survival roles. Teens can then develop family scenarios around the survival roles, act them out within the group, and discuss and process the dynamics from the psychodrama.

In all three situations, children leave the program with their own unique understanding of what alcoholism really is. They will be in a better position to use this information because they have integrated it on a level that fits with their own unique developmental timetable.

Fun and Enjoyment

Generally, children have been in school all day long, and they should not be expected to sit for long periods of time in afternoon or evening programs. The program should allow children to be mobile and be fun as well as informational. Emphasis should be on play, regardless of the child's age. Remember that being a COA is serious business, and many are missing childhood and cannot be kids outside of the group, since many COAs never have the opportunity to relax and have fun. Besides, children learn a lot through play.

Child Centered

The programs should employ words and concepts children can understand. When talking about the family roles and defenses used to survive active alcoholism, for example, terms can be translated to children as wearing masks and building walls. Toys and materials should be available at the kid's level— not on high shelves. Effective programs take a wholistic, child-centered approach, encompassing the physical, cognitive, social, emotional, and spiritual areas of development. Programmatically translated, these areas become physical exercise, movement, and play; problem solving and coping; social interaction, sharing ideas, and getting along with others; dealing with feelings, defenses, self-worth; and continued healing and personal growth in recovery.

Curriculum Design

The child's treatment should come from the inside out—not from the outside in. The COA curriculum, with general plans, routines, and goals, should follow the spontaneous swing and style of the child. Curriculum activities should include both planned and unplanned time with flexibility built in for spontaneous needs of children. Conscientious group leaders can become so focused on covering all their points that they neglect the individual needs of the child. Every child should not be doing the same things at the same time.

An effective curriculum provides free choice so that children select from a variety of activities to reach a particular goal and can pace themselves at their own developmental rate. Program planners can keep the program fresh by tapping into the children's own creativity while using a minimum of workbooks or canned curricula. Activities should be varied, diverse, multisensory, and should encourage self-expression. A good example is using children's favorite rock songs and letting them write the lyrics as they apply to the specific curriculum theme. For example, "Kids Just Want to Be Safe" is sung to the tune of Cyndi Lauper's "Girls Just Want to Have Fun" and the tune of "Wake Me Up Before You Go Go" is adapted as "It's Not Our Fault, No No No No. We Didn't Make Our Parents Drink That Mojo" (Moe & Pohlman 1988).

Thematic Focus

Thematic approaches are helpful, especially for younger children, to integrate information in a meaningful way. Deciding upon several themes will also help organize key concepts and give the group a specific focus for each regular meeting. As illustrations, the Randolph Clinic, Inc., in Charlotte, North Carolina, has a six-week primary care program organized around one theme per week:

Week 1 deals with *Masks and Walls* that children of alcoholics erect for self-protection in response to parental drinking. Week 2 addresses *Feelings* and how to identify, express, share, and deal with feelings related to parental drinking. Week 3 revolves around *Family Disease and Family Roles* and helps children to understand the role(s) they play and why they play those roles. Week 4 deals with *The Three C's* and the fact that children did not cause, cannot control, and cannot cure parental alcoholism. Week 5 centers around *Self-image,* in which children are taught to affirm themselves and others, to problem solve, and to do good things for themselves. Week 6 concludes the curriculum with the message of *You are Not Alone,* which helps them understand what a support network is and how to reach out to others in various ways for support in dealing with the disease of alcoholism.

The Charlotte Treatment Center has a similar five-week program with accompanying themes:

Week 1: *Understanding Feelings*

Week 2: *Alcoholism/Chemical Dependency Is a Family Disease*

Week 3: *Kids Can Cope*

Week 4: *Families Can Recover*

Week 5: *Kids Are Special*

Weekly Format

Establishing a regular program format will give kids a certain amount of security and predictability during weekly sessions. An example of one type of weekly schedule follows:

6:00–6:30	Arrival and outside/inside play
6:30–6:45	Snack
6:45–7:00	Bathroom break
7:00–8:00	Curriculum theme activity and discussion
8:00–9:00	Film, storytelling, board game, or other activity, followed by discussion
9:00	Departure

There is no single best format. Practitioners must consider time constraints for each session, program goals, and individual leadership styles in devising their own format to best match their needs.

Rules

All programs need ground rules and children adjust better when they have choices within limits. Rules should be designed for children, not grownups. Programs must avoid too many "don'ts," as children get enough of these at home. Program leaders who spend an inordinate amount of time giving orders to children, refereeing disputes, demanding silence, and enforcing rules have a serious problem and should ask for outside help. While rules are essential, they should not have to be overly emphasized. Certain rules should be included in all programs, such as group confidentiality, listening as other group members talk, and being on time. Practitioners should avoid stating rules in negative ways such as "don't be late" or "no sharing of information outside the group." Positive statements always work best and more clearly get the point across. The box on page 160 presents a checklist that practitioners can use to assess whether their treatment interventions are appropriately tailored for children.

Tips for Practitioners

Aside from the basic treatment strategies discussed in this chapter, there are numerous points practitioners should keep in mind in working with children of alcoholic parents.

A Check for Tailored Treatment

The following questions ask pertinent information about programs for children of alcoholic parents. If your answer to all ten questions is "yes," then your curriculum has the major components for a tailored treatment program.

1. Is there a match between program content and the child's developmental level?

2. Are children grouped according to developmental interests and abilities?

3. Is the curriculum integrated around meaningful topics rather than served in piecemeal fashion?

4. Does the program address the whole child by providing experiences in the physical, cognitive, social, emotional, and spiritual domains?

5. Is the curriculum fun and interesting and does it include times for play and the release of the inner child?

6. Are key points, toys, equipment, and space child-centered rather than adult-centered?

7. Are children permitted to make choices that allow them to become actively involved and to process information at their own rate and in their individual style?

8. Does the curriculum employ a variety of activities and materials that tap children's self-expression through multisensory approaches?

9. Are there general rules and limits that are reasonable and geared to children's developmental status?

10. Are there major program goals with flex-time and spontaneity built in along the way?

Disseminate Information

Provide families with books and pamphlets on alcoholism, especially those that discuss the effects on children. Where appropriate, sharing the results of research studies could be beneficial to parents. This might include the detrimental effects on children who have alcoholic parents and the positive effects of early treatment intervention on these children. Other media such as filmed vignettes, pamphlets, or books can be useful informational tools for other uninformed professionals in your workplace, and for parents and children.

An easy and effective way of disseminating information to alcoholic families is to establish a lending library where newsletters, magazines, pamphlets, and books are catalogued and can be checked out on a regular basis. A corner of a classroom, a waiting area, health room, lounge, or other underused area can house the collection in a minimal amount of space. Reading of these materials promotes knowledge, changes attitudes, and reduces feelings of isolation. You can draw from the comprehensive list of resources in chapter 10, which provides names of filmed vignettes, organizations and their publications, and other literature for adults as well as for children.

Address Individual Differences

It is important to remember that children of alcoholics are not a homogeneous population and the depth and degree to which each child experiences difficulty is a function of individual differences. Although group context is the preferred treatment strategy for kids, do not lose sight of their uniqueness and that they will need some individual attention.

Help Children Center Themselves

Achieving and maintaining balance is the goal of all human beings. Most children of alcoholics are off balance by virtue of their unbalanced upbringing. Imbalance is perpetuated by the adoption of any addictions that can throw us off center. My own imbalance came about from workaholism. For others it may be excessive eating, cleaning, substance abuse, and so forth. If we think of the child as a physical, mental, social, emotional, and spiritual system that functions as a harmonious whole, we must be balanced in all component parts for the whole to optimally sustain itself.

You can help children become balanced or well-rounded. Teachers, counselors, and other school personnel are in an especially advantageous position because of the lengthy daily contact they have with children. A child who studies too much may be encouraged to socially interact with other kids. A child who suffers from poor self-concept can be put in leadership roles that are likely to lead to successful experiences and to result in accolades from peers. A child who excels in athletics may do so at the expense of his or her studies and may need direction in the academic domain. These practices are not revolutionary. Accomplished professionals, in fact, abide by them already. But capable helpers easily get sidetracked with daily humdrum routines and often forget or lose good habits that are so basic, yet so imperative.

Empower Children

Help children see themselves not as victims of alcoholism, but as survivors, which they truly are. This positive approach helps children understand that everything that has happened to them is part of a total picture of who they are. It also empowers them to continue to transform their personal lives forever—no matter how horrific an experience—into a positive end. Recovery is gradual. You can help kids be patient, while recognizing and affirming the baby steps they make in their growth.

9
Intergenerational Transmission of Alcoholism

> Their parents did not abuse alcohol, but one or more of their grand-
> parents did, and their family continues to follow the rules and behav-
> iors of an actively drinking alcoholic family. It is extremely important
> for people who come from this type of system to realize that the
> behavioral characteristics of the disease of alcoholism are transmitted
> through the family, even though the active drinking has ceased.
> —Wayne Kritsberg, *The Adult Children of Alcoholics Syndrome:
> From Discovery to Recovery*

Case 9–1

My name is Irene, and both of my grandfathers were alcoholic. There was
lots of vicious conflict in my mother's home. As a very young girl, she made
a suicide gesture, and she has spent much of her life borderline depressed. I
think her way to survive the viciousness that went on between her parents—
the name calling and the brutal verbal stuff—was to be nice and try to keep
an insulation around herself so that it affected her as little as possible. My
mother became the peacemaker in the family. She was very pleasant and had
the incredible ability to accept just about anything.

My dad became a high achiever who gets his thank-you notes out the day
after Christmas. He just does it right. A perfectionist workaholic, he holds
those same standards for everybody. If he could do it, then everybody else
ought to be able to do it and should do it. There were lots and lots of
"shoulds" in my family. He was a traveling salesman on the road constantly
working much of the time as I was growing up. No wasting of time. Both
of my parents were always busy and doing.

My parents were determined that things would be different for my
brother and me. Our family would not be like the horrible family life they
experienced as children of alcoholic parents. Alcohol was never around as
I was growing up, and my parents rarely drank. Instead, Mom became a

placater and Dad, a family hero. Both of them have always been primarily other-directed and that was reinforced in them and in myself through my family's active church involvement. It was a regular part of our life, a social as well as a religious place. The message was always taking care of other people, pride in ego, being good, and putting other people first. The fact that I was female made the layering of that message very thick. My family was a good family; they are very good people. They worked hard to send us to summer camp. They wanted to be Ozzie and Harriet and they tried real hard to be.

There was very little open conflict in my family. Everybody was always trying to do everything right—anticipating anything that could create trouble before it happened. We operated from the avoidance of conflict. My dad didn't get angry; he got sarcastic. I learned very early that the consequences of wrongdoing around my house was freeze time, a tangible chill. It was awful. I'd rather have been beaten. It was worse than a slap across the face. I always feared that if I didn't meet my parents' expectations, they would withhold their love and abandon me emotionally. That had a big effect on my self-esteem. The way to have self-esteem was to be good, to be right, to do well, to be perfect.

There was a sense of something missing. I always wished there were more closeness in the family. I never felt a sense that my parents were people to talk to or to turn to when I was in trouble. I didn't feel loved and accepted, even though I know my parents were very well-intended. They were always the last people in the world I wanted to know my real business because there was no real history of that kind of intimacy. Instead, there was more focus on the belief that "You are what you do." The adage "What would people think?" became a real measure. When I was a child, my dad gave me a dollar every time I read *How to Win Friends and Influence People* and I really internalized that book. It emphasizes the people-pleasing stuff—tuning in to others and making them feel important. What I understand now is that underneath all that kind manipulation is the basic need to control how others feel about me. That's how I can feel about myself. Today, at forty-two, I still struggle with whether it's okay for me to be different from others. It's been okay for other people to be different from me, but the issue of my being different from them is based on a security within myself that I'm okay even if others don't like me.

I still don't know how to deal with sarcasm. My response to my father's cold sarcasm was to be crushed inside and not to react in a way that would let him know that I was hurt. In fact my mother and I both ate a lot and became overweight to deal with our stuffed feelings. It was also a form of rebellion for me because my eating was an issue for my dad, who'd say, "Oh, you're having more potatoes?" For a long time as an adult there was no recognized conflict in my life. I bypassed any awareness of conflict and went right to accommodation so as not to have conflict. Being accepting and understanding has been one of my own coping devices, being a good girl, a good daughter, doing all the things you're supposed to do. If I wanted Chinese and you wanted Mexican, I was willing to give up Chinese, no problem! I became exactly like my mother—a placater.

The major disadvantage of being the grandchild of alcoholics is that there is no obvious dysfunction in my immediate family to point to as the reason for my discontent, lack, and frustration. So the logical conclusion I arrived at was that there's something wrong with me. It's my fault. It cannot be them. Christ, my parents are fine, upstanding, righteous people. So there must be something wrong with me for wanting to have intimate, feeling conversations and relationships and for feeling like I wasn't loved or accepted.

My understanding of adult children issues has helped me to clarify my own confusion. Now I understand how my mom and dad became who they are and therefore why I have some of the feelings I have. With that awareness has come a sense of more choice that I don't have to always be a placater simply because that was what I learned. I can learn that it's okay to be tougher and can learn that it's okay for me to disagree, be angry, or for your behavior not to be acceptable to me. As an adult, I have learned that there is something to be said for clearing the air in relationships. Not only is conflict normal but it is okay and sometimes even very productive. If I had children, the biggest thing I would hope to do would be to promote an atmosphere of intimacy, of being able to really talk. I would see myself as the kind of mother who would want to hear how your day went and would want to talk more about how I felt and how my children felt.

— Irene, age forty-two

Intergenerational Transmission of Alcoholism

The transmission of alcoholism from parent to child to grandchild is an intriguing and complex issue, as the case of Irene illustrates. Children of alcoholics comprise 60 percent of all patients in chemical dependency programs (Liepman, White & Nirenberg 1986). Although it is clear that alcoholism is carried in families, the degree to which hereditary and environmental factors contribute to this transmission is unclear. Scientists are still trying to untangle the puzzle of how the disease is transmitted. Researchers have found that both genetic predisposition and family dynamics play major roles in perpetuating the disease. During the 1980s, for example, genetic research revealed overwhelming support in favor of biochemical differences in children of alcoholics, compared to children of nonalcoholics. But the evidence is equally convincing that alcoholism is perpetuated in a generational cycle from parent to child and from grandparent to grandchild, not just genetically but also environmentally, because of certain behavioral patterns that piggyback the disease and carry it forth.

Actress and recovering alcoholic Margaux Hemingway (1988) spoke of following in the alcoholic footsteps of her famous grandfather. She felt that she was living the life of Ernest Hemingway for a time:

> I think alcohol drove my grandfather to suicide, but I'm still alive because I did something about it. (p. 95)

Family Dynamics

A principal school of thought on the transmission of addictions is that the disease alters the operation of the family system, rendering it dysfunctional. The dysfunctions are passed on to future generations, not necessarily through alcoholism, but through dysfunctional family dynamics. According to Ann Smith (1988), author of *Grandchildren of Alcoholics:*

> Many of us have heard others ask the question, "Why do I identify with adult children of alcoholics when my parents didn't drink?" The answer lies not in the family's addiction or lack of it, but in the codependent family dynamics which are subtly passed on from one generation to the next (p. 3)

Through the family operation—its rules, beliefs, and behavior patterns—codependency is passed on to further generations, even though chemical dependency is not. Irene is a case in point. Codependency was passed on to Irene's parents. And, although they never drank, they continued the dysfunctional cycle by passing it on to Irene through the daily operation of the family. Despite the fact that Irene's parents were not alcoholic, the rules of "don't talk," "don't trust," and "don't feel" applied throughout her childhood. Her well-intended parents grew up with these rules and inadvertently passed the disease to their daughter through the disguised roles of family hero and placater. Food and work addictions replaced the grandparents' alcoholism. Irene developed the identical traits of a child reared in an active alcoholic home. The big difference is that children of alcoholics, once grown, have the experience of active drinking and active family dysfunction to point to as the source of their problems. But grandchildren of alcoholics do not have those markers and thus suffer greater confusion.

Irene was never told about the grandpaternal alcoholism and accidentally discovered it as an adult: "I had early memories of the awful smell of bourbon and cigars as a little girl sitting on my grandfather's lap. To this day I hate that smell." Aside from these early memories, however, Irene had nothing overt to identify as the source of her discontent, emptiness, and frustration. Still, the symptoms were there. "It kills me to be a disappointment. Oh! It just kills me if I let someone down. It's a carryover of what will people think and what will they do if I don't meet their standards. And I still have a terrible fear of abandonment." Irene said she overcompensated for the "don't trust" rule by becoming too trusting:

> I'm still not very good at figuring out who's trustworthy and who's not. I have to take a massive abuse of mistrust before I will learn to mistrust a person. I too often laid myself open too much and too soon and ended up hurt and resentful and a lot of self-doubt about not being smart enough on how to discriminate who to trust and how much.

Feelings of intimacy were always missing in Irene's family. After her first therapy group, it was she who introduced hugging into her family, followed by saying "I love you," which she still has to say first, if it is said at all.

Family Types

Irene's account is substantiated by Wayne Kritsberg (1985), who has observed what he calls the adult children of alcoholics syndrome—common personality traits that originate from common dysfunctional family experiences (see box on page 168). He suggests that this syndrome is directly related to being raised in an unsafe, dysfunctional, alcoholic family system. Kritsberg describes four types of alcoholic families that can transmit the disease to future generations.

Famity Type 1 contains an active alcoholic in all three generations of the family: grandparent, grandparent's child, and grandchild. In *Family Type 2* the active alcoholic family member has stopped drinking. Although active alcoholism has been arrested, without treatment, the family dysfunction will continue to carry the disease. The grandparent, for instance, may be an alcoholic who stops drinking. But the family remains untreated, and the disease is transmitted to the second-generation children and third-generation grandchildren who will recreate the dysfunctional dynamics of the alcoholic family when they have families of their own, even if they never drink.

Family Type 3 resembles Irene's family structure. This type occurs when active drinking has been removed from the family for one generation or more. Suppose, for example, that a grandfather was an alcoholic but his daughter and her spouse were teetotalers. Their children (the grandchildren) are still at high risk for addiction because of the continuation of dysfunctional family dynamics and adherence to the rules and behaviors of the actively drinking alcoholic household of the past.

Family Type 4 is one with no previous history of alcoholism. Grandparents from both sides of the family are abstainers but one of their children

Common Characteristics of Adult Children of Alcoholics

Children who grow up in severely dysfunctional families where parents are alcoholics usually have many adult personality traits in common. Adult children of alcoholics who identify with many or all of the following characteristics may find some comfort in knowing they are not alone. This list of characteristics can be a guide for personal healing. Those who learned these behaviors in a dysfunctional, unhealthy family can learn how to change them through a personalized program of recovery.

Adult children of alcoholics:

_____ 1. guess at what is normal.

_____ 2. have difficulty in following a project through from beginning to end.

_____ 3. lie when it would be just as easy to tell the truth.

_____ 4. judge themselves without mercy.

_____ 5. have difficulty having fun.

_____ 6. take themselves very seriously.

_____ 7. have difficulty with intimate relationships.

_____ 8. overreact to changes over which they have no control.

_____ 9. constantly seek approval and affirmation.

_____ 10. feel that they are different from other people.

_____ 11. are either extremely responsible or irresponsible.

_____ 12. show extreme loyalty, even in the face of evidence that the loyalty is undeserved.

_____ 13. look for immediate rather than deferred gratification.

_____ 14. lock themselves into a course of action without giving serious consideration to alternate behaviors or possible consequences.

_____ 15. seek tension and crisis and then complain about the results.

_____ 16. avoid conflict or aggravate it, rarely dealing with it.

_____ 17. fear rejection and abandonment, yet reject others.

_____ 18. fear failure, but sabotage their success.

_____ 19. fear criticism and judgment, yet criticize and judge others.

_____ 20. manage time poorly, and do not set priorities in a way that works well for them.

Adapted from Woititz 1983.

becomes alcoholic even though the alcoholic's spouse does not drink and has no family history of alcoholism. The grandchildren will have adult children issues with which to deal and be at high risk for dysfunctional behaviors themselves.

Analysis of these four family types provides two convincing arguments regarding family transmission of alcoholism: (1) Although active drinking is not present, the effects of alcoholism on the family can persist; (2) Untreated, the alcoholic family system will recreate itself generation after generation (Kritsberg 1985). Where alcoholism is in one's family history, ACOA issues will exist.

Family Rituals

Another body of research suggests that the existence of certain family customs is associated with the transmission of alcoholism. Researchers Steven Wolin, Linda Bennett, and their colleagues (1980) studied transmitter and nontransmitter families to determine why transmission of alcoholism occurred in some families and not in others. They discovered that the disruption of family rituals in alcoholic families contributes to the transmission of the disease. Rituals such as family celebrations, family traditions, and patterned family interactions are the glue that holds the family fabric together and give it meaning and an identity of its own. When one or both parents are alcoholic and family rituals—such as family meals, birthdays, holidays, vacations, and graduations—are abandoned or altered during periods of heavy drinking, alcoholism is likely to be transmitted to children. Failing to respond to intoxicated parents as they abandon participation in rituals, transmitter families accept the demise of family rituals. In contrast, nontransmitter families reject or confront the drinking parent and protect the rituals by refusing to allow alcoholism to interfere. Nontransmitter families in which rituals remain intact are less likely to pass on the disease, even when drinking is heavy. Families that stick together and present a united front are less likely to transmit alcoholism to the next generation.

Developmental Passages for Children of Alcoholics

Another popular view on alcohol transmission holds that family dysfunction, caused by parental alcoholism, interferes with the natural progression of personality development from birth. The nature of childhood experiences, strategies of coping, and ways of understanding and reacting to parental alcoholism depend upon children's ages at the onset of parental drinking problems (Wilson & Orford 1978). The earlier in life a child is exposed to parental alcoholism, the more severe are the side effects. Parental drinking begins to affect children in infancy. Research confirms that youngsters reared in alcoholism from infancy are likely to have more serious social and psychological adjustment problems than children who face parental alcoholism for the first time in adolescence (Morehouse & Scola 1986; Werner 1986).

Developmentally, there is a natural time when all humans struggle with the same emotions that children of alcoholics experience in greater intensity and depth. At certain sensitive times in childhood, youngsters are more susceptible to develop the dysfunctional traits associated with adult children of alcoholics. During each developmental period, personality crises naturally occur that must be resolved in a positive way for healthy development to continue (Erikson 1963) (see table 9–1). When people fail to resolve a crisis in a particular stage, they will still go on to the next stage, but they cannot completely resolve the crisis in this new stage until crises of earlier stages have been resolved. It is possible to "go back" at a later time and work through the conflict, but it is more difficult.

For children of alcoholics, the crisis at each stage is multiplied, and passing the test much more difficult. Active parental alcoholism at any one of these sensitive times during the lifespan can impair the successful resolution of the crisis and passage to the next developmental stage.

Infancy

Children living in active parental alcoholism at birth will be negatively affected by the disease in many ways. Those whose mothers drank during prenatal development can be FAS babies and suffer permanent neurological and cognitive deficits. Aside from prenatal influences, successful resolution of the conflict of *trust versus mistrust* depends upon the quality of the parent-infant relationship.

Infants are dependent on their caregivers to *consistently* gratify their needs for food, security, love, and touching. If infants are fed when hungry, if their cries are answered within a reasonable time, if their discomforts are removed, and if they are loved, cuddled, played with, and talked to, they will begin to feel that the world is a safe place and that they can trust others to care for them. When their needs are not met in a loving adult-child relationship, or if needs are inconsistently met, they will grow to mistrust their world and those in it. Because of consistent care, trustful children develop a general "feeling" that their caregivers are accessible and responsive, while those who receive inconsistent care are mistrustful and unsure that their caregivers will be there when they need them. In active alcoholic families, infant trust is challenged from the first day of life because parents are too consumed with alcoholism to provide adequate support and nurturance to children. The inconsistency, neglect, and abuse that characterize many alcoholic homes give children an overriding sense of mistrust, insecurity, and separation anxiety. They learn very early that they cannot count on anything. These

Table 9–1
Erikson's Eight Stages of Personality Development

Developmental Period	Age	Personality Crisis Stage
Infancy	Birth to 1 year	Trust vs. Mistrust
Toddlerhood	1 to 3 years	Autonomy vs. Shame/Doubt
Early Childhood	4 to 5 years	Initiative vs. Guilt
Middle Childhood	6 to 11 years	Industry vs. Inferiority
Adolescence	12 to 18 years	Identity vs. Role Confusion
Young Adulthood	19 to 34 years	Intimacy vs. Isolation
Middle Adulthood	35 to 64 years	Generativity vs. Self-Absorption
Older Adulthood	65 to death	Integrity vs. Despair

infantile feelings build across the lifespan and are transformed into problems that many children of alcoholics have with intimacy, insecure relationships, and fear of abandonment in adulthood. Unless treatment intervention occurs, difficulty trusting others and abandonment anxiety will become an integral and lifelong part of their personalities. The inability to trust also extends to one's self, opinions, and confidence.

Toddlerhood

Toddlerhood ushers in the struggle between *autonomy versus shame and doubt*. At this stage children develop abilities to manage and control their bodies and their world. They learn such self-control as walking, dressing, feeding, and toileting. They no longer need to depend on adults to carry them or push them in a stroller. They can move about by themselves and climb, push, and pull to get things without asking. Along with this new-found ability to control themselves and their surroundings, children develop autonomy and a will of their own. They express a desire to make independent choices and decisions that often conflict with parental wishes. Sometimes unwanted help or demands from adults are met with negativism and resistance from toddlers. Conflicts centering around the basic routines of eating, sleeping, and elimination are unavoidable at this age.

Children who develop a healthy sense of autonomy have parents who are patient and supportive, especially during conflict. Their parents praise them for using self-control and making good choices. A positive sense of self and a healthy outlook on control develop when adults encourage autonomy while lovingly and consistently setting firm, reasonable limits. Toddlers develop a sense of shame or doubt about their abilities when their newly discovered independence is restricted, discouraged, or poorly guided. Shame and doubt and problems with control arise from children in alcoholic homes when they witness parents who lack self-control, who scold and criticize them for making poor choices and mistakes, or who deny them opportunities to make choices and develop self-control. Children of alcoholics develop self-doubt about their abilities to manage their lives and to stand on their own two feet. Rigid parental demands and oppressive rules without some room for choices lead to codependency. Toddlers who live in active alcoholism where autonomy cannot be exercised begin to show the marks of codependency during this stage. As adults, they have difficulty making decisions and often marry people who will make decisions for them. Without treatment, they will carry issues around control and negative attitudes toward authority into their adult personalities. They overreact—become angry and sad—to situations in which they have no control or in which the future is unknown, and they fear and resent authority figures.

Early Childhood

It is during this stage that children struggle with the conflict between *initiative and guilt.* Children must internalize right from wrong and adhere to the rules of society. Parents generally require children to assume more responsibility for supervising themselves, their pets, and their toys at this age. Hitting others and stealing are prohibited. Such rules are internalized in the conscience. Trouble typically arises as free-spirited, initiating children must learn to control their own behavior and follow the rules of society. Reality testing, a critical lesson, is difficult at this stage because children view the world as magical and cannot think logically. Imagination, fantasy, and fairy tales are the child's reality at this stage, so it is typical for children to have difficulty separating reality from fantasy. This developmental characteristic makes reality testing in alcoholic homes doubly problematic, because children are often told that what they saw didn't really happen or was not as bad as they perceived it to be. The line between reality and imagination becomes blurred and children become confused. They often decide that their fantasy world offers a gift of escape, which they overuse to cope with the harsh reality of alcoholic family conflict. Rules of right and wrong change daily in unpredictable alcoholic homes so that children never understand what the rule for today is. They also have trouble predicting what is appropriate from one situation to the next and may feel guilty for thoughts and behaviors that others consider perfectly proper.

This stage is also characterized by egocentrism when children believe they cause everything that happens to them. They feel guilty because they believe their parent drinks because of something they did, perhaps not putting away all of their toys or not eating all of their mashed potatoes. In alcoholic homes, being responsible for toys is extended to taking on adult responsibilities such as getting your own meals and getting yourself to school on time. As adults, children who have trouble at this stage will not be able to distinguish what normal is and will feel they are to blame for their parent's drinking. They may become overly responsible for others and blame themselves for others' failures. They have guilt feelings when they stand up for themselves, and so they give in to others, putting others' needs before their own. Failure to successfully resolve this stage results in children and adults who overcontrol themselves by obeying all the rules of their restrictive consciences without meeting their own needs, in order to avoid guilt. Such persons are also often intolerant of others who do not rigidly adhere to their strict set of rules.

Middle Childhood

School-age children have moved to a stage of personality development that involves the struggle between *industry versus inferiority,* in which success comes with the child's feeling productive and competent. Failure comes with feelings of inadequacy. Whether a child develops industry or inferiority is strongly influenced by the support and feedback that comes from important adults and peers. Feelings of worth and industry come when children's efforts and products are recognized and approved by others. Accomplishments come from doing well in school, learning new skills as playing musical instruments, or achieving distinctions in Scouts or other civic organizations.

When frequent failure or disapproval are common, as in most alcoholic homes, children may come to believe that the results of their work are not worthwhile and that they themselves have low self-worth. Poor work habits and feelings of uselessness are sometimes the consequence. In adulthood, these people have difficulty following through on projects or they are prone to procrastination. On the other extreme, some children in alcoholic homes get stuck in this stage and spend the rest of their lives trying to prove to themselves and to others that they are competent and worthwhile. They become overly serious and do not know how to have fun. Achievement becomes a compulsion and external accomplishments become sources of self-esteem. They may become high achievers in school and prized workaholics in their careers, but inside they feel driven, unhappy, and worthless. Although their standards are unrealistic, they judge themselves and others harshly for not meeting them. Nothing they accomplish can ever be good enough to change these feelings of incompetence, except for the completion of a good recovery program.

Adolescence

Identity versus role confusion is the struggle during adolescence. It is a time to struggle for a sense of self as well as an outlook on life that is acceptable to the teenager and society. Resolving this conflict involves satisfactory answers to many questions: "Who am I?" "Where am I going?" "What will I do with my life?" Adolescents who have resolved the struggle develop a positive identity and move into adulthood knowing who they are and where they are going. They find a fit between who they are and what society wants them to be.

This fit is impossible for children of alcoholism who have been unsuccessful at the previous stages. Lacking the inward resources to affirm their own worth, they become approval seekers. They constantly change their values to gain the affirmation of others or lose their identity in another person altogether. A backlog of unresolved residue from previous stages interferes with the identity crisis and leads to role confusion, negative self-concept, and doubts about the future:

> As teenagers, they are unable to develop adequately the social skills and attitudes necessary for separating from the family and establishing their own identity. As they limp into adulthood, they often leave a trail of poor relationships and they have difficulties with intimacy. They often feel unable to meet life's challenges adequately, even when they are. They feel different; they feel frightened; and they feel misunderstood. (Gravitz 1985, 15–16)

This confusion is sometimes exaggerated when children of alcoholics turn to substance abuse, delinquent or psychotic behavior, or suicide attempts to deal with their failure at resolving personal issues. A fifteen-year-old girl, whose parents are both addicted, drew what she wished her parents *would not* do at home (see figure 9–1).

Adulthood

It is not until children of alcoholics reach adulthood that many of the dysfunctional characteristics from their upbringing start to demand resolution. A lifetime of unresolved issues make healthy and happy relationships extremely difficult. *Intimacy versus isolation* becomes the struggle in young adulthood. Unmet needs are stockpiled. Difficulty being intimate is the hallmark at this stage because stuffed feelings from childhood impair the ability to feel or express emotions. Feelings of being different and isolated from other people are also commonly reported by young adult children. Seldom do they trace this difficulty to parental alcoholism.

Adult children of alcoholics unconsciously are attracted to one another because they feel less isolated and more at home with those who were also raised in codependency and chemical dependency. They confuse love with pity and are prone to care for codependent people whom they can pity and rescue. They tend to help and seek out victims and are attracted by that weakness in love and friendships. Marriages and friendships typically occur

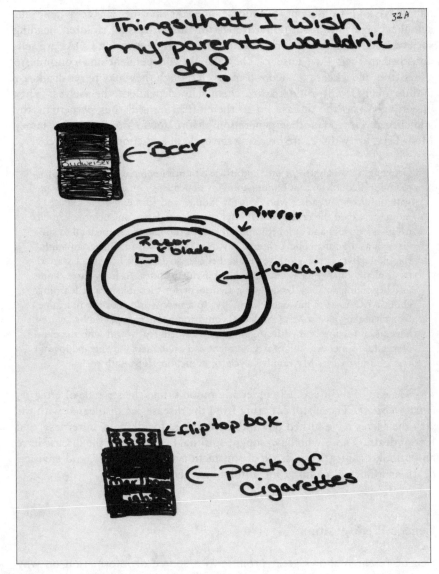

Figure 9–1. A fifteen-year-old girl's expression of what she wishes her parents would not do.

with others who are children of alcoholics, substance abusers, or members of dysfunctional families.

Middle adulthood brings the conflict of *generativity versus self-absorption*. Untreated, the disease of alcoholism continues to eat away at the happiness and fulfillment of middle age. At a time in life when self-actualization comes from doing things for others, raising children, leading society, and making the world a better place, nonrecovering COAs are self-absorbed in their own misery. They remain codependent and continue to suffer from the disease of alcoholism, even though they may never drink. By midlife many adult children are chemically dependent themselves. They unwittingly pass the disease on to their offspring and thus perpetuate the addiction cycle to another generation. More fortunate ones, like Jamey McCullers, forty-three, are breaking the cycle of addiction through recovery:

> Growing up was hard for me, and it wasn't until I entered a treatment program for alcoholism that I understood my dependency on alcohol. I grew up with an alcoholic father who beat my mother and tormented the kids. My mother escaped the craziness with her own dependency on such prescribed drugs as Librium and amphetamines. I knew I too had to escape it all to survive, so as a young child I entered my own fantasy world. But as an adult, I couldn't live in the world of make-believe, so I drank instead. I started using alcohol in my teens and marijuana in my twenties. At forty-three, I am just beginning to live. Undergoing treatment for alcoholism and learning about ACOA issues has opened my eyes to a new world. For the first time I am facing my past sober. Childhood confusion has been replaced by awareness and direction in my life. Again I can view the real world with the eyes of a child—sober eyes full of wonderment and excitement—living and loving every minute of it. My family's cycle of addiction stops with me!

The end of the lifecycle in older adulthood brings the struggle of *integrity versus despair*. Those still suffering from the disease are displeased with the way their lives have turned out and are destined for despair, bitterness, and fear of death. Those who have sought spiritual healing from the disease have an outlook of integrity, a sense of satisfaction with their lives, and envision death as a normal ending to a fulfilling existence.

Genetic Predisposition

Genetic research shows great promise as a source of information on why alcohol runs in families. Scientists have isolated inherited factors from environmental factors by studying differences among identical and fraternal twins and among adopted children. That research was carried a step further by later physiological studies that tried to pinpoint the exact transmitter of alcoholism among some kids and not others. These studies have examined metabolism, brain activity, and other neuropsychological factors as possible mediators of the disease.

Twin Studies

The early twin investigations compared the incidence of alcoholism among identical twins (who have the same genetic makeup) with fraternal twins (who have only about half the same makeup in common). A Swedish study in which one twin in each pair was alcoholic, reported that identical twins were more similar for alcoholism than fraternal twins (Kaij 1960). A greater likelihood existed that if one identical twin was alcoholic, the other would be too. This trend, however, was not as prevalent among fraternal twins. A second study analyzing Veterans Administration records also supported an inherited predisposition to alcohol (Hrubec & Omenn 1981). Identical twins in the study were not only more likely to share the disease of alcoholism than the fraternal twins, but also to have more organic manifestations of the disease such as alcoholic cirrhosis and psychosis.

Adoption Studies

Scientific efforts of the early 1970s continued to untangle inherited and environmental factors associated with alcoholism. A series of adoption studies were launched by an investigation that originally sought to determine if full siblings would more often be alcoholic than half siblings (Schuckit, Goodwin & Winokur 1972). Findings revealed no real differences in alcoholism between the two groups. But when researchers studied half siblings from broken homes separately, the significance of biological factors was striking. Even when raised separately from their parents, a larger portion of half siblings with alcoholic biological parents became alcoholics themselves, compared to half siblings without alcoholic parents.

With the groundwork laid, an entire body of adoption research confirmed the contributing influences of genetic factors to alcoholism. Adoption studies from three different nations—Denmark, Sweden, and the United States—reported the existence of similar inherited themes (Bohman 1978; Bohman, Sigvardsson & Cloninger 1981; Cadoret, Cain & Grove 1980; Cloninger, Bohman & Sigvardsson 1981; Goodwin, Schulsinger, Hermansen, Guze & Winokur 1973; Goodwin 1985). Sons of alcoholics were four times more likely to become alcoholic than sons of nonalcoholics, whether raised by their alcoholic biological parents or by nonalcoholic adoptive parents. Adopted sons reared by nondrinking parents were just as likely to become alcoholic as sons reared by alcoholic biological parents. By contrast, sons of nonalcoholic biological parents, adopted by alcoholic parents, did not become alcoholic at an unusually high rate. Adopted daughters with alcoholic biological mothers were three times more likely to become alcoholic than other women, even when reared from an early age by nondrinking parents.

Physiological Research

Most physiological research has studied high-risk candidates for alcoholism, usually children of alcoholics, who are still too young to have developed the disease. Metabolic research has revealed that children of alcoholics, ranging in age from eight to thirteen, had lower zinc levels than children of non-alcoholic parents. This finding suggests that before any alcohol ingestion, children of alcoholics have the same zinc deficiency that manifests itself in the chronic adult alcoholic population (Kern, Hassett & Collipp 1981). Zinc deficiency has been associated with cerebellar dysfunction, learning disabilities, and schizophrenia. This deficiency suggests school-age children may already be physiologically prepared for alcoholism and supports other research that indicates abnormalities in alcohol metabolism in adult children of alcoholics (Schuckit & Rayses 1979).

When intoxicated, adult sons of alcoholics also have lower levels of the hormone prolactin in their bloodstreams than do sons of nonalcoholics (Schuckit, Gold & Risch 1987). It takes more alcohol for sons of alcoholics to become inebriated, and they have less ability to detect the effects of alcohol than their peers (Schuckit 1984a,b,c). It is believed that prolactin may ultimately provide clues about the development of alcoholism and act as an early warning signal for those at risk. The presence of blood chemicals also has been effective in distinguishing adult alcoholics from nonalcoholics and may someday serve as a basis for spotting children who are at high risk of becoming alcoholics when they grow up (Tabakoff et al. 1988).

Several studies suggest that neuropsychological deficits predispose children to alcoholism. Findings indicated, for example, that sons of alcoholics are deficient in emotional self-regulation, planning, memory, perceptual-motor functioning, and language processing in comparison to sons of non-alcoholics (Tarter et al. 1984). Researchers attributed these differences to defects in the prefrontal cortex of the brain, resulting in neurotransmitter disequilibrium at the biochemical level. Scientists observed brain abnormalities (for example, rapid EEG activity) resembling that of adult alcoholics to be more common among sons of alcoholics than among sons of nonalcoholics (Begleiter, Porjesz & Bihari 1984; Gabrielli et al. 1982).

Lynn Hennecke (1984) found that *stimulus augmenting* (that is, perception that something is of greater magnitude than it really is, including sensitivity to pain, sound, and light) is higher in children of alcoholic fathers than children of sober fathers. Augmenting is believed to reflect a biochemical deficiency in the brain and is prevalent among alcoholics. Augmenters drink to reduce the augmenting tendency, which preexists the active phase of alcoholism. Other studies have also cited more neuropsychological disorders in adults with family histories of alcoholism than in the average person. One such study reported that adults with alcoholic family histories had more difficulty than adults without such histories in performing abstract problem solving and perceptual motor tasks (Schaeffer, Parsons & Yohman 1984). Contrasting these findings, other data report that poor neuropsychological performance among COAs was not upheld and, in fact, they scored as well or better than nonCOAs (Workman-Daniels & Hesselbrock 1987).

As the box on page 180 indicates, the evidence linking inheritance to alcoholism is strong. That does not necessarily mean, however, that children of alcoholics are biologically doomed and that all COAs will become alcoholics. Many COAs, approximately two-thirds in fact, never have problems with alcohol. Although all pieces of the puzzle are not yet in place, scientists suggest that genes somehow combine with what happens throughout life to cause alcoholism. Researchers are beginning to uncover different types and degrees of alcoholism that originate from interactions of genetic and environmental factors (Cloninger, Bohman & Sigvardsson 1981). Even children who carry a genetic predisposition can live a healthy lifestyle, free of chemical abuse. But regardless of whether alcoholism resides in our genes, family patterns, or a combination of both, when parents drink, hope and help are available for children who can recover from the disease.

Genograms

Adults can trace the transgenerational prevalence of addictions in their family tree. Information from genograms will indicate a high or low incidence of alcoholism and other dysfunctional behaviors but will not tell you whether the behaviors were transmitted through heredity or environment. You can complete the genogram in the box on page 181 by providing the names of family members on both sides of the family. Once all the blanks are filled in, place an "A" next to the names of those people you know who have experienced alcohol and other drug problems. Indicate with an "E" the names of those people you know have experienced eating disorder problems. Mark with a "P" the names of those people you know who were physical abusers and/or were abused. Place an "I" next to the names of those people you know who were incest abusers and/or incest victims. Indicate with an "O" the names of those people you know who experienced other identifiable dysfunctions, and name the problem.

Evidence Supporting a Genetic Link to Alcoholism

- Incidence of alcoholism is greater among identical than fraternal twins. [1,2]

- Alcoholism occurs more often among adopted children, separated from biological alcoholic parents at birth, than among adopted children without family histories of alcohol. [3,4,5,6,7,8,9]

- Adopted daughters and sons of alcoholics are three to four times more likely to become alcoholics than adopted children of non-alcoholics. [3,4]

- Grandsons of alcoholic grandfathers are three times more prone to alcoholism than grandsons of nonalcoholic grandfathers. [10]

- Children of alcoholics are metabolically more prone to alcoholism than children of nonalcoholics. [11,12,13,14]

- Even when alcoholics have not consumed alcohol for years, their blood chemistry is different from that of nonalcoholics. [15]

- Neurological differences among children of alcoholics, compared to nonalcoholics, predispose them to become alcoholics as adults. [16,17,18,19,20]

Sources: 1. Kaij 1960; 2. Hrubec & Omenn 1981; 3. Bohman, Sigvardsson & Cloninger 1981; 4. Goodwin et al. 1973; 5. Cadoret & Gath 1978; 6. Cadoret, Cain & Grove 1980; 7. Cloninger, Bohman & Sigvardsson 1981; 8. Goodwin et al. 1974; 9. Goodwin et al. 1977; 10. Kaij & Dock 1975; 11. Kern et al. 1981; 12. Schuckit & Rayses 1979; 13. Schuckit, Gold & Risch 1987; 14. Schuckit 1984; 15. Tabakoff et al. 1988; 16. Tarter, Hegedus & Goldstein 1984; 17. Hennecke 1984; 18. Schaeffer, Parsons & Yohman 1984; 19. Gabrielli et al. 1982; 20. Begleiter, Porjesz & Bihari 1984.

A New Beginning

As this book draws to an end, I would like to leave you with the message that it is really just the beginning. The grassroots children of alcoholics movement will continue to grow nationwide as children, young and grown, become aware of issues that lend clarity to their history with the disease of alcoholism and start them on the road to a new life's beginning. This newly found knowledge is call for a celebration that, as one recovering child exclaimed, "makes me want to shout it from the mountaintops!"

COAs are survivors. They have many positive traits and remarkable skills that helped them triumph against incredible odds. That in itself is

Genogram

Mother's Side

Maternal Grandparents _____   _____
                              Grandmother   Grandfather

Name Aunts with Spouses

Aunt _____Spouse _____

   Children _____   _____

   _____   _____

Aunt _____Spouse _____

   Children _____   _____

   _____   _____

Aunt _____Spouse _____

   Children _____   _____

   _____   _____

Name Uncles with Spouses

Uncle _____Spouse _____

   Children _____   _____

   _____   _____

Uncle _____Spouse _____

   Children _____   _____

   _____   _____

Uncle _____Spouse _____

   Children _____   _____

   _____   _____

Father's Side

Paternal Grandparents _____ _____
                                Grandmother   Grandfather

Name Aunts with Spouses

    Aunt _____Spouse _____

        Children _____ _____

                  _____ _____

    Aunt _____Spouse _____

        Children _____ _____

                  _____ _____

    Aunt _____Spouse _____

        Children _____ _____

                  _____ _____

Name Uncles with Spouses

    Uncle _____Spouse _____

        Children _____ _____

                  _____ _____

    Uncle _____Spouse _____

        Children _____ _____

                  _____ _____

    Uncle _____Spouse _____

        Children _____ _____

                  _____ _____

Your Parents

Mother _____

Second Husband (Stepfather) _____

Father _____

Second Wife (Stepmother) _____

Sisters and Brothers (Include Yourself)

    Yourself _____ Spouse _____

        Children _____ _____

                _____ _____

   Sister/Brother _____ Spouse _____

        Children _____ _____

                _____ _____

   Sister/Brother _____ Spouse _____

        Children _____ _____

                _____ _____

   Sister/Brother _____ Spouse _____

        Children _____ _____

                _____ _____

   Sister/Brother _____ Spouse _____

        Children _____ _____

                _____ _____

   Sister/Brother _____ Spouse _____

        Children _____ _____

                _____ _____

_____

Excerpted from *Repeat After Me* by Claudia Black (1985). Used with permission.

reason to celebrate. They grow up with many gifts they bestow on others, among which are help and hope for a brighter future. Without ACOAs, the human services field would collapse. The discovery of being a child of an alcoholic is a joyous occasion that brings with it a wondrous sense of hope for growth and fulfillment. It is a second chance at self-discovery, an exciting life adventure. Every alcoholic childhood—no matter how devastating—is an opportunity for personal and spiritual transformation that can bring an exceptional tone to the quality of life.

As more and more practitioners become aware of the complexity of alcoholism and its powerful effects upon kids, they will have a chance to contribute to the self-actualization of millions of children. I would like to close with a poem I wrote that expresses my wish, my hope, and my belief that all children of alcoholics—whether six, sixteen, or sixty—can find their true selves through recovery. With the help of millions of committed practitioners in the helping professions, this wish, hope, and belief will be realized.

Children of Recovery

Searching—earnestly and secretly—the sacred quest,

Engulfs their being and carries them,

Lowering them deeply to the core of their essence,

Faltering as they question, affirm, and love what they discover!

With Love,

Bryan Robinson

10

Resources for Working with Children of Alcoholics

> There are only two lasting bequests we can give our children—one is roots, the other wings.
>
> —Hodding Carter

T his chapter contains annotations of books for adults and children, unpublished research reports, organizations, periodicals, audiovisuals, therapeutic games, curriculum materials, and publications for practitioners interested in research, counseling and social work, education, program development, and the popular press—all pertaining to children from alcoholic families.

Books for Adults

Many books have been written about and for children of alcoholic families. Some books emphasize the childhood years, while others focus on adulthood when the impact of an alcoholic upbringing continues to be felt. I have organized readings in the following list by their emphasis into one of the following categories: Children of Alcoholics, Adult Children of Alcoholics, Alcoholic/Dysfunctional Families, Autobiographical, and Fiction.

Children of Alcoholics

Ackerman, Robert. (1986). *Growing in the shadow: Children of alcoholics.* Pompano Beach, Florida: Health Communications. The book is divided into four parts and addresses children of alcoholics from childhood to adulthood. Written for anyone who has an interest in or who is currently working with children of alcoholics.

Ackerman, Robert. (1983). *Children of alcoholics: A guidebook for educators, therapists, and parents* (2nd Ed.). Holmes Beach, Florida: Learning Publications. The author describes what it is like to be a child of an alcoholic and presents suggestions for educators, therapists, and parents. A comprehensive list of resources and materials is included in the appendixes.

Ackerman, Robert. (1987). *Children of alcoholics: Bibliography & resource guide* (3rd Ed.). Pompano Beach, Florida: Health Communications. A complete bibliography and resource on children of alcoholics, including youngsters and adult children.

Black, Claudia. (1982). *It will never happen to me.* Denver, Colorado: M.A.C. Publications. This book shares some of the experiences of children of alcoholics, explains the process of what happens and what can be done to both prevent and handle these problems.

Chandler, Mitzi. (1987). *Whiskey's song: An explicit story of surviving in an alcoholic home.* Pompano Beach, Florida: Health Communications. Told in verse, this is a story of a life of chaos, pathos, and survival of a child growing up in an alcoholic family where violence and neglect are everyday occurrences.

Cork, Margaret. (1969). *The forgotten children.* Ontario, Canada: General Publishing Company. Based on her interviews with 115 children, this pioneering work answers some of the unresolved questions pertaining to children in families where there is alcoholism.

Deutsch, Charles. (1982). *Broken bottles, broken dreams: Understanding and helping the children of alcoholics.* New York: Teachers College Press. This book explores the problems children experience in alcoholic homes and ways of helping them cope.

Gravitz, Herbert. (1985). *Children of alcoholics handbook: Who they are, what they experience, how they recover.* South Laguna, California: The National Association for Children of Alcoholics. (25-page pamphlet). Provides for the lay person a clear understanding on the important issues relating to being raised in an alcoholic home.

Hammond, Mary. (1985). *Children of alcoholics in play therapy.* Pompano Beach, Florida: Health Communications. An overview of how play can be an integral vehicle for working with children of alcoholics. Topics include the structure of the play environment, necessary equipment, and techniques to use in play intervention.

Lewis, David, & Williams, Carol. (1986). *Providing care for children of alcoholics: Clinical and research perspectives.* Pompano Beach, Florida: Health Communications. Aimed at professionals who work with children of alcoholics, this book provides clinical insights and research findings.

Moe, Jerry, & Pohlmen, Don. (1988). *Kids power: Healing games for children of alcoholics.* Sequoia Hospital District, Whipple & Alameda, Redwood City, California 94062. An excellent resource of games and activities to help kids learn about parental alcoholism and how to cope with it on a daily basis. Includes music, art, puppets, and many innovative approaches such as "The Wheel of Misfortune."

Morehouse, Ellen, & Scola, Claire. (1986). *Children of alcoholics: Meeting the needs of the young COA in the school setting.* South Laguna, California: The National Association for Children of Alcoholics. (30-page pamphlet). Written for the professional in the school system, this pamphlet describes the COA and offers advice on how to help these children.

Pickens, Roy. (1986). *Children of alcoholics.* Center City, Minnesota: Hazelden. Reviews research on children of alcoholics and the emotional and medical problems that result. Implications for treatment and prevention are also presented.

Richards, Tarpley, Tuohey, Martha & Petrash, Patricia. (1987). *Children of alcoholics: A guide for professionals.* South Laguna, California: National Association for Children of Alcoholics. A pamphlet for practitioners involved in facilitating the recovery of children of alcoholics.

Seixas, Judith, & Youcha, Geraldine. (1985). *Children of alcoholism: A survivor's manual.* New York: Crown Publishers. Shows what happened in childhood to make adult children as they are. Also presents ideas on what to do about dysfunctional behaviors.

Veenstra, Susan. (1987). *Children of alcoholic parents: A handbook for counselors and teachers.* Cleveland, Ohio: Alcoholism Services of Cleveland. A guide for professionals in creating a system of identification, intervention, and treatment for children in the schools.

Adult Children of Alcoholics

Ackerman, Robert. (1987). *Let go and grow.* Pompano Beach, Florida: Health Communications. An in-depth study of the different characteristics of adult children of alcoholics followed up with guidelines for recovery.

Ackerman, Robert. (1987). *Same house different homes: Why adult children of alcoholics are not all the same.* Pompano Beach, Florida: Health communications. A study of over one thousand adults who grew up in dysfunctional homes and how the findings can produce positive solutions for adult children of alcoholics.

Black, Claudia. (1985). *Repeat after me: A step-by-step workbook for adult children of alcoholics to set a new course in their personal lives.* Denver, Colorado: M.A.C. (1850 High Street, Denver, Colorado 80218). Written to help ACOAs recognize how their present lives are influenced by the past, to help them release the parts of the past that they would like to put behind them, and to take responsibility for how they live their lives today.

Cermak, Timmen. (1988). *Evaluating and treating adult children of alcoholics: A guide for professionals.* Minneapolis, Minnesota: The Johnson Institute. Presents an integrated approach to evaluating and treating adult children of alcoholics. A theoretical framework for understanding adult children characteristics and problems and specific guidelines for initial interviews and clinical evaluations.

Cermak, Timmen. (1985). *A primer on adult children of alcoholics.* Pompano Beach, Florida: Health Communications. This booklet is written on adult children of alcoholics and identifies issues and steps to recovery. The analogy between Post Traumatic Stress Syndrome and growing up in alcoholism is discussed.

Curtin, Paul. (1986). *Tumbleweeds: A therapist's guide to treatment of adult children of alcoholics.* Rutherford, New Jersey: Perrin & Treggett Booksellers. A brief guide with tips on therapeutic issues.

Dean, Amy. (1987). *Making changes: How adult children can have healthier, happier relationships.* Center City, Minnesota: Hazelden. Brings the awareness and the tools necessary for changing unhealthy ways of interacting with others that were derived from living in an alcoholic home.

Friel, John, & Friel, Linda. (1988). *Adult children: The secret of dysfunctional families.* Pompano Beach, Florida: Health Communications. Defines the problems of dysfunctional families, analyzes the characteristic symptoms and offers guidelines to live healthy, happy lives now.

Gravitz, Herbert, & Bowden, Julie. (1986). *Guide to recovery: A book for adult children of alcoholics.* Pompano Beach, Florida: Health Communications. Answers more than 75 questions typically asked by adult children of alcoholics and presents a description of the stages of recovery from the effects of parental alcoholism.

Health Communications. (1988). *Bread and roses: A poetry anthology for adult children.* Pompano Beach, Florida: Health Communications. This book is a series of poems by adult children who have survived childhood in an alcoholic home. Their word-pictures in poems are sometimes graphically violent, at other times gentle, forgiving, and always touching.

Kritsberg, Wayne. (1985). *The ACOA syndrome, from discovery to recovery.* Pompano Beach, Florida: Health Communications. The foundations for healing the wounds of an alcoholic-influenced childhood are laid in this book.

Lerner, Rokelle. (1985). *Daily affirmations for adult children of alcoholics.* Pompano Beach, Florida: Health Communications. This book provides a daily source of inspiration to change the distorted and undermining messages of childhood in an alcoholic family.

McConnell, Patty. (1986). *A workbook for healing adult children of alcoholics.* New York: Harper & Row. The workbook is divided into two parts: "The Hurt," in which the reader is invited to explore childhood experiences with adulthood awareness and "The Healing," which suggests that the reader can change behaviors by modifying feelings and defenses.

Marlin, Emily. (1987). *HOPE: New choices and recovery strategies for adult children of alcoholics.* New York: Harper & Row. The author shows how all adult children of alcoholics have similar legacies, helps them reexamine the past to better understand themselves, and presents strategies for self-change.

Middleton-Moz, Jane, & Dwinell, Larie. (1986). *After the tears: Reclaiming the personal losses of childhood.* Pompano Beach, Florida: Health Communications. A child raised in an alcoholic environment will perpetuate an alcoholic legacy even if they never drink. This book shows readers how to mourn the loss of childhood and recapture their self-worth.

Perrin, T.W. (1985). *This new day: Daily affirmations for adult children of alcoholics.* Rutherford, New Jersey: Thomas W. Perrin, Inc. An inspirational reading for each day of the year, these affirming messages are used by many adult children in their recovery process.

Robinson, Bryan. (1989). *Work addiction: Hidden legacy of adult children of alcoholics.* Pompano Beach, Florida: Health Communications. Explores the disease of workaholism and how it destroys relationships and kills people. Provides help for adult children of alcoholics for whom work has become their drug of choice.

Rosellini, Gayle. (1982). *Taming your turbulent past: A self-help guide for adult children.* Pompano Beach, Florida: Health Communications. This practical book is directed at troubled adult children who are capable of happiness and how to achieve it. It deals with anger and the power of forgiveness, fear and self-esteem, unhappiness, and tyranny of always needing to please.

Smith, Ann. (1988). *Grandchildren of alcoholics: Another generation of co-dependency.* Pompano Beach, Florida: Health Communications. Pinpoints the problems of those living in families where a grandparent is or was an alcoholic and where the parents are therefore children of alcoholics with the resulting dysfunctional parenting skills.

Wegscheider-Cruse, Sharon. (1985). *Choicemaking.* Pompano Beach, Florida: Health Communications. For those recovering from codependency, the author integrates her personal experiences as a child of alcoholic parents with professional knowledge to foster spiritual transformation.

Wegscheider-Cruse, Sharon. (1985). *Understanding me.* Pompano Beach, Florida: Health Communications. Helps readers in their quest for self-understanding and self-respect.

Wegscheider-Cruse, Sharon. (1987). *Learning to love yourself: Finding your self-worth.* Pompano Beach, Florida: Health Communications. The author points out that self-esteem is not inherited but learned. She presents, step-by-step, how self-worth can be developed.

Whitfield, Charles L. (1987). *Healing the child within: Discovery and recovery for adult children of dysfunctional families.* Pompano Beach, Florida: Health Communications. Defines, describes, and discovers how we can find our child within and gently heal and nurture it until we can reach the role of spirituality within our child and live the free life we were meant to live.

Woititz, J.G. (1987). *Home away from home: The art of self sabotage.* Pompano Beach, Florida: Health Communications. Raises and answers such questions as What are the best jobs for ACOA's? Do all ACOAs end up as workaholics? How can they prevent burnout?

Woititzt, Janet. (1985). *Struggle for intimacy.* Pompano Beach, Florida: Health Communications. Reveals the barriers to trust and intimacy learned early in life by children of alcoholics. Tips for rebuilding intimacy in adult relationships are provided.

Woititz, Janet. (1983). *Adult children of alcoholics.* Pompano Beach, Florida: Health Communications. This best-selling book is an excellent overview to the insights of how upbringing in chemically dependent families can be carried into adulthood and what can be done to change these patterns.

Wood, Barbara. (1987). *Children of alcoholism: The struggle for self and intimacy in adult life.* New York: New York University Press. A look at COA issues through traditional psychological theories. Also a reinterpretation of the survival roles.

Alcoholic/Dysfunctional Families

Bepko, Claudia, & Krestan, JoAnn. (1985). *The responsibility trap: A blueprint for treating the alcoholic family.* New York: The Free Press. Presents a treatment plan that includes the alcoholic as well as all family members.

Bradshaw, John. (1988). *The family: A revolutionary way of self-discovery.* Pompano Beach, Florida: Health Communications. Guides the reader out of dysfunction and proposes how problems within the family can be remedied.

Brown, Stephanie. (1985) *Treating the alcoholic family: A developmental model of recovery.* New York: Wiley. Focuses on how practitioners can best understand and meet the needs of the person who is addicted to alcohol. A major section is also included on treating the family of alcoholics.

Goodwin, Donald. (1976). *Is alcoholism inherited?* New York: Oxford University Press. Addresses the age-old nature/nurture question of genetic predisposition versus environmental influences. Surveys the research on both sides of the issue.

Meagher, David. (1987) *Beginning of a miracle: How to intervene with the addicted or alcoholic person.* Pompano Beach, Florida: Health Communications. Step-by-step instructions on what can be done to stop the alcoholic or addicted person from his or her downward spiral.

O'Gorman, Patricia, & Oliver-Diaz, Philip. (1987). *Breaking the cycle of addiction: A parent's guide to raising healthy kids.* Pompano Beach, Florida: Health Communications. Especially for parents or prospective parents who were raised in addicted or dysfunctional families, this book helps break the compulsion that is frequently passed on through family dynamics.

Orford, J., & Harwin, J. (1982). *Alcohol and the family.* New York: St. Martin's Press. Covers how alcohol affects the entire family and examines treatment needs for everyone concerned.

Perez, Joseph. (1986). *Coping within the alcoholic family.* Muncie, Indiana: Accelerated Development Publishers. Explores the emotional deprivations experienced by family members when one is an alcoholic. An important focus is on the children of alcoholics. This book is intended for family members as well as counselors and therapists who treat alcoholic families.

Porterfield, Kay. (1985). *Keeping promises: The challenge of a sober parent.* Center City, Minnesota: Hazelden. A one-day-at-a-time approach to the parenting challenges faced by people recovering from chemical dependency.

Steinglass, Peter. (1988). *The alcoholic family*. New York: Basic Books. Over ten years of study into alcoholism in the family is presented. Covers understanding, treatment, and research into alcoholism.

Subby, Robert. (1987). *Lost in the shuffle: The co-dependent reality*. Pompano Beach, Florida: Health Communications. Written for those who seek to understand the condition of codependency, the problems, the pitfalls, the unreal rules the codependent lives by, and the way out of the diseased condition to recovery.

Wegscheider, Sharon. (1980). *Another chance: Hope and health for the alcoholic family*. Palo Alto, California: Science and Behavior Books. Integrates family therapy and alcoholism and explains and exposes the feelings and frustrations of family members living with an alcoholic.

Wegscheider, Sharon. (1976). *The family trap*. Palo Alto, California: Science & Behavior Books. Identifies and describes the survival roles family members play when living with an alcoholic.

Autobiographical

Burnett, Carol. (1986) *One more time*. New York: Random House. A touching and candid account of the famous entertainer's alcoholic childhood and how it affected her life as a grownup.

Crews, Harry. (1983). *A childhood: The biography of a place*. New York: Morrow. A biography of the novelist's tumultuous, alcoholic upbringing and the long-lasting effects it had on his life and career.

Dean, Amy. (1987). *Once upon a time: Stories from adult children*. Center City, Minnesota: Hazelden. Twenty adult children share their stories revealing the problems they had to overcome in their alcoholic upbringing to free themselves of their past.

LeBoutillier, Megan. (1987). *Little miss perfect*. Denver, Colorado: Claudja Inc. The author describes her efforts to survive her alcoholic home and a means for others to move beyond their past into healthy adulthood.

Scales, Cynthia. (1986). *Potato chips for breakfast*. Rutherford, New Jersey: Perrin & Treggett Booksellers. An autobiography of a sixteen-year-old girl with two alcoholic parents. A story of tragedy and triumph.

Somers, Suzanne. (1988). *Keeping secrets*. New York: Warner Books. A retrospective and candid account of how alcoholism robbed this celebrity of her childhood. It reminded me a lot of my own.

V., Rachel. (1987). *Family secrets*. New York: Harper & Row. Life stories of adult children of alcoholics are given to help millions of people recover from the ill effects of growing up in an alcoholic household.

Fiction

Anderson, Peggy. (1988). *Coming home: Mending memories for adult children of alcoholics*. Seattle Washington: Glen Abbey Books. This story concerns a healing experience between a recovering father and his daughter.

Heckler, Jonellen. (1986). *A fragile peace*. New York: G.P. Putnam. This novel tells of a family's journey through the agonizing torture of a father's alcoholism.

Nilsen, Mary. (1985). *When a bough breaks: Mending the family tree*. Center City, Minnesota: Hazelden. This novel follows a family that enters a five-day treatment program and relates its dramatic and exciting changes.

Books for Children and Adolescents

Al-Anon. (1977). *What's "drunk" mama?* New York: Al-Anon Family Group Headquarters. Deals with a little girl's feelings about her father's alcoholism. Presents the problems through the child's eyes and presents the concepts of Alateen and Al-Anon. The story ends with the father going to AA.

Anders, Rebecca. (1978). *A look at alcoholism*. Minneapolis, Minnesota: Lerner. Provides factual information about alcohol and drinking.

Balcerzak, Lois. (1981). *Hope for young people with alcoholic parents*. Center City, Minnesota: Hazelden Foundation. Helps kids deal with their feelings of hurt, fear, embarrassment, and confusion that stems from parental drinking.

Bissell, L., & Watherwax, R. (1982). *The cat who drank too much*. Bantam, Connecticut: Bibulophile Press. An alcoholic cat named Willoughby is the main character of this story. Shows all the problems of alcoholism through the cat's behaviors.

Berger, Gilda. (1982). *Addiction: Its causes, problems, and treatments.* New York: Watts. This thorough overview of addiction covers abuse of and dependence on alcohol, caffeine, food, tobacco, legal and illegal drugs. Discusses the psychological, genetic, and physical causes and effects of addiction.

Black, Claudia. (1979). *My dad loves me, my dad has a disease: A workbook for children of alcoholics.* Denver, Colorado: MAC Publishers. WRITE: MAC, 1850 High Street, Denver, Colorado 80218. A workbook for children of alcoholics that is designed to help them work through and better understand alcoholism as well as their own feelings. The basic premise is that alcoholism is a disease. Illustrations were created by children up to age fourteen.

Brooks, Cathleen. (1981). *The secret everyone knows.* Center City, Minnesota: Hazelden. This story for children and adolescents expresses feelings commonly experienced by children of alcoholics and offers suggestions for honestly coping with problems in the home. The author's true story lets kids know they are not alone.

Brooks, Jerome. (1973). *Uncle Mike's boy.* New York: Harper Press. A father's drinking causes many psychological problems for an eleven-year-old boy.

Brown, Michael. (Ed.). (1986). *Letters from the children of alcoholic parents.* Charlotte, North Carolina: Randolph Clinic, Inc. A series of moving letters and illustrations written by children of alcoholic parents, revealing their pain, hurt, frustration, and anger. WRITE: The Randolph Clinic, Inc., 100 Billingsley Road, Charlotte, N.C. 28211.

Childhelp U.S.A. (1983). *How could Momma say she loved us?* Woodland Hills, California: Childhelp U.S.A. In this ten-page booklet, a fourteen-year-old boy describes his attempts to protect his younger siblings and himself from his alcoholic mother's neglect.

DiGiovanni, Kathe. (1986). *My house is different.* Center City, Minnesota: Hazelden. This storybook for children ages six and up, interprets the twelve steps of recovery. Joe and his dog Fuzzy travel down Rainbow Road and encounter a variety of creatures and adventures that help Joe learn how he can feel good about himself even if his dad continues to drink.

Duggan, Maureen. (1988). *Mommy doesn't live here anymore.* Weaverville, North Carolina: Bonnie Brae Publications. For children who suffer from parental alcoholism, this is a true, comforting story written by a mother. Especially written for professional use with six- to twelve-year-olds who have one parent who is alcoholic.

Guy, Rosa. (1979). *The disappearance.* New York: Delacorte Press. A powerful story for teenagers about a black sixteen-year-old named Imamu and his wino mother who live in poverty and alcoholism. Shows how the adolescent never stops loving his mother and returns to help her with her disease.

Hammond, Mary, & Chestnut, Lynnann. (1987). *My mom doesn't look like an alcoholic*. Pompano Beach, Florida: Health Communications. A story written about living in an alcoholic family, told through the eyes of a nine-year-old child. This well-illustrated book can be read by parents to their children or by children themselves.

Hastings, Jill, & Typpo, Marion. (1984). *An elephant in the living room.* Minneapolis, Minnesota: Comp Care. When children live in a family where drinking is a problem, it's a lot like living with an elephant in the living room that no one talks about. The book's purpose is to help children realize they are not alone, understand that alcoholism is a disease, learn to express their feelings, improve self-esteem, make decisions, and seek support. Written for children ages seven to early adolescence.

Hip, Earl. (1988). *Fighting invisible tigers: A student guide to life in the jungle.* Minneapolis, Minnesota: The Johnson Institute. Talking teens' language and using cartoon humor and quotes from famous people, the author explains what stress is and how to handle it. Intended as a preventive measure for alcohol and drug abuse, this book emphasizes being the best person you can be.

Hornik, Edith. (1974). *You and your alcoholic parent.* New York: Association Press. Uses questions and answers to address topics of interest to teens to prepare them for circumstances that might arise in an alcoholic family.

Hornik-Beer, Edith. (1985). *A teenager's guide to living with an alcoholic parent.* Center City, Minnesota: Hazelden. Teenagers' questions and anxieties about parental alcoholism are answered in this book. Family arguments, unkept promises, and misdirected responsibilities are discussed.

Hyde, Margaret. (1978). *Know about alcohol.* New York: McGraw. Emphasizes the dangerous consequences of drinking. Also includes a question-and-answer section with vignettes that allow individual responses.

Jance, Judith. (1986). *Welcome home. A child's view of alcoholism.* Washington D.C.: Franklin Publishers. Tad's father is a problem drinker. This book not only informs the child about alcoholism, but emphasizes that he or she is not to blame. Ages five to eleven.

Jones, Penny. (1983). *The brown bottle.* Center City, Minnesota: Hazelden. This brief little story is about a caterpillar named Charlie who discovers a bottle of alcohol and spends many hours inside because of the pleasant feelings he gets. Spending time there begins to fill all his time, eventually becomes his home and ultimately his doom.

Johnson Institute. (1987). *A story about feelings coloring book*. Minneapolis, Minnesota: Johnson Institute. Using cartoon characters from the film "A Story About Feelings," this coloring book helps children gain a clearer understanding of chemical dependence and the role that feelings play in their lives.

Kenny, K., & Krull, H. (1980). *Sometimes my mom drinks too much*. Milwaukee, Wisconsin: Raintree Children's Books. Details Maureen's account of her mother's drinking and the feelings the child has around the drinking and the disease of alcoholism. Several embarrassing situations are depicted in which the mother is drunk and the father tries in vain to shield the child. In this instance a caring teacher comes to the support of the child.

Kranyik, M. (1985). *Coping with adult problems when you're still a kid*. Mount Dora, Florida: KIDSRIGHTS. Addresses the special problems of kids who must assume adult responsibilities because of stress, both parents working, divorce, alcoholism, and other crises.

Lee, Essie, & Israel, Elaine. (1975). *Alcohol and you*. New York: Julian Messner. Gives vignettes about the tragedy of alcohol. Uses cartoons to illustrate points on the devastation of the disease.

Leiner, Katherine. (1987). *Something's wrong in my house*. New York: Watts. Stories about children growing up in alcoholic homes.

Leite, Evelyn, & Espeland, Pamela. (1988). *Different like me: A book for teens who worry about their parents' use of alcohol/drugs*. Minneapolis, Minnesota: The Johnson Institute. Looks at the problem from the kids' point of view. Written especially for teens who are concerned, confused, scared, and angry because their parents abuse alcohol and drugs.

Mathis, Sharon. (1974). *Listen for the fig tree*. New York: The Viking Press. A story for teens about a black sixteen-year-old blind girl named Marvina, who rises above her disability to help her alcoholic mother, who feels defeated by the disease.

Melquist, Elaine. (1974). *Pepper*. Frederick, Maryland: Fredrick County Council on Alcoholism. A heart-warming story told through the eyes of a dog, Pepper, whose master is alcoholic. Pepper describes how he felt when his master neglected him and treated him badly when drunk.

Miner, Jane. (1982). *A day at a time*. Maleato, Minnesota: Crestwood House. Anger, fear, and denial of a little girl whose father is alcoholic are described in this story. The little girl eventually attends Alateen and is able to understand and cope with her father's illness.

Nelville, Emily Cheney. (1975). *Garden of broken glass.* New York: Dela-corte Press. A story of a thirteen-year-old boy and how he copes with his mother's alcoholism. Shows the roles the boy and his siblings take on as a result of parental alcoholism.

Operation Cork. (1983). *Winthrop and Munchie talk about alcohol.* La Jolla, California: Operation Cork. (Write: Operation Cork, 8939 Villa La Jolla Drive, Suite 203, La Jolla, California 92037). A story of two cartoon characters, Winthrop and Munchie, who carry on a simple conversation about drinking that young children can understand. The story goes on to explain problems alcoholism can bring and contains illustrations that kids can color.

Pegors, T. (1983). *Learn about alcohol* and *Learn about alcoholism.* Center City, Minnesota: Hazelden. These two pamphlets present the facts on alcoholism in a straightforward way, showing the effects of alcohol on the body and providing illustrations to bring the content alive.

Porterfield, Kay. (1985). *Coping with an alcoholic parent.* New York: Rosen Group. Over seven million children in the United States live in families where one or both parents are alcoholics. This reassuring book helps teens deal with problems and take care of themselves when things aren't right at home. For ages thirteen to eighteen.

Rattray, Jamie, Howells, Bill, & Siegler, Irving. (1982). *Kids and alcohol: Facts and ideas about drinking and not drinking.* Hollywood, Florida: Health Communications. Myths about alcoholism are included along with the facts that debunk them. Also includes techniques for exploring feelings and ways to take care of yourself and deal with feelings when a parent drinks.

Ryerson, Eric. (1987). *When your parent drinks too much: A book for teen-agers.* New York: Warner Books. Breaks through the isolation and reaches out to teenage children of alcoholics by putting them in touch with those best able to help—other children of alcoholics. Draws on ideas from Al-Anon and Alateen.

Seixas, Judith. (1977). *Alcohol: What it is, what it does.* New York: Green-willow Books. Includes chapters giving facts about alcohol, the disease concept, and reasons for drinking. Illustrated with cartoon-style pictures, the book concludes with the message that kids have a choice.

Seixas, Judith. (1979). *Living with a parent who drinks too much.* New York: Greenwillow Books. This book was written especially for children living in a situation where parents are alcoholic. It offers insight into the behaviors of the family members and offers strategies for coping with the environment.

Silverstein, Shel. (1976). *The missing piece.* New York: Harper & Row. What the missing piece finds on its search for wholeness is told in this fable that gently probes the nature of trying to fit in and not feel so different. Illustrated by line drawings, the missing piece sets out to find what's missing and to search for fulfillment.

Snyder, Anne. (1975). *First step.* Center City, Minnesota: Hazelden Foundation. Shows how Alateen helps children deal with their parent's drinking. In this story a girl learns to cope with her mother's alcoholism with the aid of Alateen.

Summers, James. (1966). *The long ride home.* Philadelphia: Westminster Press. A brother and sister, high school age, must cope with their father's alcoholism, which prevents them from carrying on an ordinary social life.

Special Reports

This section includes governmental and advocacy reports that have relevance for program developers, child advocates, researchers, and practitioners nationwide.

Blume, S. (1985). *Report of the conference on prevention research.* New York: Children of Alcoholics Foundation, Inc. Summarizes a conference on prevention research held in New York City in December 1984. High priority research needs and proposed strategies to improve prevention research were identified.

Children of Alcoholics Foundation. (1982). *Report of the children of alcoholics foundation.* New York: Children of Alcoholics Foundation, Inc. Presents an extensive review of the literature, identifies roles for professionals including educators, mental health workers, and health care workers, and discusses issues in identification. Recommends high priority areas of research. Sobering children's art illustrates the inner pain these children suffer.

Children of Alcoholics Foundation. (1984). *Report of the conference on research needs and opportunities for children of alcoholics.* New York: Children of Alcoholics Foundation, Inc. Summarizes the conclusions of a Conference on Research Needs and Opportunities for Children of Alcoholics in New York City in April 1984. High priority research opportunities were identified, strategies were recommended, and areas of research were reviewed.

Cramer, P. (1977). *An educational strategy to impact the children of alcoholic parents: A feasibility report.* Arlington, Virginia: National Center for Alcohol Education. ERIC ED 199 190. Examines areas in which supportive services can be provided to children of alcoholic parents within a school setting. Concludes that the school staff is the best resource to provide needed care.

National Institute on Alcohol Abuse and Alcoholism. (1981). *Services for children of alcoholics.* Research Monograph 4. Washington, D.C.: U.S. Printing Office. Document Number: HE 208315:4. Reports on a symposium about children from alcoholic homes. Deals with identification, intervention, prevention, and treatment issues.

Office for Substance Abuse Prevention. (1988). *Children of alcoholics: Kit for kids, parents, therapists, and helpers.* Rockville, Maryland: National Clearinghouse for Alcohol and Drug Information. This package includes four kits directed to four audiences: kids, parents, therapists, and helpers. The kit is free and can be copied at will.

Russell, M., Henderson, C., & Blume, S.B. (1985). *Children of alcoholics: A review of the literature.* New York: Children of Alcoholics Foundation, Inc. A comprehensive review of the research on children of alcoholics, presenting an excellent overview and synthesis of current knowledge on the topic.

Waite, B.J., & Ludwig, M.J. (1985). *A growing concern: How to provide services for children of alcoholic families.* Rockville, Maryland: National Institute on Alcohol Abuse and Alcoholism. Enlightens caregivers on how to identify, intervene, treat, and prevent further problems with children of alcoholics. Also includes sections on training caregivers, referral and support resources, cultural factors, and research directions.

Woodside, M. (1982). *Children of alcoholics.* New York: Children of Alcoholics Foundation, Inc. Examines the problems and needs of children of alcoholics through literature review and interviews with programs providing services for children from chemically dependent families and site visits to eleven programs. The report was presented to Governor Hugh Carey and Joseph Califano, special counselor on alcoholism and drug abuse.

Woodside, M. (1986). *Children of alcoholics on the job.* New York: Children of Alcoholics Foundation, Inc. Aimed at corporations and businesses, this report includes a general overview of children of alcoholics, preliminary findings by various companies, problems parental alcohol abuse can cause employees, results of the first nationwide survey of Corporate Medical Directors and Employee Assistance Programs on this issue, and practical, cost-free recommendations for action.

Organizations

This section details the major organizations concerned with alcoholism as it pertains to children and chemically dependent families. I have divided the organizations into two types: resource organizations and professional organizations. Resource organizations provide such services as dissemination of information on the incidence and effects on children of alcoholic parents, methods of supporting children in such homes, legislative advocacy efforts for these children, replication models for programs, and other types of technical assistance in the area of alcoholism and the family. Professional organizations are national associations of professionals dedicated to the improvement of those who work with children and adolescents. These organizations generally charge membership dues, publish their own journals, and sponsor an annual meeting where members gather for seminars, speeches, and workshops.

Resource Organizations

Addiction Research Foundation, 33 Russell Street, Toronto, Ontario Canada M5S 2S1. Conducts and promotes research in alcoholism and other addictions; conducts programs for and methods of treatment and rehabilitation of alcoholics and other addicts; disseminates information about alcoholism and other addictions through public education and prevention.

Adult Children of Alcoholics Central Service Board, P.O. Box 3216, 2522 West Sepulveda Blvd., Suite 200, Torrance, California 90505. A twelve-step, twelve-tradition suggested program of recovery/discovery for adults who were raised in an alcoholic family. The board was formed on November 10, 1984 by the independent meetings in California and an interim World Service Organization was formed on January 19, 1986. The office now serves as a clearinghouse for information to, from, and about the growing fellowship of adult children of alcoholics around the world.

Alcoholics Anonymous, P.O. Box 459, Grand Central Station, New York, New York 10163. A fellowship of men and women who share their experience, strength and hope with each other that they may solve their common problem and help others recover from alcoholism. The only requirement for membership is a desire to stop drinking.

Al-Anon/Alateen Family Group Headquarters, Inc., P.O. Box 182, Madison Square Station, New York, New York 10159-0182. A nationwide fellowship of young people, usually teenagers, whose lives have been affected by alcoholism in a family member or close friend. Help is offered by sharing of personal experiences, strength and hope.

American Council for Drug Education, 5820 Hubbard Drive, Rockville, Maryland 20852. The council's goal is to communicate the latest valid information on psychoactive drugs, including alcohol, to the public at large.

Center for Alcohol Studies, Rutgers University, P.O. Box 969, Piscataway, New Jersey 08854. The multifaceted mission of the center includes research education, clinical services, and information services. The center serves as an international source of information on alcohol studies.

Children of Alcoholics Foundation, Inc., 31st Floor, 200 Park Avenue, New York, New York 10166. A nonprofit, public organization created to assist this country's 28 million children of alcoholic parents. The primary goals of the foundation are to raise awareness of the intergenerational links in the disease of alcoholism, help reduce the suffering and pain by those from alcoholic homes, and prevent future alcoholism.

Children's Defense Fund. 122 C Street, N.W., Washington, D.C. 20001. Publishes information on prevention problems, issues, and news regarding children of all ages. A newsletter and booklets are available for child advocates, community leaders, public health workers, and others interested in improving the lives of children.

Co-Dependents Anonymous, National Service Office, Co-Dependents Anonymous, P.O. Box 5508, Glendale, Arizona 85312-5508. Co-Dependents Anonymous is a fellowship of men and women whose common problem is an inability to maintain functional relationships. CODA bases its meetings on AA's twelve steps and twelve traditions. Its meetings are open to those who feel they are in a codependent relationship and feel overly responsible for others' feelings and behaviors.

Families Anonymous, P.O Box 528, Van Nuys, California 91408. For relatives and friends concerned about the use of drugs or related behavioral problems. Uses the twelve steps of Alcoholics Anonymous to help families recover.

Families in Action Drug Information Center, 3845 North Druid Hills Road, Suite 300, Decatur, Georgia 30033. Educates the public about the dangers of drug abuse by disseminating accurate, timely information.

Just Say No Foundation, 1777 North California Blvd., Suite 210, Walnut Creek, California 94596. A nonprofit organization that provides a national link for all "Just Say No" clubs through the distribution of materials, information, fundraising, and by providing technical assistance and onsite training.

National Clearinghouse for Alcohol and Drug Information, P.O. Box 2345, Rockville, Maryland 20852. Provides information and services to anyone with questions or concerns about any type of drug problem, including alcohol abuse, illicit drug use, and misuse of prescription drugs. Printed materials, references and referrals, and media are available through the clearinghouse.

National Council on Alcoholism, Inc., 12 West 21st Street, New York, New York 10010. A national nonprofit organization combating alcoholism, other drug addictions, and related problems. Major programs include prevention and education, public information, public policy advocacy, medical/scientific information, conferences and publications.

National Federation of Parents for Drug-Free Youth (NFP), 8730 Georgia Avenue, Suite 200, Silver Spring, Maryland 20910. A nonprofit organization committed to raising a generation of drug-free youth. Its principal objective is to assist in the formation and support of local parent and youth groups in communities across America to eliminate drug and alcohol use among youth.

National Institute on Alcohol Abuse and Alcoholism, 5600 Fishers Lane, Rockville, Maryland 20852. Provides a focus in the federal effort to increase knowledge and promote effective strategies to deal with economic, social, and human devastation associated with alcohol abuse and alcoholism. It is committed to promoting and carrying out the long-term basic and applied research required to accomplish treatment, training, and prevention programs.

National Women's Christian Temperance Union, 1730 Chicago Avenue, Evanston, Illinois 60201. A nonprofit, nonpartisan, interdenominational organization, dedicated to the education of our nation's citizens, especially our youth, on the harmful effects of alcoholic beverages, other narcotic drugs, and tobacco on the human body and the society in which we live.

U.S. Journal, 3201 S.W. 15th Street, Deerfield Beach, Florida. Publishes alcohol-related information and three periodicals: *The U.S. Journal of Drug and Alcohol Dependence; Chemical Dependency;* and *Grassroots,* a comprehensive alcohol and drug information service.

Professional Organizations

Association for Childhood Education International, 11141 Georgia Avenue, Suite 200, Wheaton, Maryland 20902. A professional medium for those concerned with the education and well-being of children from infancy through early adolescence: classroom teachers, teachers in training, teacher educators, parents, day care workers, librarians, supervisors, administrators, and other practitioners.

Association for the Care of Children's Health, 3615 Wisconsin Avenue, N.W., Washington, D.C. 20016. Formerly the Association for the Care of

Children in Hospitals, this organization is committed to humanizing health care for children, adolescents, and their families.

Child Study Association of America, 9 East Eighty-ninth Street, New York, New York 10028. Concerned with the study and development of young children and the environments that affect them.

Child Welfare League of America, 67 Irving Place, New York, New York 10003. Concerned with any facet of social policy that bears on the welfare of youth and their families. Its membership is composed of professionals who work for child and family welfare through administration, supervision, casework, group work, community organization, teaching, or research.

National Association for Children of Alcoholics, 31582 Coast Highway, Suite B, South Laguna, California 92677. A national nonprofit organization founded in 1983 to support and serve as a resource for children of alcoholics of all ages and for those in a position to help them. NACOA believes that children of alcoholics deserve the understanding, information and help they need to break out of their isolation and silence.

National Association of Social Workers, 2 Park Avenue, New York, New York 10016. NASW is composed of caseworkers in the field of social welfare, many of whom work with chemically dependent families.

National Council on Family Relations, 1910 West County Road B., Suite 147, Saint Paul, Minnesota 55113. NCFR is dedicated to furthering all aspects of family life in terms of program development, education, and research.

National Association for the Education of Young Children, 1834 Connecticut Avenue, N.W., Washington, D.C. 20009-5786. NAEYC offers professional development opportunities to early childhood educators designed to improve the quality of services to children from birth through age eight—the critical years of development.

National PTA, 700 North Rush Street, Chicago, Illinois 60611. A professional organization for parents, teachers, and others concerned with bridging the gap between home and school for the welfare of the nation's children.

Society for Research in Child Development, 5801 Ellis Avenue, Chicago, Illinois 60637. A professional platform for researchers and theoreticians interested in the study and development of children from infancy to adolescence.

Periodicals

This section highlights the major periodicals in the field that publish articles pertaining to alcoholism, chemically dependent families, and children of alcoholic parents. I have classified the periodicals list into three types: professional journals, popular magazines, and newsletters. Professional journals are usually, but not always, sponsored by a professional organization and refereed by experts in the field; their content tends to be academic and research based in nature. Popular magazines are generally written for the lay person in a casual style and sometimes lack a sound scientific basis. Nevertheless, many of the magazines listed here publish articles by top experts in the field. Newsletters are published by professional and resource organizations to keep readers up to date.

Newsletters

The Addiction Newsletter. Published monthly, this newsletter serves as a resource exchange for professionals in preventing and treating alcoholism and drug abuse. Manisses Communications Group, Inc. P.O. Box 3357, Wayland Square, Providence, Rhode Island 02906-0357.

Alateen Talk. Alateens' own bimonthly newsletter keeps the groups informed of interesting events shared by individual Alateen members, Alateen groups, Alateen conferences and Alateen sponsors. P.O. Box 182, Madison Square Station, New York, New York 10159-0182.

Inside Al-Anon. Alateen groups receive this bulletin, which includes a regular feature article about Alateen and news and notes concerning Al-Anon and Alateen worldwide. P.O. Box 182, Madison Square Station, New York, New York 10159-0182.

COA Review. An international newsletter for those concerned about children of alcoholics. Thomas Perrin, Inc., P.O. Box 423, Rutherford, New Jersey 07070.

Grapevine. The international monthly journal of Alcoholics Anonymous. It presents the experiences and opinions of AA members and others interested in AA's recovery program. P.O. Box 459, Grand Central Station, New York, New York 10163.

Our Voice. A newsletter about chemical dependency and treatment in the gay and lesbian community. The Pride Institute, 14400 Martin Drive, Eden Prairie, Minnesota 55344.

NACA Network. Quarterly newsletter for the National Association for Children of Alcoholics announcing the latest in national movements, research, conferences, and other national news. 31582 Coast Highway, Suite B, South Laguna, California 92677.

Prevention Parentline. A quarterly publication of the National Federation of Parents for Drug-Free Youth. The Editor, NFP, 8730 Georgia Avenue, Suite 200, Silver Spring, Maryland 20910.

U.S. Journal of Drug and Alcohol Dependence. The only monthly national trade newspaper for addictions professionals. The U.S. Journal, Inc., 3201 S.W. 15th Street, Deerfield Beach, Florida 33442.

Professional Journals

The ACA Journal. American Council on Alcoholism, Inc., 8501 LaSalle Road, Suite 301, Towson, Maryland 21204. Published quarterly by the American Council on Alcoholism, this journal presents the latest information in the field of alcoholism.

Addictive Behaviors: An International Journal. Pergamon Journals, Inc., Maxwell House, Fairview Park, Elmsford, New York 10523. Published quarterly, the journal publishes original research, theoretical papers, and critical reviews in the area of substance abuse. Attention is given to alcohol, drug abuse, smoking and eating disorders.

Alcohol Health & Research World. The Editor, P.O. Box 2345, Rockville, Maryland 20852. A quarterly journal produced by the National Institute on Alcohol Abuse and Alcoholism that brings current research in an easily readable format.

Alcoholism Treatment Quarterly. The Haworth Press, 12 West 32nd Street, New York, New York 10001. This practical journal is the practitioner's quarterly for individual, group, and family therapy. It provides a balance of practice-oriented material along with selective publication of data-based research.

Child Abuse and Neglect: The International Journal. International Society for Prevention of Child Abuse and Neglect, c/o Pergamon Journals, Fairview Park, Elmsford, New York 10523. Published quarterly by the International Society for Prevention of Child Abuse and Neglect, the journal provides a multidisciplinary forum on the prevention and treatment of child abuse and neglect, including sexual abuse.

International Journal of Addictions. The Editor, 417 Garces Drive, San Francisco, California 94132. An international journal that reports the latest research in the area of alcohol and other human addictions.

Journal of Alcohol and Drug Education. Journal Executive, 1120 East Oakland, P.O. Box 10212, Lansing, Michigan 48901. Published three times a year, the journal reports various educational philosophies and differing points of view regarding alcohol and drugs. Teacher experience, experiments, materials, techniques, and procedures all are possible topics.

Journal of Chemical Dependency Treatment. The Haworth Press, 12 West 32nd Street, New York, New York 10001. Published biannually, this journal provides focused thematic issues dealing with practical clinical topics for drug abuse/substance abuse counselors and treatment professionals, covering both maintenance and drug-free philosophies.

Journal of Drug Issues. P.O. Box 4021, Tallahassie, Florida 32315-4021. Published quarterly, this journal provides a forum for discussion of drug policy issues. Includes timely and critical commentaries on social, legal, political, economic, historical, and medical issues related to drug policy making.

Journal of Studies on Alcohol. Center of Alcohol Studies, Rutgers University, P.O. Box 969, Piscataway, New Jersey 08854. Published bimonthly at the Center of Alcohol Studies, this journal contains original research reports that contribute significantly to fundamental knowledge about alcohol, its use and misuse, and its biomedical, behavioral, and sociocultural effects.

Journal of Substance Abuse Treatment. Editorial Office, Drug Treatment and Education Center, Dept. of Psychiatry, North Shore University Hospital, 400 Community Drive, Manhasset, New York 11030. Published quarterly, the journal features original contributions and articles on the clinical treatment of substance abuse and alcoholism. Directed toward treatment practitioners in both public and private sectors.

Professional Counselor. 12729 N.E. 20th, Suite 12, Bellevue, Washington 98005. Published bimonthly and serving the alcohol and drug addictions field, the journal gives special tips to counselors.

Popular Magazines

Alcoholism: The National Magazine. The Editor, *Alcoholism Magazine,* Box C19051, Seattle, Washington 98109. Published bimonthly by Alcom, Inc., this magazine is for recovered alcoholics, professionals in the field, family and friends of still-drinking alcoholics.

Alcoholism and Addiction Magazine. P.O. Box 31329, Seattle, Washington 98103. Published bimonthly, this magazine presents information on chemical dependence and other addictions in a slick format and readable style for the lay person.

Changes. The U.S. Journal, Inc., 3201 S.W. 15th Street, Deerfield Beach, Florida 33442. For and about children of alcoholics. Began circulation in January of 1986 and is published six times a year.

Focus on Chemically Dependent Families. The U.S. Journal, 3201 S.W. 15th Street, Deerfield Beach, Florida 33442. The first magazine that devotes its entire contents to the effects of chemical dependency on families and children in the United States.

The Forum. Al-Anon Family Group Headquarters, Inc. 1372 Broadway, New York, New York 10018-6106. The international monthly journal of Al-Anon. A publication for, about, and written by family members who have been affected by alcoholism.

Audiovisuals

This section includes the burgeoning numbers of audiovisuals on family alcoholism, particularly as it relates to children of alcoholic parents. I have organized these resources by type of audiovisual and have included 16mm films, videotapes, filmstrips, audiocassettes, therapeutic games and curriculum materials.

16mm Films

Alcohol, Drugs or Alternatives. Shows the freedom of choice as an alternative to drug and alcohol dependence. Order from: Sandler Institutional Films, Inc., 3490 East Foothill Boulevard, P.O. Box 5667, Pasadena, California 91107. (30 mins.)

All Bottled Up. Animated film showing what happens when feelings about alcoholic parents are kept bottled up inside. Narrated by adolescents expressing their feelings about alcoholic parents. Order from: Aims Instructional Media Services, Inc., Hollywood, California 90028. (11 mins.) (For school-age and adolescent youngsters.)

Another Chance. Features Sharon Wegscheider-Cruse and focuses on the anguish and ultimate emotional breakthrough of an adult child of an alcoholic who experiences the "reconstruction process." Examines forms of counseling for family members of alcoholics. Order from: Health Communications, 3201 S.W. 15th Street, Deerfield Beach, Florida 33442 (30 mins.)

A Step In Time. A fantasy story about a child of an alcoholic mother who meets a time traveler who shows him the future and the choices he has in how he reacts to the situation. Best for preadolescent and adolescent children. Order from: Southerby Productions, Inc. 5000 East Anaheim Street, Long Beach, California, 90804. (29 mins.)

A Story About Feelings. An animated film of children's drawings that come to life as the children narrate them. Feelings deal with smoking and chemical dependency and how you can feel good without addictions. Order from: The Johnson Institute, 7151 Metro Blvd., Minneapolis, Minnesota 55435. (10 mins.) (For younger children.)

A Slight Drinking Problem. Portrays the wife of an alcoholic husband and how she learns to cope with the alcoholism through Al-Anon. Order from: Southerby Productions, Inc., 5000 E. Anaheim Street, Long Beach, California 90804. (28 mins.)

Children of Denial. Features Claudia Black speaking about the three "no's" children learn in alcoholic families: (1) Don't feel (2) Don't tell (3) Don't trust. Order from: MAC, 1850 High Street, Denver, Colorado 80218. (28 mins.)

Family Matters. Vignettes of five different families that show how they are affected by an addicted family member and how they cope with the problem. Order from: Hazelden Press, Pleasant Valley Road, Center City, Minnesota 55012-0176. (30 mins.)

Family Trap. Explores the roles played by members of an alcoholic family. Features Sharon Wegscheider-Cruse. Order from: Onsite Training, 2820 West Main Street, Rapid City, South Dakota 57702. (30 mins.)

Hope For the Children. A training film for practitioners giving clear guidelines for handling children of alcoholic parents. Covers the years from five to twelve and the problems kids have growing up in chemically dependent homes. Order from: Health Communications, 3201 S.W. 15th Street, Deerfield Beach, Florida 33442. (28 mins.)

Life Father, Like Son. Jim tries to approach his father about his drinking but the father becomes belligerent when the topic is brought up. The film suggests methods of rehabilitation and sources of help. Order from: National Audiovisual Center, General Services Administration, Washington, D.C. 20409. (15 mins.)

Lots of Kids Like Us. This is an excellent film to introduce the notion of alcoholism as a family disease to children. The setting is a camp where many children are grappling with their parents' alcoholism. The adult leaders show the kids that their parents have a disease and that the children did not cause, cannot control, and cannot cure the disease. Order from: Gerald T. Rogers Productions, Inc., 5225 Old Orchard Road, Suite #6, Skokie, Illinois 60077. (30 mins.)

My Father's Son. A film of three generations confronted with chemical dependency. It follows sixteen-year-old Michael, the son of an alcoholic, trying to lead a normal life amid the chaos of a dysfunctioning family. Order from: Gerald T. Rogers Productions, Inc., 5225 Old Orchard Road, Suite #6, Skokie, Illinois 60077. (33 mins.)

She Drinks a Little. Teenage Cindy has an alcoholic mother whose drinking is destroying both of their lives. The film explains and endorses Alateen. Order from: Learning Corporation of America, 1350 Avenue of Americas, New York, New York 10019. (31 mins.)

Soft Is the Heart of a Child. Deals with the effect of alcoholism on children in a family. Shows different roles children adopt to survive an alcoholic family: Hero, Mascot, Scapegoat, and Lost Child. This touching film is a *must* for introducing the concept of family dysfunction in alcoholic homes. Order from: Operation CORK/PGP, 138 B Avenue, Coronado, California 92118. (28 mins.)

Sounds of Silence. In this touching film, Claudia Black talks with children of alcoholics, both young and adult, from violent homes. They tell about the abuse that runs rampant in their alcoholic homes. Dr. Black encourages them to talk about the violent acts rather than to pretend it doesn't happen or never happened at all. Order from: ACT Productions, 30100 Towncenter Drive, Suite 0-211, Laguna Niguel, CA 92677. (28 mins.)

Struggle for Intimacy. Dr. Janet Woititz discusses how children of alcoholics are set up for self-defeating attitudes, how they manifest themselves in relationships, and what can be done. Order from: Health Communications, Inc. 3201 S.W. 15th Street, Deerfield Beach, Florida 33442. (28 mins.)

Suffer the Children. Shows the common problems kids face growing up in alcoholism. Features Claudia Black and interviews with children speaking about their experiences. Order from: Carousel Film and Video, 241 East 34th Street, Room 304, New York, New York 10016. (30 mins.)

Trying to Find Normal. An award-winning documentary about artist Eric Fischl's battle against buried pain and trying to overcome his mother's alcoholism. Order from: Children of Alcoholics Foundation, Dept. C., P.O. Box 4185, Grand Central Station, New York, New York 10163. (20 mins.)

Videotapes

A Story About Feelings. Effective, eye-catching film for three- to eight-year-olds. Presented mainly in cartoon form, it helps them understand the role that feelings play in their lives. Helps children understand that some people drink, smoke, and use drugs to change their feelings. Order from: The Johnson Institute, 7151 Metro Boulevard, Minneapolis, Minnesota 55435. (10 mins.)

Children of Alcoholics. Designed for use with therapists, counselors, and other professionals, this video discusses important dynamics for the child of alcoholism. Offers valuable guidance to the parents and helping professionals. Order from: KIDSRIGHTS, 3700 Progress Boulevard, P.O. Box 851, Mount Dora, Florida 32757. (38 mins.)

Children of Alcoholics. Portrays the dysfunctional behaviors that develop in alcoholic families, with special emphasis on children. Sharon Wegscheider narrates on the roles and potential for change. Order from: Onsite Training and Consulting, Inc., 2820 West Main Street, Rapid City, South Dakota 57702. (30 mins.)

Children of Alcoholics: Choices for Growth. Featuring Dr. Robert Ackerman before a live audience discussing the effects of parental alcoholism on children of alcoholics who are now adults. Appropriate for anyone raised in an alcoholic home and for those who work with them. Order from: KIDS-RIGHTS, 3700 Progress Boulevard, P.O. Box 851, Mount Dora, Florida 32757. (55 mins.)

Drinking Parents. Twenty million children living in homes with alcoholic parents are often subjected to violence, abuse, and neglect. The special problems of these children are brought to light in this film. Victimized children and their parents give case history accounts of how they coped. Order from: Coronet/MTI Film & Video, 108 Wilmot Road, Deerfield, Illinois 60015. (10 mins.)

If Someone in Your Family Drinks . . . Helps youngsters who may be growing up in an alcoholic family system to understand the situation and see how it affects their behavior. Recommends specific things they can do to make things better for themselves. For ages ten to fifteen. Order from: KIDS-RIGHTS, 3700 Progress Boulevard, P.O. Box 851, Mount Dora, Florida 32757. (30 mins.)

Parents with Alcoholism: Kids with Hope. Shows how a parent's alcoholism affects the rest of the family. Helps teens who blame themselves for their parent's drinking. Shows how to cope; provides kids with hope. Ages fourteen to eighteen. Order from: KIDSRIGHTS, 3700 Progress Boulevard, P.O. Box 851, Mount Dora, Florida 32757. (30 mins.)

Strong Kids, Safe Kids. Henry Winkler and cohosts John Ritter and Mariette Hartley are joined by Scooby Doo, Yogi Bear, and The Flintstones in this special family guide to protecting children against sexual abuse. Order from: Mass Media Ministries Films and Videos, 2116 North Charles Street, Baltimore, Maryland 21218. (42 mins.)

Roles. Claudia Black presents the four family roles she writes about in her book *It will never happen to me:* The responsible child, the adjuster, the placater, and the acting-out child. Order from: MAC, 1850 High Street, Denver, Colorado 80218. (30 mins.)

Twelve Steps, The Video. A completely new approach for families touched by alcoholism. Based on the twelve steps, this film serves to motivate and provide spiritual strength for living life fully and joyously, one day at a time. Beta and VHS. Order from: Perrin & Treggett Booksellers, P.O. Box 190, 5 Glen Road, Rutherford, New Jersey 07070.

The Summer We Moved to Elm Street. A nine-year-old girl's feelings are explored in an environment of emotional neglect. The child must take greater responsibility and adjust to a new neighborhood in the midst of problems caused by parental conflicts and a nonsupportive, alcoholic father. Beta and VHS. Order from: CRM-McGraw-Hill Inc., P.O. Box 641, Del Mar, California 92014. (28 mins.)

Where's Shelley? A stimulating story about ordinary children nine to eleven years old faced with a situation where alcohol and drugs are available for their use. Without moralizing, the film helps children understand factors that can affect their decisions about using alcohol and drugs. Order from: The Johnson Institute, 7151 Metro Boulevard, Minneapolis, Minnesota 55435. (10 mins.)

Filmstrips and Audiocassettes

Children of Alcoholic Parents. Part 1 identifies the scope of the problem in terms of the adults who overuse alcohol and the negative effects on the children. Part 2 suggests some of the causes for excessive abuse of alcohol by parents and shows recent trends in treatment programs for children. Order from: Multi-Media Productions Inc., Box 5097, Stanford, California 94305. (17 mins.)

Claudia Black: Don't Talk, Don't Trust, Don't Feel. An album of four audio cassettes of Claudia Black discussing the major issues from her books: "It will never happen to me"; "Don't talk, don't trust, don't feel"; "The adult child"; and "The progression of roles." Order from: Hazelden Educational Materials, Pleasant Valley Road, Box 176, Center City, Minnesota 55012-0176.

Codependent No More. An audio cassette that explores the issues of living as a codependent in an alcoholic home. Order from: Hazelden Educational Materials, Pleasant Valley Road, Box 176, Center City, Minnesota 55012-0176.

For Adult Children of Alcoholics and Those Who Love Them. Examines the ACOA syndrome, explains how to assess your own family of origin, explores the relationship between feelings and recovery, defines the characteristic problem ACOAs have in relationships, and provides examples of successful redirection. Order from: The Johnson Institute, 7151 Metro Boulevard, Minneapolis, Minnesota 55435. Six tapes in this series.

Growth Stages and Adult Children of Alcoholics. Robert Ackerman explores stages of growth through childhood, adolescence, and into adulthood and the ways these stages are influenced by being the child of an alcoholic. Order from: Access Audiotape, Thomas Perrin, Inc., P.O. Box 423, Rutherford, New Jersey 07070.

Hiding the Truth. Introduces the Snyder family. Illustrates the roles other family members took on to avoid facing the problem of Mr. Snyder's drinking. The enabler, scapegoat, and the mascot are portrayed. Order from: Sunburst Communications, Room RL15, 101 Castleton Street, Pleasantville, New York 10570-9971. Also available on videocassette. (Grades five through nine.)

Hope for Adult Children of Alcoholics. An album of four audiocassettes created especially for adult children of alcoholics. Topics include: Fulfillment in Recovery; Decisions and Choices; Adult Relationships; Stages of Growth; Grief and Loss; The Twelve Steps and ACOA; Reflections Side 1; and Reflections Side 2. Order from: Hazelden Educational Materials, Pleasant Valley Road, Box 176, Center City, Minnesota 55012-0176.

Breaking the Pattern. Describes an alcoholic family and the roles played within it. Explains why it is difficult for a young person living in an alcoholic family system to see the problem. Suggests steps to improve the situation. Order from: Sunburst Communications, Room RL15, 101 Castleton Street, Pleasantville, New York 10570-9971. Also available on videocassette. (Grades five through nine.)

Hope for Adult Children of Alcoholics. Includes four audiocassettes on workshop lectures and personal stories of some of the most respected speakers on children of alcoholics issues today. Speakers include Earnie Larsen, Robert Subby, and Barbara Naiditch. Order from: Hazelden Educational Materials, Pleasant Valley Road, Box 176, Center City, Minnesota 55012-0176.

Trouble at Home. Helps young people understand and cope with the fear, anger, and resentment when alcoholism, divorce, unemployment or other family problems exist. Order from: Sunburst Communications, Room RL15, 101 Castleton Street, Pleasantville, New York 10570-9971. Also available on videocassette. (Grades five through nine.)

Therapeutic Games

Drugs/Alcohol: Play It Straight. This board game has three decks of cards, five pawns, and one die and is played in the Monopoly format. Players must make decisions and choices and correctly answer questions about drugs and alcohol to progress through the game. The winner is the first player to land exactly on the *winner* space by using the choice cards wisely, dealing with the consequences of decisions and answering questions. Order from: Goodwin-Geier Products, P.O. Box 1971, Tuscaloosa, Alabama 35403.

The Adult Children Game. This board game provides a safe setting to process issues related to players' childhood stories. Group sharing and hugs are included in the design and all ages can play. Order from: Sobriety Publications, P.O. Box 30773, Tucson, Arizona 85751.

The Stamp Game. Developed by Claudia Black, this board game helps players to better identify, clarify, and discuss feelings. It is especially useful with children because it gives them a concrete focus that fosters the process in a nonthreatening way. Appropriate for older children and adolescents; 60–90 minute time frame. Order from: MAC, 1850 High Street, Denver, Colorado 80218.

The Just Say No Game. A board game for children between ages seven and fourteen that helps them form a peer group which supports saying "no" to drugs. A total of 144 cards pose open-ended questions and encourage discussions which are different every time the game is played. Order from: Lifegames, Inc., 57 Acorn Court, Walnut Creek, California 94595.

Response. This therapeutic game was created for those recovering from chemical dependency and for their families. It can also be played with those recovering from eating disorders, relationship addictions, and other dependencies. Order from: SunLu Company, 1656 Boston Place, Fayetteville, Arkansas 72703.

Satisfy! A Relationship Repair Manual and Board Game. This board game is for adults to help them keep their relationships vital and healthy. Five basic communication techniques and how to use them and a structure in which players can practice the techniques make up the board game. Order from: Libra Publishers, Inc., 3089C Clairemont Drive, Suite 383, San Diego, California 92117.

Sobriety. Appropriate for teenagers and adult children of alcoholics, this board game helps treatment personnel assess the coping skills of alcoholism and substance abuse patients, as well as to provide problem drinkers with simulations of actual situations in which to try new coping skills. Order from: Therapeutic Innovations, Inc., P.O. Box 6630, Reno, Nevada 89513-6630.

Talk Alcohol With Kids (TAWK). A five-color vinyl board game played by adult and child that enhances communication and awareness for children of alcoholics. It helps establish an environment of discovery and dialogue, uncover unexposed fears, feelings, and questions, make treatment more enjoyable and comfortable for child and adult, and enhance a positive attitude about treatment for child and family. Order from: TAWK, 3703 North Main Street, Rockford, Illinois 61103.

Mandala: The Parenting Game. Players rear an imaginary child from conception to adolescence and must deal with many pitfalls of being an alcoholic parent. Good for recovering parents or for recovering adult children of alcoholics who are striving to separate the disease of alcoholism from what is normal child development and who want to break the disease cycle. Order from: Dr. Bryan Robinson, Department of Human Services, University of North Carolina, Charlotte, North Carolina 28223.

The Ungame. This board game helps children accept and understand themselves and others while having fun. Gives kids a chance to share their ideas as well as their feelings. It can be played in groups of two to six with people of all ages. A 45–60 minute time frame. Order from: P.O. Box 6382, Anaheim, California 92806.

Curriculum Materials

Alba, James, and Colello, Thomas. *Life Positive: A Model for Drug Intervention and Health Promotion.* A curriculum guide and training manual to help make children acutely aware of the external realities of drugs and alcohol and their misuse and at the same time to help them become emotionally equipped to handle this. Essentially this educational approach aims to prevent drug abuse in youth. Order from: Sunburst Communications, 39 Washington Avenue, P.O. Box 40, Pleasantville, New York 10570-9971.

BABES (Beginning Alcohol and Addictions Basic Education Studies). This unique curriculum is a primary prevention program designed to give very young preschool children and early elementary children a lifetime of protection from substance abuse. The purpose of BABES is to enable children to learn and practice living/loving skills and make positive early decisions about the use of alcohol and other drugs. The program includes seven colorful hand puppets, seven story books, flash cards and worksheets, and cassette tapes for each of the seven lessons. Order from: BABES, 17330 Northland Park Court, Southfield, Missouri 48075.

Buxbaum, Ann, and Gussin, Gilda. *Self-Discovery: Alcohol and Other Drugs Using Skills to Make Tough Choices.* This self-discovery course allows students to develop and practice self-discovery skills and strategies. Self-discovery strategies are ways to feel good and cope with problems without hurting oneself or others. The strategies provide new choices for students so they will be less pressured to engage in unhealthy behaviors. Order from: Management Sciences for Health, 165 Allandale Road, Boston, Massachusetts 02130.

Children Are People. This is an excellent curriculum designed especially to assist school professionals and other concerned adults to develop early prevention and intervention programs for children of alcoholic parents. Order from: The Johnson Institute, 7151 Metro Blvd., Minneapolis, Minnesota 55435 or from Children Are People, 493 Selby Avenue, St. Paul, Minnesota 55102.

Hipp, Earl, and Schmitz, Connie. (1988). *A Teacher's Guide to Fighting Invisible Tigers: A Course in Lifeskills Development for Students Grades 6–12.* Designed for use with *Fighting Invisible Tigers,* this guide offers a complete twelve-session course for teens on stress management and lifeskills. Recommended for chemical dependence counselors, prevention specialists, teachers, youth workers, mental health professionals, and other practitioners who work with children and adolescents. Order from: B.L. Winch & Associates, 45 Hitching Post Drive, Bldg. 25, Rolling Hills Estates, California 90274-4297.

Kids Are Special. A program that serves young children (ages four to seventeen) of alcoholic parents. A ten-week curriculum composed of small structured, closed groups and covering such topics as chemical dependency, family disease, feelings, defenses, problem solving, and specialness. Order from: Kids Are Special, 525 Race Street, San Jose, California 95126.

Lerner, Rokelle, and Naiditch, Barbara. *Children Are People Support Group Training.* A comprehensive guide with exercises, creative projects, and lesson plans needed to conduct support groups for children of alcoholics between ages five and twelve. Order from: Health Communications, 3201 S.W. 15th Street, Deerfield Beach, Florida 33442.

Making Friends, Making Choices. Fifty-three lesson plans, including thirty illustrated work sheets, are designed to promote students' decision making and interpersonal skills. Alcohol use and family alcoholism are explored in relation to self-concept, friendship, and decision making. Order from: Alcohol Education and Training Center, 520 Main Street, Waltham, Massachusetts 02154.

McDaniel, Sandy, and Bielen, Peggy. *Project Self-Esteem: A Parent Involvement Program for Elementary-Age Children.* A curriculum for guidance counselors and teachers showing how to implement activities that enhance self-esteem. Order from: B.L. Winch & Associates, 45 Hitching Post Drive, Bldg. 25, Rolling Hills Estates, California 90274-4297.

Paper People. A school-based substance abuse program for children in the primary grades. Paper People are paper bag puppets made and used by the children. The *Paper People* kit contains all the materials necessary to implement prevention programs for teachers, parents, and eight lessons for children. Order from: The Knopf Company, Inc., 1126 South Main Street, Plymouth, Michigan 48170.

Solberg, Melanie, Simpson, Dorothy, and Ferguson, Lorraine. *A Better Chance (ABC).* ABC provides educational and support services for children affected by someone else's chemical dependency and is recommended for grades four through eight. The fifteen-session format uses the twelve-step recovery philosophy in a child-appropriate manner and in a peer-group experience. The ABC kit includes a comprehensive manual and all materials needed to start a group and/or hold ABC training workshops. Order from: New Start Program, St. Joseph Hospital and Trauma Center, 172 Kinsley Street, Nashua, New Hampshire 03061.

Tainey, Phyllis. (1988). *Adult children of alcoholics.* This workshop model was developed to meet the needs of individuals who have grown up in alcoholic families and continue to be affected into adulthood by the experience. Order from: Family Service America, 11700 West Lake Park Drive, Milwaukee, Wisconsin 53224.

Professional Library

This section provides an extensive bibliography of selected readings for practitioners who wish to pursue their study on children of alcoholics in more detail. I have drawn the following bibliography from professional journals and subdivided it into four interest areas: research, treatment, education, and popular press. Additional citations can be found in the reference list at the end of this book.

Research

Beardslee, W.R., Son, L., & Vaillant, G.E. (1986). Exposure to parental alcoholism during childhood and outcome in adulthood: A prospective longitudinal study. *British Journal of Psychiatry, 149,* 584–591.

Black, C., Bucky, S.F., & Wilder-Padilla, S. (1986). The interpersonal and emotional consequences of being an adult child of an alcoholic. *The International Journal of the Addictions, 21,* 213–232.

Boham, M., Cloninger, R., Von Knorring, A.L., & Sigvardsson, S. (1984). An adoption study of somatoform disorders. *Archives of General Psychiatry, 41,* 872–878.

Bohman, M., Sigvardsson, S., & Cloninger, R. (1981). Maternal inheritance of alcohol abuse. *Archives of General Psychiatry, 38,* 965–969.

Brooks, K.F. (1983, September/October). Adult children of alcoholics . . . psychosocial stages of development. *Focus on Family,* 34–36.

Cadoret, R.J., Cain, C.A., & Grove, W.M. (1980). Development of alcoholism in adoptees raised apart from alcoholic biologic relatives. *Archives of General Psychiatry, 37,* 561–563.

Cadoret, R.J., & Gath, A. (1978). Inheritance of alcoholism in adoptees. *British Journal of Psychiatry, 132,* 252–258.

Cadoret, R.J., Troughton, E., & O'Gorman, T.W. (1987). Genetic and environmental factors in alcohol abuse and antisocial personality. *Journal of Studies on Alcohol, 48,* 1–8.

Callan, V.J., & Jackson, D. (1986). Children of alcoholic fathers and recovered alcoholic fathers: Personal and family functioning. *Journal of Studies on Alcohol, 47,* 180–181.

Clair, D., & Genest, M. (1987). Variables associated with the adjustment of offspring of alcoholic fathers. *Journal of Studies on Alcohol, 48,* 345–355.

Cloninger, R., Bohman, M., & Sigvardsson, S. (1981). Inheritance of alcohol abuse. *Archives of General Psychiatry, 38,* 861–868.

Cotton, N.S. (1979). The familial incidence of alcoholism: A review. *Journal of Studies on Alcohol, 40,* 89–1027.

Cutter, C.G., & Cutter, H.S. (1987). Experience and change in Al-Anon family groups: Adult children of alcoholics. *Journal of Studies on Alcohol, 48,* 29–32.

DiCicco, L., Davis, R., & Orenstein, A. (1984). Identifying the children of alcoholic parents from survey responses. *Journal of Alcohol and Drug Education, 30,* 1–17.

Donovan, J.M. (1986). An etiologic model of alcoholism. *American Journal of Psychiatry, 143,* 1–11.

El-Guebaly, N., & Offord, D.R. (1977). The offspring of alcoholics: A critical review. *The American Journal of Psychiatry, 134,* 357–365.

El-Guebaly, N., & Offord, D.R. (1979). On being the offspring of an alcoholic: An update. *Alcoholism: Clinical and Experimental Research, 3,* 148–157.

Ervin, C.S., Little, R.E., Streissguth, A.P., & Beck, D.E. (1984). Alcoholic fathering and its relation to child's intellectual development: A pilot investigation. *Alcoholism: Clinical and Experimental Research, 8,* 362–365.

Famularo, R., Stone, K., Barnum, R., & Wharton, R. (1986). Alcoholism and severe child maltreatment. *American Journal of Orthopsychiatry, 56,* 481–485.

Frances, R.J., Timm, S., & Bucky, S. (1980). Studies of familial and non-familial alcoholism. *Archives of General Psychiatry, 37,* 564–566.

Goodwin, D.W. (1985). Alcoholism and genetics: The sins of the fathers. *Archives of General Psychiatry, 42,* 171–174.

Goodwin, D.W., Schulsinger, F., Knop, J., Mednick, S., & Guze, S.B. (1977). Alcoholism and depression in adopted-out daughters of alcoholics. *Archives of General Psychiatry, 34,* 751–755.

Goodwin, D.W., Schulsinger, M.D., Knop, J., Mednick, S., & Guze, S.B. (1977). Psychopathology in adopted and nonadopted daughters of alcoholics. *Archives of General Psychiatry, 34,* 1005–1009.

Haberman, P.W. (1966). Childhood symptoms in children of alcoholics and comparison group parents. *Journal of Marriage and the Family, 28,* 152–154.

Hegedus, A.M., Alterman, A.I., & Tarter, R.E. (1984). Learning achievement in sons of alcoholics. *Alcoholism: Clinical and Experimental Research, 8,* 330–333.

Hennecke, L. (1984). Stimulus augmenting and field dependence in children of alcoholic fathers. *Journal of Studies on Alcohol, 45,* 486–492.

Hughes, J.M. (1977). Adolescent children of alcoholic parents and the relationship of Alateen to these children. *Journal of Consulting and Clinical Psychology, 45,* 946–947.

Jacob, T., Favorini, A., Meisel, S.S., & Anderson, C.M. (1978). The alcoholic's spouse, children and family interactions: Substantive findings and methodological issues. *Journal of Studies on Alcohol, 39,* 1231–1251.

Jones-Saumty, D.L., Parsons, O.A., & Fabian, M.S. (1980). Familial alcoholism, drinking behavior, and neuropsychological performance in alcoholic women. *Alcohol Technical Reports, 9,* 29–34.

Kammeier, M.L. (1971). Adolescents from families with and without alcohol problems. *Quarterly Journal on the Study of Alcohol, 32,* 364–372.

Keltner, N.L., McIntyre, C.W., & Gee, R. (1986). Birth order effects in second-generation alcoholics. *Journal of Studies on Alcohol, 47,* 495–497.

Kern, J.C., Hassett, C.A., Collipp, P.J., Bridges, C., Solomon, M., & Condren, R.J. (1981). Children of alcoholics: Locus of control, mental age, and zinc level. *Journal of Psychiatric Treatment and Evaluation, 3,* 169–173.

Klinge, V. (1983). A comparison of parental and adolescent MMPIs as related to substance use. *The International Journal of the Addictions, 18,* 1179–1185.

Kroll, P.D., Stock, D.F., & James, M.E. (1985). The behavior of adult alcoholic men abused as children. *Journal of Nervous and Mental Disease, 173,* 689–693.

Knop, J., Teasdale, T.W., Schulsinger, F., & Goodwin, D.W. (1985). A prospective study of young men at high risk for alcoholism: School behavior and achievement. *Journal of Studies on Alcohol, 46,* 273–277.

Kosten, T.R., Rounsaville, B.J., & Kleber, H.D. (1985). Parental alcoholism in opioid addicts. *The Journal of Nervous and Mental Disease, 173,* 461–468.

Krauthamer, C. (1979). Maternal attitudes of alcoholic and nonalcoholic upper middle class women. *The International Journal of the Addictions, 14,* 639–644.

Kritsberg, W. (1984, November/December). Chronic shock and emotional numbness in adult children of alcoholics. *Focus on Family,* 24–25, 40.

Marcus, A. (1986). Academic achievement in elementary school children of alcoholic mothers. *Journal of Clinical Psychology, 42,* 372–376.

McKenna, T., & Pickens, R. (1983). Personality characteristics of alcoholic children of alcoholics. *Journal of Studies on Alcohol, 44,* 688–700.

McKenna, T., & Pickens, R. (1981). Alcoholic children of alcoholics. *Journal of Studies on Alcohol, 42,* 1021–1029.

Merikangas, K.R., Weissman, M.M., Prusoff, B.A., Pauls, D.L., & Leckman, J.F. (1985). Depressives with secondary alcoholism: Psychiatric disorders in offspring. *Journal of Studies on Alcohol, 46,* 199–204.

Miller, D., & Jang, M. (1977). Children of alcoholics: A twenty-year longitudinal study. *Social Work Research and Abstracts, 13,* 23–29.

Moos, R.H., & Billings, A.G. (1982). Children of alcoholics during the recovery process: Alcoholic and matched control families. *Addictive Behaviors, 7,* 155–163.

Nardi, P.M. (1987). Power and control in families of alcoholism. *Journal of Alcohol and Drug Education, 32,* 14–18.

Parker, D.A., & Harford, T.C. (1987). Alcohol-related problems of children of heavy-drinking parents. *Journal of Studies on Alcohol, 48,* 265–268.

Penick, E.C., Powell, B.J., Bingham, S.F., Liskow, B., Miller, N.S., & Read, M.R. (1987). A comparative study of familial alcoholism. *Journal of Studies on Alcohol, 48,* 136–146.

Pilat, J.M., & Jones, J.W. (1985). Identification of children of alcoholics: Two empirical studies. *Alcohol Health and Research World, 9,* 27–33.

Prewett, M.J., & Spence, R. (1981). Attribution of causality by children with alcoholic parents. *The International Journal of the Addictions, 16,* 367–370.

Rimmer, J. (1982). The children of alcoholics: An exploratory study. *Children and Youth Services Review, 4,* 365–373.

Schaeffer, K.W., Parsons, O.A., & Yohman, J.R. (1984). Neuropsychological differences between male familial and nonfamilial alcoholics and nonalcoholics. *Alcoholism: Clinical and Experimental Research, 8,* 347–351.

Schuckit, M.A., Goodwin, D., & Winokur, G. (1972). A study of alcoholism in half siblings. *American Journal of Psychiatry, 128,* 1132–1136.

Schuckit, M.A. (1984). Relationship between the course of primary alcoholism in men and family history. *Journal of Studies on Alcohol, 45,* 334–338.

Schuckit, M.A. (1984). Subjective responses to alcohol in sons of alcoholics and control subjects. *Archives of General Psychiatry, 41,* 879–884.

Schulsinger, F., Knop, J., Goodwin, D.W., Teasdale, T.W., & Mikkelsen, U. (1986). A prospective study of young men at high risk of alcoholism. *Archives of General Psychiatry, 43,* 755–760.

Steinhausen, H.C., Gobel, D., & Nestler, V. (1984). Psychopathology in the offspring of alcoholic parents. *Journal of the American Academy of Child Psychiatry, 23,* 465–471.

Steinhausen, H.C., Nestler, V., & Huth, H. (1982). Psychopathology and mental functions in the offspring of alcoholic and epileptic mothers. *Journal of the American Academy of Child Psychiatry, 21,* 268–273.

Tabakoff, B., Hoffman, P.L., Lee, J.M., Saito, T., Willard, B., & Leon-Jones, F. (1988). Differences in platelet enzyme activity between alcoholics and nonalcoholics. *New England Journal of Medicine, 318,* 134–139.

Tarter, E. (1987). Vulnerability to abuse. *Journal of Drug Issues, 17,* 69–71.

Tarter, E., Hegedus, A.M., Goldstein, G., Shelly, C., & Alterman, A.I. (1984). Adolescent sons of alcoholics: Neuropsychological and personality characteristics. *Alcoholism: Clinical and Experimental Research, 8,* 216–222.

Tarter, R.E., Hegedus, A.M., & Gavaler, J.S. (1985). Hyperactivity in sons of alcoholics. *Journal of Studies on Alcohol, 46,* 259–261.

Tittmar, H.G. (1982). Some problems inherent in natal alcoholism. *Journal of Psychiatric Treatment and Evaluation, 4,* 165–171.

Udayakumar, G.S., Mohan, A., Shariff, I.A., Sekar, K., & Eswari, C. (1984). Children of the alcoholic parent. *Child Psychiatry Quarterly, 17,* 9–14.

Utne, H.E., Hansen, F.V., Winkler, K., & Schulsinger, F. (1977). Alcohol elimination rates in adoptees with and without alcohol parents. *Journal of Studies on Alcohol, 38,* 1219–1223.

Venugopal, M. (1985). Emotional problems of the children of alcoholic fathers. *Child Psychiatry Quarterly, 18,* 114–117.

Werner, E.E. (1986). Resilient offspring of alcoholics: A longitudinal study from birth to age eighteen. *Journal of Studies on Alcohol, 47,* 34–40.

West, M.O., & Prinz, R.J. (1987). Parental alcoholism and childhood psychopathology. *Psychological Bulletin, 102,* 204–218.

Wilson, C., & Mulhall, D.J. (1983). Describing relationships in families with alcohol problems. *British Journal of Addiction, 78,* 181–191.

Wilson, C., & Orford, J. (1978). Children of alcoholics: Report of a preliminary study and comments on the literature. *Journal of Studies on Alcohol, 39,* 121–142.

Wolin, S.J., Bennett, L.A., Noonan, D.L., & Teitelbaum, M.A. (1980). Disrupted family rituals: A factor in the intergenerational transmission of alcoholism. *Journal of Studies on Alcohol, 41,* 199–214.

Workman-Davis, K.L., & Hesselbrock, V.M. (1987). Childhood problem behavior and neuropsychological functioning in persons at risk for alcoholism. *Journal of Studies on Alcohol, 48,* 187–192.

Treatment

Adler, R., & Raphael, B. (1983). Children of alcoholics. *Australian and New Zealand Journal of Psychiatry, 17,* 3–8.

Bingham, A., & Bargar, J. (1985). Children of alcoholic families. *Journal of Psychosocial Nursing, 23,* 13–15.

Black, C. (1979). Children of alcoholics. *Alcohol Health and Research World,* (Fall), 23–27.

Cermak, T.L., & Brown, S. (1982). Interactional group therapy with the adult children of alcoholics. *International Journal of Group Psychotherapy, 32,* 375–388.

Chafetz, M.E., Blane, H.T., & Hill, M.J. (1971). Children of alcoholics: Observations in a child guidance clinic. *Quarterly Journal of Studies on Alcoholism, 32,* 687–698.

Davis, R.B., Johnston, P.D., DiCicco, L., & Orenstein, A. (1985). Helping children of alcoholic parents: An elementary school program. *The School Counselor, 33,* 357–363.

Deckman, J., & Downs, B. (1982). A group treatment approach for adolescent children of alcoholic parents. *Social Work with Groups, 5,* 73–77.

DiCicco, L., Davis, R.B., Hogan, J., MacLean, A., & Orenstein, A. (1984). Group experiences for children of alcoholics. *Alcohol Health and Research World, 8,* 20–24.

Einstein, S. (1980). Project outreach: An experimental support system intervention program. *The International Journal of the Addictions, 15,* 1–37.

Goodman, R.W. (1987). Adult children of alcoholics. *Journal of Counseling and Development, 66,* 162–163.

Hawley, N.P., & Brown, E.L. (1981). The use of group treatment with children of alcoholics. *Social Casework: The Journal of Contemporary Social Work, 62,* 40–46.

Hecht, M. (1973). Children of alcoholics are children at risk. *American Journal of Nursing, 73,* 1764–1767.

Hecht, M. (1977). A cooperative approach toward children from alcoholic families. *Elementary School Guidance and Counseling, 11,* 197–203.

Held, B.S., & Heller, L. (1982). Symptom prescription as metaphor: A systemic approach to the psychosomatic-alcoholic family. *Family Therapy, 9,* 133–145.

Heller, K., Sher, K.J., & Benson, C.S. (1982). Problems associated with risk overprediction in studies of offspring of alcoholics: Implications for prevention. *Clinical Psychology Review, 2,* 183–200.

Manning, D.T. (1987). Books as therapy for children of alcoholics. *Child Welfare, 66,* 35–41.

MacDonald, D.I., & Blume, S.B. (1986). Children of alcoholics. *American Journal of Diseases of Children, 140,* 750–754.

McElligatt, K. (1986). Identifying and treating children of alcoholic parents. *Social Work in Education, 9,* 55–69.

Miller, N. (1983). Group psychotherapy in school setting for adolescent children of alcoholics. *Group, 7,* 34–40.

Morehouse, E.R. (1979). Working in the schools with children of alcoholic parents. *Health and Social Work, 4,* 145–162.

Morehouse, E.R. (1986). Counseling adolescent children of alcoholics in groups. In R.J. Ackerman (Ed.). *Growing in the shadow.* Pompano Beach, Florida: Health Communications.

Owen, S.M., Rosenberg, J., & Barkley, D. (1985). Bottled-up children: A group treatment approach for children of alcoholics. *Group, 9,* 31–42.

Perrin, T.W. (1985, November/December). Recovery skills for COAs: The care and management of flashbacks. *Alcoholism and Addiction, 15.*

Perrin, T.W. (1986, January/February). Charity being formed to aid children of moms in treatment. *Alcoholism and Addiction, 49.*

Priest, K. (1985). Adolescents' response to parents' alcoholism. *Social casework: Journal of Contemporary Social Work, 66,* 533–539.

Regan, J.M., Connors, G.J., O'Farrell, T.J., & Wyatt, C.J. (1983). Services for the families of alcoholics: A survey of treatment agencies in Massachusetts. *Journal of Studies on Alcohol, 44,* 1072–1075.

Richards, T.M. (1979). Splitting as a defense mechanism in children of alcoholic parents. *Currents in Alcoholism, 7,* 239–244.

Sloboda, S.B. (1974). The children of alcoholics: A neglected problem. *Hospital and Community Psychiatry, 25,* 605–606.

Steinglass, P. (1980). A life history model of the alcoholic family. *Family Process, 19,* 211–226.

Triplett, J.L., & Arneson, S.W. (1983). Working with children of alcoholics. *Pediatric Nursing, 5,* 317–320.

Wanck, B. (1985, September). Treatment of adult children of alcoholics. *Carrier Foundation Letter,* 1–6.

Whitfield, C.L. (1980). Children of alcoholics: Treatment issues. *Maryland State Medical Journal, 29,* 86–91.

Education

Black, C. (1986). Alcoholism and family violence. *Alcoholism and Addiction Magazine,* January-February, 46–47.

Bowles, C. (1968). Children of alcoholic parents. *American Journal of Nursing, 68,* 1062–1064.

Brisbane, F.L. (1985). Using contemporary fiction with black children and adolescents in alcoholism treatment. *Alcoholism Treatment Quarterly, 2,* 179–197.

Brooks, K.F. (1983, September/October). Adult children of alcoholics: Psychosocial stages of development. *Focus on Family,* 34–36.

Campbell, J.D. (1988). Children of alcoholics: The silent victims. *Learning Magazine, 16,* 45–48.

DiCicco, L., Deutsch, C., Levine, G., Mills, D., & Unterberger, H. (1977, July/August). A school-community approach to alcohol education. *Health Education, 4,* 11–13.

Donovan, B.E. (1981). A collegiate group for the sons and daughters of alcoholics. *Journal of the American College Health Association, 30,* 83–86.

Enzer, C.H. (1986). The children of alcoholic parents. *The Ohio State Medical Journal, 82,* 519.

Eve, S.I. (1985). Takin' care of business and family. *Focus on Family* (November/December), 24–25.

Fassler, D.G. (1987). Children's books about alcoholism. *Childhood Education, 55,* 188–194.

Gress, J.R. (1988). Alcoholism's hidden curriculum. *Educational Leadership, 45,* 18–19.

Hindman, M. (1975–76). Children of alcoholic parents. *Alcohol Health and Research World* (Winter), 2–6.

Kritsberg, W. (1984, November/December). Chronic shock and emotional numbness in adult children of alcoholics. *Focus on Family*, 24–25, 40.

Manning, D.T. (1987). Books as therapy for children of alcoholics. *Child Welfare, 66*, 35–43.

McAndrew, J.A. (1985). Children of alcoholics, school intervention. *Childhood Education, 61*, 343–345.

Nardi, P.M. (1981). Children of alcoholics: A role-theoretical perspective. *Journal of Social Psychology, 115*, 237–245.

National Institute on Alcohol Abuse. (1986). Helping children from alcoholic families: Approaches and caregivers. *Children Today, 15*, 13–16.

Newlon, B.J., & Furrow, W.V. (1986). Using the classroom to identify children from alcoholic homes. *The School Counselor, 33*, 286–291.

Robinson, B.E. (1988/June-July). Wearing mommy's apron, filling daddy's shoes. Children of alcoholic parents: Latchkey kids by default. *Focus on Chemically Dependent Families, 11*, 22–23, 39.

Robinson, B.E. (1989). Identifying preschool children of alcoholic parents. *Alcohol Health and Research World.*

Robinson, B.E. (1989). The teacher's role in working with children of alcoholic parents. *Young Children, 44.*

Schall, J. (1986). Alcoholism: When a parent drinks a child struggles. *Instructor, XLV*, 54–57.

Triplett, J.L., & Arneson, S.W. (1978). Children of alcoholic parents: A neglected issue. *Journal of School Health, 48*, 596–599.

Triplett, J.L., & Arneson, S.W. (1986). Coping with parental alcoholism. *ACEI Exchange Newsletter, 54*, 1.

Waters, F.E., & Twaite, J.A. (1986). Test your COA quotient. *Changes, 1*, 14–19.

Weddle, C.D., & Wishon, P.M. (1986). Children of alcoholics: What we should know; how we can help. *Children Today, 15*, 8–12.

Woodside, M. (1986). Children of alcoholics: Breaking the cycle. *Journal of School Health, 56*, 448–449.

Woodside, M. (1983). Children of alcoholic parents: Inherited and psychosocial influences. *Journal of Psychiatric Treatment and Evaluation, 5*, 531–537.

Popular Press

Hibsch, Marcia, & Gage, Diane. (1984, October). Emotional hangover: Growing up with an alcoholic parent. *McCall's Magazine*, 161–162.

Jaworski, Margaret. (1986, April 15). Bitter legacy: Growing up with alcoholism. *Family Circle,* 18–20.

Lake, A. (1986, September). Living under the influence. *Redbook,* 138–140, 178–181.

Leerhsen, Charles. (1988, January 18). Alcohol and the family: Growing up with alcoholic parents can leave scars for life. *Newsweek Magazine,* 62–68.

Marks, Jane. (1986, March). The children of alcoholics. *Parents Magazine,* 104–108, 194–198.

Rozen, Leah, & Bonnie Johnson. (1988, April 18). Breaking the bonds of silence: Children of alcoholics. *People Magazine, 29,* 100–110.

Stark, Elizabeth. (1986). Forgotten victims: Children of alcoholics. *Psychology Today, 21,* 58–62.

Strong, Maggie. (1986, March). Children of the bottle. *Glamour,* 84–87.

Vernon, Jodi. (1985, April). Children of alcoholics. *Kiwanis Magazine,* 34–36.

Appendix
Answers to the COAT

Y ou should know the answers to most of these questions if you have finished reading the book. But in case you couldn't wait and peeked before reading the chapters, all the statements are myths about children of alcoholics and thus all the answers are false. The accurate version of each statement is written below beside the number corresponding to the myth that it debunks.

1. There are 28 million children of alcoholics in the United States—7 million of whom are under eighteen years of age.

2. Without help, children of alcoholics carry low self-esteem, anxiety, depression, compulsive need to control, and inability to establish and maintain trusting and intimate relationships into adulthood.

3. One of the biggest myths is that once alcoholic parents stop drinking, their children will readjust automatically. But children need treatment of their own to deal with the dysfunctional behavior patterns that have already developed.

4. As adults, children of alcoholics are at high risk for being alcoholics, workaholics, compulsive eaters, gamblers, spenders, and sex and drug addicts.

5. Children cannot control or cure their parents' alcoholism. Their best approach is to get help for themselves and to take responsibility for their own behaviors, but not to take on someone else's responsibilities, especially when it could enable that person's drinking.

6. While there are common patterns, all children are affected by alcoholism differently. Birth order, sex of child, sex of alcoholic parent, age of child, socioeconomic status, whether both parents drink, and whether the parent is in recovery or still drinking are all factors that determine child outcomes.

7. Children often feel guilty and blame themselves for their parents' drinking and think they can get them to stop if they try hard enough.

8. Parental inconsistency and unpredictability are hallmarks of alcoholism that propel children into a cyclone of confusion and anxiety.

9. Compared to nonalcoholic homes, more dysfunction occurs in alcoholic homes, characterized by conflict, deception, lies, mixed messages, poor cohesion, disruption, and violence.

10. Children of alcoholics tend to isolate themselves from their peers, have few friends, and have difficulty trusting others as well as forming intimate and lasting relationships.

11. Alcoholism plays a significant role in 90 percent of the reported child abuse cases.

12. Children of alcoholics have lower grades and lower scores on standardized achievement tests than children of nonalcoholics.

13. Children learn very early to deny to themselves and others that a parent has a drinking problem. Even when they know, they try to hide it and keep it a secret.

14. Things *are* as bad as they seem, maybe worse. The most damaging thing an adult can do to a child of an alcoholic is to minimize or deny that child's perception of the experience.

15. It is difficult but not impossible to identify preschool children of alcoholics. Astute professional observations of daily routines, playtime, emotional adjustment, and parent-child relationships can yield a pattern of possible alcohol-related problems.

16. An estimated 95 percent of children of alcoholics pass through elementary and high schools and are never identified or treated. The majority of these children do not show any negative outward signs of alcoholism and, in fact, function competently while hiding their pain inside.

17. A higher concentration of adult children of alcoholics is found in the helping professions and the field of alcoholism than in any other occupational group.

18. Most alcohol treatment programs in the United States have focused their attention on the alcoholic and spouse and have involved the children only in relation to the alcoholic's recovery.

19. Alcoholism runs in families. Despite the torment they encounter when young, adult children are four times more likely to become alcoholics than children from sober homes, and they frequently marry someone who becomes alcoholic.

20. Practitioners are as powerless over alcohol as the parents. Neither they nor the children can control the parent's drinking. Still, teachers,

counselors, social workers, the clergy and others can help children of alcoholics, simply by being supportive of the child, validating their perceptions and feelings, and providing them with healthy experiences and relationships.

Computing and Interpreting Your COAT Score

Give yourself 5 points for each statement you checked as false. The higher your COAT score, the more you know about children of alcoholics. The lower your score, the less you know about them. The following key will help you interpret your score:

A score from 0 to 30 —You are **uninformed** about children of alcoholics. Read the book, if you haven't already. If you have, read it again.

A score from 35 to 65 —You are **moderately informed** about children of alcoholics, but you missed a lot, too. Read back over the major highlights of the book.

A score from 70 to 100 —You are very **informed** about children of alcoholics. Either you were already trained in chemical dependence or you learned a lot from reading this book. Pass the book on to a friend.

References

Ackerman, R. (1983). *Children of alcoholics: A guidebook for educators, thera-pists, and parents* (2nd Ed.). Holmes Beach, Florida: Learning Publications.
———. (1987). *Same house, different homes: Why adult children of alcoholics are not all the same.* Pompano Beach, Florida: Health Communications.

Adler, R., & Raphael, B. (1983). Children of alcoholics. *Australian and New Zealand Journal of Psychiatry, 17,* 3–8.

Ainsworth, M.D., Blehar, M.C., Waters, E., & Wall, S. (1978). *Patterns of attachment: A psychological study of the strange situation.* Hillsdale, New Jersey: Erlbaum.

Anthony, E.J. (1978). A new scientific region to explore. In E. J. Anthony C. Koupernik, & C. Chiland (Eds.) *The child and his family: Vulnerable children,* Vol. 4. New York: Wiley.

Aronson, H., & Gilbert, A. (1963). Preadolescent sons of male alcoholics. *Archives of General Psychiatry, 8,* 47–53.

Aronson, M., Kyllerman, M., Sable, K.G., Sandin, B., & Olegard, R. (1985). Children of alcoholic mothers: Developmental, perceptual and behavioral characteristics as compared to matched controls. *Acta Paediatrica Scandanavia, 74,* 27–35.

Barnard, C.P., & Spoentgen, P.A. (1987). *Alcoholism Treatment Quarterly, 3,* 47–65.

Baumrind, D. (1967). Child care practices anteceding three patterns of preschool behavior. *Genetic Psychology Monographs, 75,* 43–48.

Beardslee, W.R., Son, L., & Vaillant, G.E. (1986). Exposure to parental alcoholism during childhood and outcome in adulthood: A prospective longitudinal study. *British Journal of Psychiatry, 149,* 584–591.

Begleiter, H., Porjesz, B., & Bihari, B. (1984). Event-related brain potentials in boys at risk for alcoholism. *Science, 225,* 1493–1496.

Bell, B., & Cohen, R. (1981). The Bristol Social Adjustment Guide: Comparison between the offspring of alcoholic and nonalcoholic mothers. *British Journal of Clinical Psychology, 20,* 93–95.

Bepko, C., & Krestan, J.A. (1985). *The responsibility trap: A blueprint for treat-ing the alcoholic family.* New York: The Free Press.

Biek, J. (1981). Screening test for identifying adolescents adversely affected by a parental drinking problem. *Journal of Adolescent Health Care, 2,* 107–113.

Bingham, A., & Bargar, J. (1985). Children of alcoholic families. *Journal of Psychosocial Nursing, 23*, 13–15.

Black, C. (1987, November 10–11). Young and adult children of alcoholics. Seminar presented by the Randolph Clinic. Charlotte, North Carolina.

———. (1986). Alcoholism and family violence. *Alcoholism and Addiction Magazine.* (Jan.–Feb.), 46–47.

———. (1982). *It will never happen to me!* Denver, Colorado: MAC Publications.

———. (1979). Children of alcoholics. *Alcohol Health and Research World* (Fall). 23–27.

Black, C., Bucky, S.F., & Wilder-Padilla, S. (1986). The interpersonal and emotional consequences of being an adult child of an alcoholic. *The International Journal of Addictions, 21*, 213–232.

Bly, R. (1987). In Rachel V. (Ed.) *Family secrets.* New York: Harper & Row.

Bohman, M. (1978). Some genetic aspects of alcoholism and criminality: A population of adoptees. *Archives of General Psychiatry, 35*, 269–276.

Bohman, M., Cloninger, R., Von Knorring, A.L., & Sigvardsson, S. (1984). An adoption study of somatoform disorders. *Archives of General Psychiatry, 41*, 872–878.

Bohman, M., Sigvardsson, S., & Cloninger, R. (1981). Maternal inheritance of alcohol abuse. *Archives of General Psychiatry, 38*, 965–969.

Booz-Allen & Hamilton, Inc. (1974). *Final report on the needs of and resources for children of alcoholic parents.* Rockville, Maryland: National Institute on Alcohol Abuse and Alcoholism, Alcohol, Drug Abuse, and Mental Health Administration, U.S. Department of Health and Human Services.

Bosma, W. (1972). Alcoholism and the family: A hidden tragedy. *Maryland State Medical Journal, 21*, 34–36.

Bowles, C. (1968). Children of alcoholic parents. *American Journal of Nursing, 68*, 1062–1064.

Brenner, A. (1984). *Helping children cope with stress.* Lexington, Massachusetts: Lexington Books.

Brisbane, F.L. (1985). Using contemporary fiction with black children and adolescents in alcoholism treatment. *Alcoholism Treatment Quarterly, 2*, 179–197.

Brooks, C. (1987). Listening to the children. *Professional Counselor, 1*, 10.

Brooks, K.F. (1983, September/October). Adult children of alcoholics: Psychosocial stages of development. *Focus on Family*, 34–36.

Burnett, C. (1986). *One more time.* New York: Random House.

Cadoret, A.J., Cain, C.A., & Grove, W.M. (1980). Development of alcoholism in adoptees raised apart from alcoholic biologic relatives. *Archives of General Psychiatry, 37*, 561–563.

Cadoret, R.J., & Gath, A. (1978). Inheritance of alcoholism in adoptees. *British Journal of Psychiatry, 132*, 252–258.

Cadoret, R.J., Troughton, E., & O'Gorman, T.W. (1987). Genetic and environmental factors in alcohol abuse and antisocial personality. *Journal of Studies on Alcohol, 48*, 1–8.

Callan, V.J., & Jackson, D. (1986). Children of alcoholic fathers and recovered alcoholic fathers: Personal and family functioning. *Journal of Studies on Alcohol, 47*, 180–182.

Cermak, T.L. & Brown, S. (1982). Interactional group therapy with the adult children of alcoholics. *International Journal of Group Psychotherapy, 32,* 375–388.

Cermak, T.L. (1985). *A primer on adult children of alcoholics.* Pompano Beach, Florida: Health Communications.

Chafetz, M.E., Blane, H.T., & Hill, M.J. (1971). Children of alcoholics: Observations in a child guidance clinic. *Quarterly Journal of Studies on Alcohol, 32,* 687–698.

Clair, D., & Genest, M. (1987). Variables associated with the adjustment of offspring of alcoholic fathers. *Journal of Studies on Alcohol, 48,* 345–355.

Cloninger, R., Bohman, M., & Sigvardsson, S. (1981). Inheritance of alcohol abuse. *Archives of General Psychiatry, 38,* 861–868.

Cloninger, R., Bohman, M., Sigvardsson, S., & Knorring, A. (1984). In M. Galanter (Ed.) *Recent developments in alcoholism.* Vol. 3. New York: Plenum Press. 37–51.

Cork, M. (1969). *The forgotten children.* Ontario, Canada: General Publishing Company.

Cotton, N.S. (1979). The familial incidence of alcoholism: A review. *Journal of Studies on Alcohol, 40,* 89–1027.

Cramer, P.A. (1977). An educational strategy to impact the children of alcoholic parents: A feasibility report. Arlington, Virginia: National Center for Alcohol Education. ERIC Publications. ED 199 190.

Crews, H. (1983). *A childhood: The biography of a place.* New York: Morrow.

Cutter, C.G., & Cutter, H.S. (1987). Experience and change in Al-Anon family groups: Adult children of alcoholics. *Journal of Studies on Alcohol, 48,* 29–32.

Davis, R.B., Johnston, P.D., DiCicco, L., & Orenstein, A. (1985). Helping children of alcoholic parents: An elementary school program. *The School Counselor, 33,* 357–363.

Davis, T.S., Shanahan, P., Majchrzak, S.M., & Hagood, L. (1976, September). Recovery for the alcoholic mother and family through home-based intervention. Paper presented at the Annual Conference of the American Psychological Association, Washington, D.C.

Deckman, J., & Downs, B. (1982). A group treatment approach for adolescent children of alcoholic parents. *Social Work with Groups, 5,* 73–77.

Deutsch, C. (1982). *Broken bottles, broken dreams: Understanding and helping the children of alcoholics.* New York: Teachers College Press.

DiCicco, L., Davis, R.B., Hogan, J., MacLean, A., & Orenstein, A. (1984). Group experiences for children of alcoholics. *Alcohol Health and Research World, 8,* 20–24.

DiCicco, L., Davis, R., & Orenstein, A. (1984). Identifying the children of alcoholic parents from survey responses. *Journal of Alcohol and Drug Education, 30,* 1–17.

DiCicco, L., Deutsch, C., Levine, G., Mills, D., & Unterberger, H. (1977, July–August). A school-community approach to alcohol education. *Health Education, 4,* 11–13.

DiCicco, L. (1981). Children of alcoholic parents: Issues in identification. *Research Monograph-4, Services for children of alcoholics.* DDJS Publication No. (ADM) 81-1007. Washington, D.C.: U.S. Printing Office.

Donovan, J.M. (1986). An etiologic model of alcoholism. *American Journal of Psychiatry, 143,* 1–11.

Donovan, B.E. (1981). A collegiate group for the sons and daughters of alcoholics. *Journal of the American College Health Association, 30,* 83–86.

Einstein, S. (1980). Project outreach: An experimental support system intervention program. *The International Journal of the Addictions, 15,* 1–37.

El-Guebaly, N., & Offord, D.R. (1977). The offspring of alcoholics: A critical review. *American Journal of Psychiatry, 134,* 357–365.

———. (1979). On being the offspring of an alcoholic: An update. *Alcoholism: Clinical and Experimental Research, 3,* 148–157.

El-Guebaly, N. (1983). The offspring of alcoholics: Outcome predictors. In M. Frank (Ed.). *Children of exceptional parents.* New York: Haworth Press. 3–12.

Elkind, D. (1981). *The hurried child.* Reading, Massachusetts: Addison-Wesley.

Enzer, C.H. (1986). The children of alcoholic parents. *The Ohio State Medical Journal, 82,* 519.

Erikson, E.H. (1963). *Childhood and society* (2nd Ed.). New York: Norton.

Ervin, C.S., Little, R.E., Streissguth, A.P., & Beck, D.E. (1984). Alcoholic fathering and its relation to child's intellectual development: A pilot investigation. *Alcoholism: Clinical and Experimental Research, 8,* 362–365.

Famularo, R., Stone, K., Barnum, R., & Wharton, R. (1986). Alcoholism and severe child maltreatment. *American Journal of Orthopsychiatry, 56,* 481–485.

Fassler, D.G. (1987). Children's books about alcoholism. *Childhood Education, 66,* 188–194.

Fine, E.W., Yudin, L.W., Holmes, J., & Heinemann, S. (1976). Behavioral disorders in children with parental alcoholism. *New York Academy of Sciences Annals, 273,* 507–517.

Flake-Hobson, C., Robinson, B.E., & Skeen, P. (1983). *Child development and relationships.* New York: Random House.

Frances, R.J., Timm, S., & Bucky, S. (1980). Studies of familial and nonfamilial alcoholism. *Archives of General Psychiatry, 37,* 564–566.

Gabrielli, W., Mednick, S., Volavka, J., Pollolk, V., Schulsinger, F., & Itil, T. (1982). Electroencephalagram in children of alcoholic fathers, *Psychophysiology, 19,* 404–407.

Gabrielli, W., & Mednick, S. (1983). Intellectual performance in children of alcoholics. *Journal of Nervous and Mental Disease, 171,* 444–447.

Goodman, R.W. (1987). Adult children of alcoholics. *Journal of Counseling and Development, 66,* 162–163.

Goodwin, D.W. (1985). Alcoholism and genetics: The sins of the fathers. *Archives of General Psychiatry, 42,* 171–174.

Goodwin, D.W., Schulsinger, F., Knop, J., Mednick, S., & Guze, S.B. (1977). Alcoholism and depression in adopted-out daughters of alcoholics. *Archives of General Psychiatry, 34,* 751–755.

———. (1977). Psychopathology in adopted and nonadopted daughters of alcoholics. *Archives of General Psychiatry, 34,* 1005–1009.

Goodwin, D.W., Schulsinger, F., Moller, N., Hermansen, L., Winokur, G., & Guze, S.B. (1974). Drinking problems in adopted and nonadopted sons of alcoholics. *Archives of General Psychiatry, 31,* 164–169.

Goodwin, D.W., Schulsinger, F., Hermansen, L., Guze, S.B., & Winokur, G.

(1973). Alcohol problems in adoptees raised apart from alcoholic biological parents. *Archives of General Psychiatry, 28,* 238–242.

Gravitz, H. (1985). *Children of alcoholics handbook: Who they are, what they experience, how they recover.* South Laguna, California: The National Association for Children of Alcoholics.

Haberman, P.W. (1966). Childhood symptoms in children of alcoholics and comparison group parents. *Journal of Marriage and the Family, 28,* 152–154.

Hafen, B.Q., & Frandsen, K.J. (1986). *Youth suicide: Depression and loneliness.* Evergreen, Colorado: Cordillera Press.

Hammond, M. (1985). *Children of alcoholics in play therapy.* Pompano Beach, Florida: Health Publications.

Hastings, J., & Typpo, M. (1984). *An elephant in the living room.* Minneapolis, Minnesota: Comp Care.

Hawley, N.P., & Brown, E.L. (1981). The use of group treatment with children of alcoholics. *Social Casework: The Journal of Contemporary Social Work, 62,* 40–46.

Hecht, M. (1973). Children of alcoholics are children at risk. *American Journal of Nursing, 73,* 1764–1767.

Hegedus, A.M., Alterman, A.I., & Tarter, R.E. (1984). Learning achievement in sons of alcoholics. *Alcoholism: Clinical and Experimental Research, 8,* 330–333.

Held, B.S., & Heller, L. (1982). Symptom prescription as metaphor: A systemic approach to the psychosomatic-alcoholic family. *Family Therapy, 9,* 133–145.

Heller, K., Sher, K.J., & Benson, C.S. (1982). Problems associated with risk overprediction in studies of offspring of alcoholics: Implications for prevention. *Clinical Psychology Review, 2,* 183–200.

Hemingway, M. (1988, February 8). Quoted by Kristin McMurran. Not the vintage Margaux. *People Magazine,* 95–105.

Hennecke, L. (1984). Stimulus augmenting and field dependence in children of alcoholic fathers. *Journal of Studies on Alcohol, 45,* 486–492.

Hesselbrock, V.M., Stabenau, J.R., & Hesselbrock, M.N. (1984). In M. Galanter (Ed.) *Recent developments in alcoholism.* Vol. 3. New York: Plenum Press. 65–82.

Hindman, M. (1976). Children of alcoholic parents. *Alcohol Health and Research World* (Winter), 2–6.

Holzman, I.R. (1983). Fetal alcohol syndrome (FAS): A review. In M. Frank (Ed.) *Children of exceptional parents.* New York: Haworth Press. 13–19.

Hrubec, Z., & Omenn, G.S. (1981). Evidence of genetic predisposition to alcoholic cirrhosis and psychosis: Twin concordances for alcoholism and its biological end points by zygosity among male veterans. *Alcoholism: Clinical and Experimental Research, 5,* 207–215.

Hughes, J.M. (1977). Adolescent children of alcoholic parents and the relationship of Alateen to these children. *Journal of Consulting and Clinical Psychology, 45,* 946–947.

Jacob, T., Favorini, A., Meisel, S.S., & Anderson, C.M. (1978). The alcoholic's spouse, children, and family interactions. *Journal of Studies on Alcohol, 39,* 1231–1251.

Jalongo, M.R. (1983). Bibliotherapy: Literature to promote socioemotional growth.

The Reading Teacher, 36, 796–803.

Jaworski, M. (1986, April 15). Growing up with alcoholism. *Family Circle,* 18–20.

Jones, J.W. (1983). *The children of alcoholics screening test and test manual.* Chicago, Illinois: Camelot Unlimited.

Jones-Saumty, D.L., Parsons, O.A., & Fabian, M.S. (1980). Familial alcoholism, drinking behavior, and neuropsychological performance in alcoholic women. *Alcohol Technical Reports, 9,* 29–34.

Kaij, L., & Dock, J. (1975). Grandsons of alcoholics. *Archives of General Psychiatry, 32,* 1379–1381.

———. (1960). *Studies on the etiology and sequels of alcohol.* Lund, Sweden: University of Lund.

Kammeier, M.L. (1971). Adolescents from families with and without alcohol problems. *Quarterly Journal of Studies on Alcohol, 32,* 364–372.

Kearney, T., & Taylor, C. (1969). Emotionally disturbed adolescents with alcoholic parents. *Acta Paedopsychiatrica, 36,* 215–221.

Keltner, N.L., McIntyre, C.W., & Gee, R. (1986). Birth order effects in second-generation alcoholics. *Journal of Studies on Alcohol, 47,* 495–497.

Kern, J.C., Hassett, C.A., & Collipp, P.J. (1981). Children of alcoholics: Locus of control, mental age, and zinc level. *Journal of Psychiatric Treatment and Evaluation, 3,* 169–173.

Klinge, V. (1983). A comparison of parental and adolescent MMPIs as related to substance use. *International Journal of the Addictions, 18,* 1179–1185.

Knop, J., Teasdale, T.W., Schulsinger, F., & Goodwin, D.W. (1985). A prospective study of young men at high risk for alcoholism: School behavior and achievement. *Journal of Studies on Alcohol, 46,* 273–278.

Kosten, T.R., Rounsaville, B.J., & Kleber, H.D. (1985). Parental alcoholism in opioid addicts. *Journal of Nervous and Mental Disease, 173,* 461–468.

Krauthamer, C. (1979). Maternal attitudes of alcohol and nonalcoholic upper middle class women. *The International Journal of Addictions, 14,* 639–644.

Kritsberg, W. (1985). *The adult children of alcoholics syndrome: From discovery to recovery.* Pompano Beach, Florida: Health Communications.

———. (1984, November/December). Chronic shock and emotional numbness in adult children of alcoholics. *Focus on Family,* 24–25, 40.

Kroll, P.D., Stock, D.F., & James, M.E. (1985). The behavior of adult alcoholic men abused as children. *Journal of Nervous and Mental Disease, 173,* 689–693.

Landesman-Dwyer, S., Ragozin, A.S., & Little, R. (1979). Behavioral correlates of prenatal exposure to alcohol and nicotene. Paper presented at the Society for Research in Child Development. San Francisco, California.

Lerner, R. (1986). Codependency: The swirl of energy surrounded by confusion. In R.J. Ackerman (Ed.) *Growing in the shadow: Children of Alcoholics.* Pompano Beach, Florida: Health Communications. 113–121.

Liepman, M., White, W.T., & Nirenberg, T.D. (1986). Children of alcoholic families. In D.C. Lewis & C.N. Williams. (Eds.) *Providing care for children of alcoholics: Clinical and research perspectives.* Pompano Beach, Florida: Health Communications. 39–64.

MacDonald, D.I., & Blume, S.B. (1986). Children of alcoholics. *American Journal of Diseases of Children, 140,* 750–754.

McLachlan, J.F.C., Walderman, R.L., & Thomas, S. (1973). A study of teenagers with alcoholic parents. *Donwood Institute Research Monograph No. 3.* Toronto, Canada.

Manning, D.T. (1987). Books as therapy for children of alcoholics. *Child Welfare,* 66, 35–43.

Marcus, A.M. (1986). Academic achievement in elementary school children of alcoholic mothers. *Journal of Clinical Psychology, 42,* 372–376.

Marks, J. (1986, March). The children of alcoholics. *Parents Magazine,* 104–108, 194–198.

Matthews, K.A., & Angulo, J. (1980). Measurement of the Type A behavior pattern in children: Assessment of children's competitiveness, impatience-anger, and aggression. *Child Development, 51,* 466–475.

McAndrew, J.A. (1985). Children of alcoholics: School intervention. *Childhood Education, 61,* 343–345.

McElligatt, K. (1986). Identifying and treating children of alcoholic parents. *Social Work in Education, 9,* 55–70.

McKenna, T., & Pickens, R. (1983). Personality characteristics of alcoholic children of alcoholics. *Journal of Studies on Alcoholism, 44,* 688–700.

——. (1981). Alcoholic children of alcoholics. *Journal of Studies on Alcohol, 42,* 1021–1029.

McKenry, P.C., & Tischler, C.L. (1987). Le rapport entere l'usage de drogues et le suicide chez les adolescents. *Medecine et Hygiene, 45,* 2127–2132.

McKenry, P.C., Tischler, C.L., & Kelley, C. (1983). The role of drugs in adolescent suicide attempts. *Suicide and Life-Threatening Behavior, 13,* 166–175.

Meddin, B.J., & Rosen, A.L. (1986). Child abuse and neglect: Prevention and reporting. *Young Children, 41,* 26–30.

Merikangas, K.A., Weissman, M.M., Prusoff, B.A., Pauls, D.L., & Leckman, J.F. (1985). Depressives with secondary alcoholism: Psychiatric disorders in off-spring. *Journal of Studies on Alcohol, 46,* 199–204.

Miller, D., & Jang, M. (1977). Children of alcoholics: A twenty-year longitudinal study. *Social Work Research and Abstracts, 13,* 23–29.

Miller, N. (1983). Group psychotherapy in a school setting for adolescent children of alcoholics. *Group, 7,* 34–40.

Moe, J., & Pohlman, D. (1988). *Kids' power: Healing games for children of alcoholics.* Redwood City, California: Whipple & Alameda.

Moos, R.H., & Billings, A.G. (1982). Children of alcoholics during the recovery process: Alcoholic and matched control families. *Addictive Behaviors, 7,* 155–163.

Morehouse, E.R. (1979). Working in the schools with children of alcoholic parents. *Health and Social Work, 4,* 145–162.

——. (1986). Counseling adolescent children of alcoholics in groups. In R.J. Ackerman (Ed.) *Growing in the shadow.* Pompano Beach, Florida: Health Communications.

Morehouse, E.R., & Scola, C.M. (1986). *Children of alcoholics: Meeting the needs of the young COA in the school setting.* South Laguna, California: National Association for Children of Alcoholics.

Morehouse, E., & Richards, T. (1986). An examination of dysfunctional latency age children of alcoholic parents and problems in intervention. In R.J. Ackerman (Ed.) *Growing in the shadow.* Pompano Beach, Florida: Health Communications.

Nardi, P.M. (1987). Power and control in families of alcoholics. *Journal of Alcohol and Drug Education, 32,* 14–18.

Nardi, P.M. (1981). Children of alcoholics: A role-theoretical perspective. *Journal of Social Psychology, 115,* 237–245.

National Institute on Alcohol Abuse and Alcoholism. (1981). *Fourth Special Report to the U.S. Congress on Alcohol and Health from the Secretary of Health and Human Services.* J.R. DeLuca (Ed.) Washington, D.C.: Superintendent of Documents, U.S. Government Printing Office.

———. (1986). Helping children from alcoholic families: Approaches and caregivers. *Children Today, 15,* 13–16.

Newlon, B.J., & Furrow, W.V. (1986). Using the classroom to identify children from alcoholic homes. *The School Counselor, 33,* 286–291.

Nylander, I. (1960). Children of alcoholic fathers. *Acta Paediatrica, 49,* 1–134.

O'Gorman, P.A. (1975). *Self-concept, locus of control, and perception of father in adolescents from homes with and without severe drinking problems.* Fordham University: Unpublished doctoral dissertation.

———. (1983). Public policy and the child of the alcoholic. In M. Frank (Ed.) *Children of exceptional parents.* New York: Haworth Press. 35–41.

O'Gorman, P.A., & Oliver-Diaz, P. (1987). *Breaking the cycle of addiction: A parent's guide to raising healthy kids.* Pompano Beach, Florida: Health Communications.

Owen, S.M., Rosenberg, J., & Barkley, D. (1985). Bottled-up children: A group treatment approach for children of alcoholics. *Group, 9,* 31–42.

Pardeck, J.T., & Pardeck, J.A. (1987). Using bibliotherapy to help children cope with the changing family. *Social Work in Education, 9,* 107–116.

Parker, D.A., & Harford, T.C. (1987). Alcohol-related problems of children of heavy-drinking parents. *Journal of Studies on Alcohol, 48,* 265–268.

Parten, M.B. (1932). Social participation among preschool children. *Journal of Abnormal Psychology, 27,* 243–269.

Penick, E.C., Powell, B.J., Bingham, S.F., Liskow, B.I., Miller, N.S., & Read, M.A. (1987). A comparative study of familial alcoholism. *Journal of Studies on Alcohol, 48,* 136–146.

Pilat, J.M., & Jones, J.W. (1985). Identification of children of alcoholics: Two empirical studies. *Alcohol and Research World, 9,* 27–33.

Prewett, M.J., Spence, R., & Chaknis, M. (1981). Attribution of causality by children with alcoholic parents. *The International Journal of the Addictions, 16,* 367–370.

Priest, K. (1985). Adolescents' response to parents' alcoholism. *Social Casework: Journal of Contemporary Social Work, 66,* 533–539.

Regan, J.M., Connors, G.J., O'Farrell, T.J. & Wyatt, C.J. (1983). Services for the families of alcoholics: A survey of treatment agencies in Massachusetts. *Journal of Studies on Alcohol, 44,* 1072–1075.

Richards, T.M. (1979). Splitting as a defense mechanism in children of alcoholic parents. *Currents in Alcoholism, 7,* 239–244.

Rimmer, J. (1982). The children of alcoholics: An exploratory study. *Children and Youth Services Review, 4,* 365–373.

Roberts, K., & Brent, E. (1982). Physician utilization and illness patterns in families of alcoholics. *Journal of Studies on Alcohol, 43,* 119–128.

Robins, L.N., West, P.A., Ratcliff, K.S., & Herjanic, B.M. (1977, May). Father's alcoholism and children's outcomes. Paper presented at the Annual Medical Scientific Meeting of the National Alcoholism Forum. San Diego, California.

Robinson, B. (1989). *Work addiction: Hidden legacy of adult children of alcoholics.* Pompano Beach, Florida: Health Communications.

Robinson, B.E., (1988a). Identification of children of alcoholics. *NC-Aeyc News* (Winter), 1–8.

———. (1988b). *Psychological functioning and programmatic needs of young children of alcoholics.* Research grant funded by the Urban Institute. Charlotte: The University of North Carolina at Charlotte.

———. (1988c). Self-esteem and anxiety level among adult children of alcoholics. Unpublished manuscript. Charlotte: University of North Carolina at Charlotte.

———. (1988d/June–July). Children of alcoholics: Latchkey kids by default. *Focus on Chemically Dependent Families, 11,* 22–23, 39.

Robinson, B.E., & Fields, H. (1983). Casework with invulnerable children. *Social Work, 28,* 63–65.

Robinson, B.E., Rowland, B.H., & Coleman, M. (1989). *Home-alone kids: The working parent's complete guide to providing the best care for their child.* Lexington, Massachusetts: Lexington Books.

———. (1986). *Latchkey kids: Unlocking doors for children and their families.* Lexington, Massachusetts: Lexington Books.

Schaeffer, K.W., Parsons, O.A., & Yohman, J.R. (1984). Neuropsychological differences between male familial and nonfamilial alcoholics and nonalcoholics. *Alcoholism: Clinical and Experimental Research, 8,* 347–351.

Schall, J. (1986). Alcoholism: When a parent drinks, a child struggles. *Instructor,* XCV, 54–57.

Schuckit, M.A. (1984a). Behavioral effects of alcohol in sons of alcoholics. In M. Galanter (Ed.) *Recent developments in alcoholism.* Vol. 3. New York: Plenum Press. 11–19.

———. (1984b). Relationship between the course of primary alcoholism in men and family history. *Journal of Studies on Alcohol, 45,* 334–338.

———. (1984c). Subjective responses to alcohol in sons of alcoholics and control subjects. *Archives of General Psychiatry, 41,* 879–884.

Schuckit, M.A., Gold, E., & Risch, C. (1987). Serum prolactin levels in sons of alcoholics and control subjects. *American Journal of Psychiatry, 144,* 854–859.

Schuckit, M.A., & Rayses, V. (1979). Ethanol ingestion: Differences in blood acetaldehyde concentrations in relatives of alcoholics and controls. *Science, 203,* 54–55.

Schuckit, M.A., Goodwin, D.A., & Winokur, G. (1972). A study of alcoholism in half siblings. *American Journal of Psychiatry, 128,* 122–126.

Schulsinger, F., Knop, J., Goodwin, D.W., Teasdale, T.W., & Mikkelsen, U. (1986). A prospective study of young men at high risk for alcoholism.

Archives of General Psychiatry, 43, 755–760.

Skeen, P., & McKenry, P. (1980). The teacher's role in facilitating a child's adjustment to divorce. *Young Children, 35,* 3–12.

Sgroi, S. (1982). *Handbook of clinical intervention in child sexual abuse.* Lexington, Massachusetts: Lexington Books.

Shaywitz, S., Cohen, D., & Shaywitz, B. (1980). Behavior and learning difficulties in children of normal intelligence born to alcoholic mothers. *Journal of Pediatrics, 96,* 978–982.

Slavenas, R. (1988). The role and responsibility of teachers and child care workers in identifying and reporting child abuse and neglect. *Early Child Development and Care, 31,* 19–25.

Sloboda, S.B. (1974). The children of alcoholics: A neglected problem. *Hospital and Community Psychiatry, 25,* 605–606.

Smith, A. (1988). *Grandchildren of alcoholics.* Pompano Beach, Florida: Health Communications.

Somers, S. (1988). *Keeping secrets.* New York: Warner Books.

Stark, E. (1987, January). Forgotten victims: Children of alcoholics. *Psychology Today,* 58–62.

Steinberg, L. (1986). Latchkey children and susceptibility to peer pressure: An ecological analysis. *Developmental Psychology, 22,* 433–439.

Steinglass, P. (1980). A life history model of the alcoholic family. *Family Process, 19,* 211–226.

Steinhausen, H.C., Gobel, D., & Nestler, V. (1984). Psychopathology in the offspring of alcoholic parents. *Journal of the American Academy of Child Psychiatry, 23,* 465–471.

Steinhausen, H.C., Nestler, V., & Huth, H. (1982). Psychopathology and mental functions in the offspring of alcoholic and epileptic mothers. *Journal of the American Academy of Child Psychiatry, 21,* 268–273.

Strong, M. (1986, March). Children of the bottle. *Glamour Magazine,* 84–87.

Tabakoff, B., Hoffman, P.L., Lee, J.M., Saito, T., Willard, B., & DeLeon-Jones, J. (1988). Differences in platelet enzyme activity between alcoholics and nonalcoholics. *New England Journal of Medicine, 318,* 134–139.

Tarter, R.E., Hegedus, A.M., & Gavaler, J.S. (1985). Hyperactivity in sons of alcoholics. *Journal of Studies on Alcohol, 46,* 259–261.

Tarter, R.E., Hegedus, A.M., Goldstein, G., Shelly, C., & Alterman, A.I. (1984). Adolescent sons of alcoholics: Neuropsychological and personality characteristics. *Alcoholism: Clinical and Experimental Research, 8,* 216–222.

Thomas, A., & Chess, S. (1980). *The dynamics of psychological development.* New York: Brunner/Mazel.

Thomas, M. (1987). *Free to be a family.* New York: Bantam.

Tischler, C.L., & McKenry, P.C. (1982). Parental negative self and adolescent suicide attempts. *Journal of the American Academy of Child Psychiatry, 21,* 404–408.

Tittmar, H.G. (1982). Some problems inherent in natal alcoholism. *Journal of Psychiatric Treatment and Evaluation, 4,* 165–171.

Triplett, J.L., & Arneson, S.W. (1978). Children of alcoholic parents: A neglected issue. *Journal of School Health, 48,* 596–599.

Udayakumar, G.S., Mohan, A., Shariff, I.A., Sekar, K., & Eswari, C. (1984).

Children of the alcoholic parent. *Child Psychiatry Quarterly, 17,* 9–14.

Veenstra, S. (1987). *Children of alcoholic parents: A handbook for counselors and teachers.* Cleveland Heights, Ohio: Alcoholism Services of Cleveland.

Visintainer, P.F., & Matthews, K.A. (1987). Stability of overt type A behaviors in children: Results from a two- and five-year longitudinal study. *Child Development, 58,* 1586–1591.

Utne, H.E., Hansen, F.V., Winkler, K., & Schulsinger, F. (1977). Alcohol elimination rates in adoptees with and without alcohol parents. *Journal of Studies on Alcohol, 38,* 1219–1223.

Venugopal, M. (1985). Emotional problems of the children of alcoholic fathers. *Child Psychiatry Quarterly, 18,* 114–117.

Waters, F.E., & Twaite, J.A. (1986, January/February). Test your COA quotient. *Changes,* 14–19.

Watkins, C. (1988/March 2). Reaching adolescent COAs through student assistant programs. Presented at the National Association for Children of Alcoholics Annual Conference. New Orleans, Louisiana.

Weatherford, V. (1988, March 1). ACAs' transgenerational patterns. Paper presented at the National Association for Children of Alcoholics Conference. New Orleans, Louisiana.

Weddle, C.D., & Wishon, P.M. (1986). Children of alcoholics: What we should know; how we can help. *Children Today, 15,* 8–12.

Wegscheider, S. (1976). *The family trap.* Crystal, Minnesota: Nurturing Networks.

———. (1979). *The family trap.* Palo Alto, California: Science & Behavior Books.

Wegscheider-Cruse, S. (1985). *Choices.* Pompano Beach, Florida: Health Communications.

Weinraub, M., & Lewis, M. (1977). The determinants of children's responses to separation. *Monographs of the Society for Research in Child Development, 42,* (4, Serial No. 172).

Werner, E.E. (1986). Resilient offspring of alcoholics: A longitudinal study from birth to age eighteen. *Journal of Studies on Alcohol, 47,* 34–40.

West, M.W., & Prinz, R.J. (1987). Parental alcoholism and childhood psychopathology. *Psychological Bulletin, 102,* 204–218.

Whitfield, C.L. (1987). *Healing the child within: Discovery and recovery for adult children of dysfunctional families.* Pompano Beach, Florida: Health Communications.

———. (1980). Children of alcoholics: Treatment issues. *Maryland State Medical Journal, 29,* 86–91.

Wilson, C., & Mulhall, D.J. (1983). Describing relationships in families with alcohol problems. *British Journal of Addiction, 78,* 181–191.

Wilson, C., & Orford, J. (1978). Children of alcoholics: Report of a preliminary study and comments on the literature. *Journal of Studies on Alcohol, 39,* 121–142.

Woititz, J. (1983). *Adult children of alcoholics.* Pompano Beach, Florida: Health Communications.

Wolin, S.J., Bennett, L.A., Noonan, D.L., & Teitelbaum, M.A. (1980). Disrupted family rituals: A factor in the intergenerational transmission of alcoholism. *Journal of Studies on Alcohol, 41,* 199–214.

Wood, B.L. (1982). The COA therapist: When the family hero turns pro. ERIC

Further Readings

Chapter 1

Bradshaw, John. (1988). *On the family*. Pompano Beach, Florida: Health Communications.

Wegscheider, Sharon. (1979). *The family trap*. Palo Alto, California: Science and Behavior Books.

———. (1981). *Another chance: Hope and health for the alcoholic family*. Palo Alto, California: Science and Behavior Books.

Wood, Barbara. (1987). *Children of alcoholics: The struggle for self and intimacy in adult life*. New York: New York University Press.

Chapter 2

Beattie, Melody. (1987). *Codependent no more*. Center City, Minnesota: Hazelden.

Borba, Michele. (1978). *Self-esteem: A classroom affair*. New York: Harper & Row.

Canfield, Jack, & Wells, Harold. (1976). *100 ways to enhance self-concept in the classroom*. Englewood Cliffs, New Jersey: Prentice-Hall.

Clarke, Jean Illsley. (1980). *Self-esteem: A family affair*. New York: Harper & Row.

Felker, Donald. (1974). *Building positive self-concepts*. Minneapolis: Minnesota: Burgess.

Mack, John. (1987). *The development and sustaining of self-esteem in childhood*. New York: International Universities Press.

McDaniel, Sandy, & Bielen, Peggy. (1985). *Project self-esteem: A parent involvement program for elementary-age children*. Rolling Hills Estates, California: Jalmar Press.

Silvernail, David. (1985). *Developing positive student self-concept*. Washington, D.C.: National Education Association.

Thomas, Marlo. (1987). *Free to be a family*. New York: Bantam.

Chapter 3

Brenner, Avis. (1984). *Helping children cope with stress*. Lexington, Massachusetts: Lexington Books.

Elkind. David. (1981). *The hurried child*. Reading, Massachusetts: Addison-Wesley.

Robinson, Bryan. (1989). *Work addiction: Hidden legacy of adult children of alcoholics*. Pompano Beach, Florida: Health Communications.

Robinson, Bryan, Rowland, Bobbie, & Coleman, Mick. (1989). *Home-alone kids: The working parents' complete guide to providing the best care for their child*. Lexington, Massachusetts: Lexington Books.

————. (1986). *Latchkey kids: Unlocking doors for children and their families*. Lexington, Massachusetts: Lexington Books.

Saunders, Antoinette, & Remsberg, Bonnie. (1985). *The stress-proof child: A loving parent's guide*. New York: Holt, Rinehart, & Winston.

Sgroi, Suzanne. (1982). *Handbook of clinical intervention in child sexual abuse*. Lexington, Massachusetts: Lexington Books.

Whitfield, Charles. (1987). *Healing the child within: Discovery and recovery for adult children*. Pompano Beach, Florida: Health Communications.

Chapter 4

Hafen, Brent, & Frandsen, Kathryn. (1986). *Youth suicide: Depression and loneliness*. Evergreen, Colorado: Cordillera Press.

Morehouse, Ellen, & Scola, Claire. (1986). *Children of alcoholics: Meeting the needs of the young COA in the school setting*. South Laguna, California: National Association for Children of Alcoholics.

O'Gorman, Patricia, & Oliver-Diaz, Philip. (1987). *Breaking the cycle of addiction: A parent's guide to raising healthy kids*. Pompano Beach, Florida: Health Communications.

Porterfield, Kay. (1985). *Keeping promises: The challenge of a sober parent*. Center City, Minnesota: Hazelden.

Chapter 5

Black, Claudia. (1982). *It will never happen to me!* Denver, Colorado: MAC Publications.

Flake-Hobson, Carol, Robinson, Bryan, & Skeen, Patsy. (1983). *Child development and relationships*. New York: Random House.

Hammond, Mary. (1985). *Children of alcoholics in play therapy*. Pompano Beach, Florida: Health Communications.

Chapter 6

Ackerman, Robert. (1983). *Children of alcoholics: A guidebook for educators, therapists, and parents* (2nd Ed.). Holmes Beach, Florida: Learning Publications.

Cork, Margaret. (1969). *The forgotten children.* Ontario, Canada: General Publishing Company.

Deutsch, Charles. (1982). *Broken bottles, broken dreams: Understanding and helping the children of alcoholics.* New York: Teachers College Press.

Gravitz, Herbert. (1985). *Children of alcoholics handbook: Who they are, what they experience, how they recover.* South Laguna, California: National Association for Children of Alcoholics.

Chapter 7

Moe, Jerry, & Pohlman, Don. (1988). *Kid's power: Healing games for children of alcoholics.* (Write: Sequoia Hospital District, Whipple & Alameda, Redwood City, California 94062).

National Institute on Alcohol Abuse and Alcoholism. (1981). *Services for children of alcoholics.* (Research Monograph No. 4). Rockville, Maryland: United States Department of Health and Human Services.

Pilat, Joanne, & Jones, John. (1987). *How to develop a three-phase treatment program for children of alcoholics.* Chicago, Illinois: Camelot Unlimited.

Veenstra, Susan. (1987). *Children of alcoholic parents: A handbook for counselors and teachers.* (Write: Alcoholism Services of Cleveland, 2490 Lee Boulevard #300, Cleveland Heights, Ohio 44118).

Waite, Barbara, & Ludwig, Meredith. (1985). *A growing concern: How to provide services for children from alcoholic families.* Rockville, Maryland: National Institute on Alcohol Abuse and Alcoholism.

Chapter 8

Ackerman, Robert. (1986). *Growing in the shadow: Children of alcoholics.* Pompano Beach, Florida: Health Communciations.

New Games Foundation. (1976) *The new games book.* New York: Headlands Press.

New Games Foundation. (1981). *More new games.* New York: Dolphin, Doubleday, and Company.

Pardeck, Jean, & Pardeck, John. (1984). *Young people with problems: A guide to bibliotherapy.* Westport, Connecticut: Greenwood Press.

Rubin, R.J. (Ed.) (1978). *Bibliotherapy sourcebook.* Tucson, Arizona: The Oryx Press.

Schaefer, Charles, & Reid, Steven. (1986). *Game play: Therapeutic use of childhood games.* Somerset, New Jersey: John Wiley.

Chapter 9

Kritsberg, Wayne. (1985). *The adult children of alcoholics syndrome: From discovery to recovery.* Pompano Beach, Florida: Health Communications.

Lewis, David, & Williams, Carol. (Eds.). (1986). *Providing care for children of alcoholics: Clinical and research perspectives.* Pompano Beach, Florida: Health Communications.

Marlin, Emily. (1987). *HOPE: New choices and recovery strategies for adult children of alcoholics.* New York: Harper & Row.

Smith, Ann. (1988). *Grandchildren of alcoholics: Another generation of codependency.* Pompano Beach, Florida: Health Communications.

Woititz, Janet. (1983). *Adult children of alcoholics.* Pompano Beach, Florida: Health Communciations.

———. (1985). *Struggle for intimacy.* Pompano Beach, Florida: Health Communications.

Index

About the Author

Bryan E. Robinson is professor of child and family development at the University of North Carolina at Charlotte. He is coauthor of five other books, *Child Development and Relationships, The Developing Father, Home-Alone Kids, Latchkey Kids,* and *Teenage Fathers* and has published more than fifty articles in professional journals and popular magazines such as *Psychology Today.* Dr. Robinson's clinical practice includes work with children of alcoholics in an outpatient treatment center. He has written scripts for national television programs on child development and has appeared on national radio and television discussing children's needs.